GLOBAL SECURITY WATCH

KOREA

GLOBAL SECURITY WATCH

KOREA

A Reference Handbook

William E. Berry, Jr.

PRAEGER SECURITY INTERNATIONAL
Westport, Connecticut • London

Library of Congress Cataloging-in-Publication Data

Global security watch—Korea : a reference handbook / William E. Berry, Jr.
    p. cm.—(Global security watch, ISSN 1938–6168)
  Includes bibliographical references and index.
  ISBN 978–0–275–99484–6 (alk. paper)
1. Korea (South)—Foreign relations—Korea (North) 2. Korea (North)—Foreign relations—Korea (South) 3. Korea (North)—Foreign relations—United States. 4. United States—Foreign relations—Korea (North) 5. Nuclear nonproliferation—Korea (North) I. Title.
DS910.2.K7B47 2008
355'.0330519—dc22   2007043647

British Library Cataloguing in Publication Data is available.

Library of Congress Catalog Card Number: 2007043647
ISBN-13: 978–0–275–99484–6
ISSN: 1938–6168

First published in 2008

Praeger Security International, 88 Post Road West, Westport, CT 06881
An imprint of Greenwood Publishing Group, Inc.
www.praeger.com

Printed in the United States of America

The paper used in this book complies with the
Permanent Paper Standard issued by the National
Information Standards Organization (Z39.48–1984).

10 9 8 7 6 5 4 3 2 1

This book is dedicated to Noelle who supported my interests in East Asia every step of the way, frequently at a cost to her own career. It is our most sincere hope that when our grandchildren (Cecilia, Eliana, Raina, Jack, Mia, and Kendall) study Northeast Asia in the years to come, they will learn about a unified, peaceful, and prosperous Korea.

Contents

Preface

In July 1993, President Bill Clinton visited the ROK–South Korea (Republic of Korea) as part of a tour in Northeast Asia. During his stay in Seoul, he traveled to the DMZ (Demilitarized Zone) that separates the ROK from the DPRK–North Korea (Democratic People's Republic of Korea). Looking across the DMZ, President Clinton described the terrain he saw as one of the scariest places on earth. Now, well into the first decade of the twenty-first century and several years after the end of the Cold War, President Clinton's observation remains accurate. In fact, the argument can be made that the Korean peninsula is even more dangerous than it was in 1993 because the military forces of both the ROK and DPRK remain deployed along the 38th parallel as do military forces of the United States. In addition, the North Korean economy has largely collapsed threatening the survival of the regime in Pyongyang. Perhaps most significant, North Korea has developed and detonated a nuclear weapon, has a large arsenal of chemical weapons, and has tested missiles that may be capable of delivering both.

One of the primary purposes of this book is to address the question derived from the Clinton observation. What factors contribute to the hostility between the two Koreas when the their populations share a common recorded history of more than 2,000 years and are one of the most homogeneous peoples on the globe with the same ethnic background, culture, and language? To assist us in answering this complex question, chapter 1 will focus on the basic geography of the Korean peninsula and the origins and evolution of the Korean people. This chapter also will detail Korean history from the time of the Three Kingdoms to the unification of Korea in the seventh century under the Silla Dynasty. The efforts of successive Korean governments during the Yi Dynasty to protect Korean independence from the encroachments of China, Japan, Russia, and the Western colonial powers will also be covered. Chapter 1 will conclude with analyses of the Japanese occupation from 1910 to 1945, the division of the Korean peninsula by the United States and Soviet Union, and the devastating effects of the Korean War from 1950 to 1953.

Chapter 2 examines the political development of South Korea through the six republics from 1948 to the present with a particular emphasis on the democratization process and the development of the national security relationship with the United States The ROK has made tremendous strides moving from very authoritarian political systems after the Korean War to political pluralism and liberalization early in the twenty-first century. Similarly, chapter 3 will focus on the Kim Dynasty from Kim Il Sung who was the first leader of North Korea until his death in 1994 to the succession of Kim Jong Il, his son. This transition represents the only hereditary succession in a communist government to date. Particular attention is paid to the juche principle and the cult of personality as they influenced the succession process and concludes with some observations about possible future political developments as Kim Jong Il grows older.

Chapter 4 addresses the North Korean nuclear weapon programs from the perspective of likely DPRK motives for allocating such scarce resources over more than 30 years to develop these weapons. In order to devise an effective strategy that convinces the North Koreans to give up these weapons diplomatically, it is essential to understand the motivations behind their acquisition. Chapter 5 compares the strategies that the Clinton and Bush administrations have employed in their efforts to rid the Korean peninsula of nuclear weapons. The political, economic, and military strategies used will be evaluated and future options discussed. Chapter 6 concludes with an analysis of the evolving triangular relations between the two Koreas and the United States. The United States and ROK have a security alliance that has lasted from the end of the Korean War, but this alliance is now under some strain in part because the DPRK has had success driving a wedge between the two allies.

One final word on the organization of this book is necessary. Most of the country studies in the Praeger Security International series concentrate on just one country. In the case of the Korean peninsula, it is very difficult, if not impossible, to separate the two Koreas because they are inextricably linked by their common history, ethnicity, culture, and language. Therefore, this book will address issues related to both countries.

Note on Korean Names

For most Koreans, the surname or family name comes first with the given names following. For example, with Kim Il Sung, the founding leader of North Korea, his surname is Kim. There are a few exceptions such as Syngman Rhee, the first President of South Korea. He was born Lee Seungman, but because he spent most of the Japanese occupation years exiled in the United States, he anglicized his name to Syngman Rhee and is referred to as President Rhee.

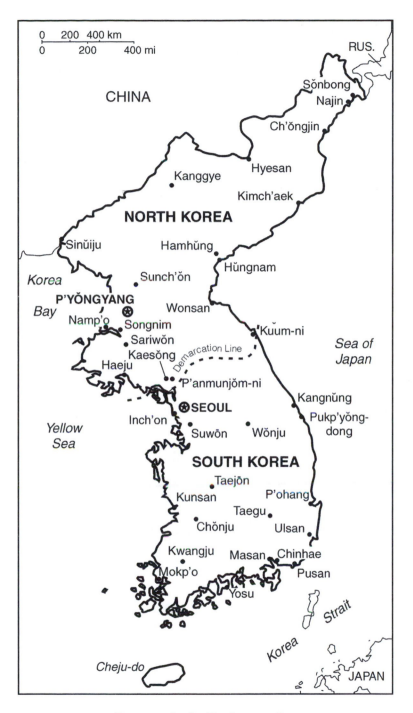

CHINA

RUS.

Sŏnbong
Najin
Ch'ŏngjin

Hyesan

Kanggye
Kimch'aek

NORTH KOREA

Sinŭiju
Hamhŭng

Hŭngnam

Korea

Sunch'ŏn

P'YŎNGYANG

Bay
Namp'o
Wonsan

Songnim
Kŭum-ni

Sariwŏn

Sea of
Japan

Kaesŏng
Demarcation Line

Haeju

P'anmunjŏm-ni

Kangnŭng

⊗SEOUL

Inch'on
Pukp'yŏng-
dong

Yellow
Sea
Suwŏn
Wŏnju

SOUTH KOREA

Taejŏn

Kunsan
P'ohang

Taegu
Chŏnju
Ulsan

Kwangju
Masan
Chinhae

Mokp'o
Pusan

Yosu

Korea
Strait

JAPAN

Cheju-do

0   200 400 km
0   200   400 mi

Cartography by Bookcomp, Inc.

CHAPTER 1

People, Geography, and History

GEOGRAPHY

One of the most critical geographic features of the Korean peninsula is that Korea is surrounded by larger, more powerful nation states. This fact has been true since the beginning of modern Korean history. China, Russia, and Japan have exercised power and competed for influence in Korea for hundreds of years. In the nineteenth and twentieth centuries, western countries such as the United States, France, and Britain joined this competition. One authority on Korea estimates that there have been more than 900 invasions of Korea over the past 2000 years, some more important than others.[1] Among the more critical were the Chinese incursion in 108 BC that established the four commanderies under China's control, the Mongol invasions in the thirteenth and fourteenth centuries, the Japanese attacks from 1592 to 1598, and the Japanese occupation from 1910 to 1945.

Of more recent significance is the division of Korea after World War II by the United States and Soviet Union and their subsequent occupations that contributed directly to the creation of the two Koreas in existence today. Although the Cold War is now long over, the historical enmities that have influenced Northeast Asia for centuries still exist as does the competition for scarce resources. Another factor leading to tension is the rise of nationalism early in the twenty-first century that complicates relations among regional powers. Added to this mix is the severe competition between North and South Korea for political legitimacy based on conflicting political and economic systems. The bottom line is that both the

Koreas experience a sense of insecurity and vulnerability that influences their relations with each other and with external powers.

The Korean peninsula shares an almost 650-mile border with China to the north along the Yalu and Tumen rivers. In the extreme northeast section of the peninsula is a slightly more than 10-mile border with Russia. To the east of Korea is Japan across the Sea of Japan (or East Sea as the Koreans refer to this body of water). The closest distance between Korea and Japan is over the Korean Strait, approximately 60 miles. To the west across the Yellow Sea is China. The 150-mile DMZ (Demilitarized Zone) divides the two Koreas and extends roughly along the 38th parallel. The Armistice Agreement at the end of the Korean War in 1953 established the DMZ. It is 2.5 miles wide and both North and South Korea have fortified their territories in close proximity to the DMZ. In the regard, the DMZ is one of the most inappropriately named pieces of real estate in the world because it is far from demilitarized. An unintended consequence of the creation of the DMZ is that it has become one of the largest wildlife sanctuaries in Asia. Whenever reunification comes to the Korean peninsula, it will be interesting to observe how the unified government handles the likely conflicting demands for development and ecological preservation in the DMZ.

The total land mass of the Korean peninsula is about 85,000 square miles, comparable to the American state of Minnesota. North Korea comprises almost 55 percent of this land mass with more than 47,000 square miles and is roughly the size of Mississippi. South Korea has an area of approximately 38,000 square miles just slightly smaller than Indiana. North Korea is endowed with more natural resources than is South Korea, but the latter is better suited to agriculture because of the milder climate and more predictable rainfall. The major natural resources in the DPRK (Democratic People's Republic of Korea) are tungsten, zinc, graphite, magnetite, iron ore, copper, gold, and hydropower. For the ROK (Republic of Korea), the major natural resources are coal, tungsten, graphite, molybdenum, lead, and hydropower.[2]

Mountains dominate the terrain of both the Koreas. This geographical feature influences not only agriculture production, but also affects political and economic developments, particularly in the ROK. For example, because of their somewhat isolated location caused by the Sobaek Mountain Range, residents of the two Cholla provinces in the southwest part of South Korea have frequently felt marginalized both politically and economically. Kim Dae Jung, a native son of Cholla, has been successful throughout his political career partly because he has been able to mobilize electoral support in his home area and work to bring development to Cholla. Regionalism is very important in ROK politics especially regarding political parties. Geography plays a significant role in the regional orientation of many political parties in South Korea as will become evident later in this book.

PEOPLE

The origins of the Korean people can be traced to Central Asia perhaps as early as the third century BC when Mongols, Ottoman Turks, Manchus, and others extended their influence over vast parts of the known world. Through the centuries, Koreans have become one of the most homogeneous populations with a common ethnicity, language, and culture. There are very few ethnic minorities in Korea, and this fact has contributed to a very strong sense of nationalism. Some visitors to Korea may believe this strong nationalism goes even further to border on xenophobia in which people or things non-Korean are looked upon as being inferior at least among parts of the population. What is fair to say is that Koreans are very proud as a people, and they should be based on their history and accomplishments.

Korean culture has been and continues to be influenced by Shamanism, a belief that good and evil spirits pervade society, Buddhism that can be traced from the fourth century, Confucianism introduced through the long relationship with China, and Christianity from foreign missionaries beginning mostly in the eighteenth century. Confucianism and neo-Confucianism are extremely important to Korean society in part because of the hierarchal nature of relationships and emphasis placed on the family. Christianity has also become very popular on the Korean peninsula particularly in the ROK, which now has the second largest Christian population in Asia after the Philippines.

South Korea has a population of approximately 49 million people. Since it is about the size of Indiana, a population of this size makes the ROK one of the most densely populated countries in the world. For anyone who has spent time in the ROK, this fact will come as no surprise especially for those who might want to take a solitary hike in the fall or visit a beach in the summer. South Korea is divided into nine provinces and seven metropolitan cities, somewhat similar to the status of Washington, DC. These cities are Seoul, Inchon, Pusan , Taegu, Taejon, Kwangju, and Ulsan. North Korea has just under 23 million people, and contrary to South Korea, has experienced much slower population growth largely because of the severe famine that has plagued the North Korean people over the past several years. The DPRK also is divided into nine provinces and has four designated municipalities. They are Pyongyang, the capital, Kaesong, Najin, and Nampo.

HISTORY

Early Korean History

As China unified under first the Qin Dynasty (232–208 BC) and then the Han Dynasty (208 BC–AD 220), its influence spread more forcefully into Korea. China's leaders were concerned about nomadic groups from Central Asia who were moving into Manchuria and Korea. To prevent these groups from causing security problems for China, the Chinese Emperor in 109 BC moved military forces into Korea and established four commanderies or military commands. The center of these commands was located at Nangnang near present day Pyongyang. These commanderies remained in place more or less for almost four centuries and served as the basis of increased Sino-Korean interactions and cultural exchanges.

Eventually, the Koreans reacted against this Chinese presence and formed what became known as the Three Kingdoms. These kingdoms were Koguryo in the northern part of the peninsula, Paekche in the southwest, and Silla in the center. The period of the Three Kingdoms lasted from about the time of Christ until AD 668. Over time, these different territorial entities came into conflict with each other. China, being an opportunistic neighbor, aligned itself with Silla since Silla appeared to be the strongest. In 660, a combined China–Silla assault defeated Paekche and then attacked Koguryo. As a result of these military victories, Silla unified the Korean peninsula under its control in 668. From that time until 1945, Korea was a unified country, a fact that Koreans both north and south of the 38th parallel continue to take great pride. However, the period of the Three Kingdoms also was very significant in forging close bonds between China and Korea. Chinese political practices, Confucian philosophy, educational methods, and Buddhist teachings all were either introduced or enhanced during these centuries.

The Silla Dynasty lasted from 668 until 936. The tributary relationship with China developed during this dynasty as particularly close ties with the Tang Dynasty progressed. Buddhism became more popular with the building of large temples and shrines around the Silla capital at Kyongju. Unfortunately, by the ninth century, Silla began to decline through internal divisions and ineffectual leadership. Wang Kon, a general who traced his roots to the Paekche Kingdom, led a successful revolt against Silla and established the Koryo Dynasty in 936. This dynasty lasted until 1392, and Wang moved its capital to Kaesong. During the Koryo period, Buddhism reached its highest point in Korea although Confucianism remained viable. Just as was the case during the Silla Dynasty, Koryo leaders established close ties with China's Song Dynasty, and the tributary relationship continued. Koreans perfected the production of celadon pottery during the eleventh and twelfth centuries, and this pottery remains a Korean specialty to the present as those who have visited after Korean know. The Koryo Dynasty also is famous for the Korean literature and poetry produced and Koreans were responsible for developing some of the first printing presses during this time.[3]

During the thirteenth century, the Mongols extended their influence not only over China but also to many other areas of the world. Korea was no exception, and in 1231, Mongol military forces defeated the Koryo army. The Mongols invaded Korea again in 1254 and forced many Koreans to join in their invasions of Japan in both 1274 and 1281. The Japanese repelled both invasions, and the

Mongols were eventually replaced by the Ming Dynasty in China beginning in 1316. Koryo leaders found themselves divided among pro-Mongol and pro-Ming groups, and conflicts among these groups ensued. One of these leaders was Yi Song Gye who defeated the other Koryo forces and thereby established the Choson (Yi) Dynasty in 1392. This dynasty survived until 1910 with its capital in Seoul.

The first century of the new dynasty represented a high point for Korean culture and politics. The fourth Choson king was Sejong who ruled from 1418 to 1450. One of King Sejong's greatest accomplishments was the development of the Korean written, phonetic alphabet (han'gul). The Choson Dynasty also was noted for the decline of Buddhism and the ascendance of neo-Confucian influence as a state philosophy. Evidence of this decline of Buddhist influence is apparent in South Korea today. If you visit a Korean museum with art from this period, you will likely see many Buddhist statues that have been disfigured. This damage can probably be traced to periods in the Choson era.

Confucian influence was evident in the emphasis placed on education, filial piety, and genealogy. Primogeniture was a common practice in which the oldest son inherited his father's land. This tradition contributed to a male dominant society that still pertains in Korea as seen, for example, in the hereditary succession in North Korea from Kim Il Sung to Kim Jong Il. Another influential group that prospered during the Choson Dynasty was the yangban (scholar-officials) who were the backbone of the Korean government and bureaucracy. In many instances, the yangban achieved their exalted status in society through hereditary considerations that tended to bind landed wealth with political power. Another dominant feature of the Choson era was the continuation of the tributary relationship with China, particularly during the Ming Dynasty. This relationship followed the Confucian principle of big brother–little brother responsibilities with Korea clearly fulfilling the younger brother's roles. Between 1637 and 1881, Korea sent more than 435 special missions to China.[4]

Late in the sixteenth century, Hideyoshi, the Japanese political leader, decided to invade mainland Asia passing through Korea. This invasion eventually was unsuccessful primarily because of the military skills of Admiral Yi Sun Sin and his famous turtle ships. He defeated the Japanese in 1598 with some assistance from China. Although Korea won this military engagement with Japan and is considered a great Korean victory to the present, the effects on the Korean and Chinese economies were devastating. The Manchus were able to take advantage of Korean and Chinese weakened conditions invading Korea in 1636 and forcing the Koreans to shift their loyalties from the Ming Dynasty to the Manchus. Korea's economic decline continued and contributed to factional strife within the Choson elite. This decline presented opportunities in Korea for western and Asian colonial powers.

The Colonial Experience

As the age of western colonialism came to Asia in the early nineteenth century, Korea was not affected initially because the colonial powers were more interested in China and to a lesser extent Japan. However, missionaries and traders began to arrive in Korea during the middle of the nineteenth century. In 1866, the General Sherman, an American merchant ship, sailed up the Taedong River near Pyongyang. An angry group of Koreans formed and attacked the ship after it ran aground. The Koreans killed all the crew members on board and destroyed the ship. In 1871, the United States decided to make amends for the loss of the General Sherman. President Ulysses Grant dispatched the Asiatic Squadron to Korea. In a battle that ensued, the Americans killed more than 600 Koreans before withdrawing.

Next came the Japanese with a naval flotilla that forced the Koreans to enter into the first of a series of unequal treaties. The Japanese and Koreans negotiated the Kanghwa Treaty in 1876 although the Koreans had little say in the specifics. This treaty opened many Korean ports to Japanese merchants and also provided extraterritorial rights to the Japanese. These rights and privileges meant that the Japanese were not subject to Korean laws while in Korea. Perhaps more important, the Kanghwa Treaty stipulated that Korea was an autonomous country. This stipulation was significant because it represented an intentional challenge to the historic tributary relationship between Korea and China and signaled that Japan meant to increase its influence in Korea. In 1882, the United States, Britain, and Germany followed the Japanese model and established extraterritorial rights in Korea.[5]

In response both to the dynastic decline and the incursions of foreigners, a reform movement gained momentum in Korea during the 1860s. This movement became known as Tonghak or Eastern Learning and concentrated largely on peasant grievances. When the Korean government was slow in responding to Tonghak demands such as to reduce taxes and stop rice exports to Japan, the movement transformed into an armed rebellion in 1894. As the conflict intensified, both China and Japan dispatched military forces to Korea. Shortly thereafter, the 1894–1895 Sino-Japanese War began with Japan achieving an overwhelming victory. In the Treaty of Shimonoseki that followed this war, Article I specifically addressed Korea. This article stated that "China recognizes definitively the full and complete independence and autonomy of Korea." By accepting this provision, China effectively ended the tributary relationship with Korea while Japan positioned itself for increased influence on the peninsula.

After its victory, Japan did indeed exercise significant influence in Korea going so far as murdering the Korean queen who the Japanese viewed as a threat to their interests. In response, Russia intervened in an effort to replace Chinese interests.

King Kojong actually moved into the Russian legation during 1896–1897. The rivalry between Japan and Russia made conflict almost inevitable, and in 1904, Japan attacked the Russian fleet at Port Arthur beginning the Russo-Japanese War that lasted until 1905.

In July 1904, American Secretary of War William Howard Taft and Japanese envoy Count Katsura entered into a signed statement that became known as the Taft–Katsura Memorandum. This document was important because in exchange for a Japanese pledge not to interfere with American involvement in the Philippines, the United States recognized Japanese suzerainty over Korea. After the Japanese defeated the Russians in 1905, the two combatants signed the Treaty of Portsmouth. In this treaty, Russia accepted that Japan "possesses in Korea paramount political, military, and economical interests" and pledged not to impede Japan's policies in Korea. In effect, Korea became a Japanese protectorate in 1905, and Japan completed the process by annexing Korea in 1910. The Japanese occupation of Korea had begun and lasted until the end of World War II in 1945. For many Koreans, the Taft–Katsura Memorandum represented a perfidious act on the part of the United States that led directly to the Japanese occupation and continued to affect relations with the Americans long after the fact.

The Japanese Occupation

The Japanese occupation of Korea from 1910 to 1945 remains one of the most controversial periods in Korean history both because of the way the Japanese conducted themselves during the occupation and the perceptions of many Koreans that the Japanese have never taken full responsibility for this conduct. Japan's political dominance was apparent during the occupation just in the numbers of its officials present in Korea and the jobs they performed. In 1910, there were 171,543 Japanese in Korea as the occupation began. By 1940, that number had increased to 708,448. Perhaps more significant was the extent to which the Japanese filled almost all the important political positions.[6] The occupation authorities proscribed the Korean language and forced Koreans to take Japanese names. The military and police presence was pervasive to ensure to the extent possible that the Koreans adhered to Japanese policies and directives.

Economically, Korea was initially important to Japan as a source of resources, particularly food, and as a destination for Japanese exports. As the occupation progressed into the 1930s, Korea's value shifted to being a source of forced labor for Japan. By 1941, almost 1.5 million Koreans were in Japan working in industry, construction, mining, and agriculture. The Japanese also forced between 100,000 and 200,000 Korean women to provide sexual favors for Japanese military forces across Asia as "comfort women."[7] Although Japan did improve Korean infrastructure by building highways, railroads, bridges, and ports, these efforts largely were designed to improve the delivery of Korean goods to Japan. From the Korean perspective, the destruction to the Korean economy and the humiliation of Korean workers during the occupation far overshadowed any infrastructure improvements.

Korean nationalism proved to be a strong force of opposition to Japan's rule. One of the most significant examples of this opposition occurred in February and March 1919. Partly in response to President Woodrow Wilson's call for self-determination as evidenced in his famous Fourteen Points presented during the deliberations of the Treaty of Versailles at the end of World War I, hundreds of thousands of Koreans demonstrated across the country against Japan's occupation demanding Korean independence. Students and religious leaders, especially representing Christian groups, drafted a Declaration of Independence and read it publicly in Seoul on March 1, 1919. The Japanese responded with overwhelming force, and Korean sources reported that more than 7,500 demonstrators were killed and approximately 45,000 were arrested.[8] From 1919 until the end of the occupation, students and religious officials acted as major resistance leaders in Korea.

However, splits developed in the Korean opposition after World War I. One of the most important of these divisions was between those who supported liberal idealism based at least in part on Woodrow Wilson's policies, and those who supported socialism based on Marx and Lenin. Leftists formed the Korean Communist Party during 1925. In Shanghai, Syngman Rhee and Kim Ku representing more centrist perspectives established the KPG (Korean Provincial Government) in 1919. In addition, thousands of Koreans joined Chinese resistance fighters in Manchuria later during the 1920s and 1930s. Kim Il Sung was among these Koreans, and his experiences as an anti-Japanese fighter provided him with much political legitimacy after World War II when he returned to Korea.[9] Despite these heroic efforts to confront the Japanese during the occupation, the occupying forces remained very much in control until the end of World War II and the dropping of the atomic bombs on Japan in August 1945.

Liberation and the Division of Korea

During World War II, President Franklin Roosevelt, Prime Minister Winston Churchill of Great Britain, and Chinese leader Chiang Kai-shek met in Cairo for a summit during late November 1943. In the Cairo Declaration issued at the conclusion of this conference, the three leaders addressed countries and territories seized by Japan and under Japanese control at that time. Regarding Korea, the Cairo Declaration stated that "the three great powers (United States, Great Britain, and China), mindful of the enslavement of the people of Korea, are determined that in due course Korea shall become free and independent."[10] The "in due course" phrase later became very controversial among Koreans because it did not provide for a specific time when Korea would gain its independence after the defeat of Japan and the end of the occupation.

At the Yalta Conference in February 1945, Soviet leader Joseph Stalin joined Roosevelt and Churchill. These leaders focused mainly on Europe and the impending occupation of Germany, but Stalin did agree to enter the war against Japan within 90 days of Germany's surrender. There was no specific mention of Korea, but apparently Roosevelt expressed his views that because Korea had been under Japanese domination for more than 35 years, he was concerned that the Koreans would not be able to govern themselves without some period of tutelage. The Yalta Declaration made reference to possible trusteeships, but no specifics were provided other than trusteeships might be applicable to "territories detached from the enemy as a result of the present war."[11] The Potsdam Conference took place in July and August 1945. After Roosevelt's death in April, Harry Truman became president and met with Stalin and Churchill at Potsdam. Similar to Yalta, the leaders did not address Korea directly. The only implied reference in the declaration was the statement that "the terms of the Cairo Declaration shall be carried out and Japanese sovereignty shall be limited to the islands of Honshu, Hokkaido, Kyushu, Shikoku and such minor islands as we determine."[12] Unfortunately for Korea, it just was not considered important enough to get more attention than it did in these two major conferences at the end of World War II.

The Soviet Union did enter the war against Japan in August 1945 as Stalin had agreed at Yalta. Soviet military units moved into Manchuria and then into northern Korea in early August. Alarmed by the Soviet advances, John McCloy of the State–War–Navy Coordinating Committee in Washington instructed two American colonels, Dean Rusk and Charles Bonesteel, to decide where the Korean peninsula should be divided so that the Soviets could be kept in the northern half and not take over all of Korea. On the day of the Japanese surrender, August 15, 1945, Rusk and Bonesteel studied a National Geographic map of Korea to find a good division point. Rusk, who would later become secretary of state in the Kennedy and Johnson administrations, related in his memoirs that Bonesteel wanted to ensure that Seoul remained in the American sector. When they tried to find some natural geographic line such as a river, they could find none. Rusk and Bonesteel then selected the 38th parallel as the dividing line between the two halves of Korea, and the Soviets accepted this division somewhat to the American surprise.[13] There was no consultation with any Korean representatives prior to the Truman administration making this critical decision.

Once the United States and Soviet Union decided to divide Korea, the United States needed to designate military forces to secure its half since Soviet forces already were present north of the 38th parallel. The 24th Corps of the 10th Army under the command of Lieutenant General John R. Hodge was the unit selected. The 24th Corps had been engaged in difficult fighting against the Japanese on

Okinawa and was preparing for the invasion of the main islands of Japan. Hodge's forces were designated to go to Korea primarily because since they were located on Okinawa, they could be transported to Korea quickly. The 24th Corps left Okinawa on September 5, 1945 and arrived in Seoul 3 days later.

General Hodge and his forces had no preparation for the occupation before they arrived in Seoul, and few of them knew anything about Korea. This lack of preparation contrasted sharply with the preparation for the occupation of Japan that had begun years earlier and is another indicator that Korea was not a major concern for the United States. This lack of planning increased the already significant difficulties Hodge would confront in Korea as the Japanese began a rapid withdrawal after their surrender. Shortly after his arrival, Hodge established the USAMGIK (U.S. Army Military Government in Korea) that became the primary American governing organization in Korea from 1945 until 1948. Not only was Hodge and his staff unprepared for the occupation, but so was the American government in Washington. The State Department did not send its first policy guidance to Hodge until January 1946 and its first detailed political policy directive until July of that year.[14] Although perhaps understandable since the Japanese surrender came more quickly than expected because of the dropping of the atomic bombs on Hiroshima and Nagasaki, the lack of preparation and the mistakes associated with the occupation would have major implications for United States–Korean relations and Korean governance in the years ahead.

When Koreans became aware of the "in due course" provision in the Cairo Declaration, many of them began to make serious preparations for the end of the Japanese occupation and what they hoped would become Korean independence. As early as 1919, Koreans in exile had established the Korean Provisional Government in Shanghai so that at least the initial planning could begin for eventual independence. After Japan's surrender, the Japanese governor general appointed Lyuh Woon Hyung to assist in maintaining order in Korea and begin organizing to take political control. Lyuh was a missionary-trained school teacher with a slightly left of center political orientation. He and some of his supporters formed the Preparatory Committee for Korean Independence later in August 1945, and this committee then called for a national convention. At this convention, delegates from across the country established the KPR (Korean People's Republic) in early September just days before General Hodge arrived in Seoul.

The KPR represented a cross section of Koreans from both the left and right of the political spectrum although leftist influence was more in evidence particularly involving topics such as land reform and social equality. As an example of the efforts to provide some sort of balance, Syngman Rhee became the KPR's first chairman although he did not give his approval for this selection and had not returned to Korea from exile in the United States. Lyuh Woon Hyung became vice chairman.[15] For the Koreans involved in forming the KPR, they hoped that if they established some sort of political organization prior to the arrival of the Americans, this would assist with early independence.

Lyuh and his colleagues were mistaken in this assumption. When General Hodge arrived in Korea in early September 1945, he relied on the Japanese to maintain order. This decision was not well received by most Koreans who despised the Japanese occupiers. As Hodge began to cultivate ties with Koreans, he tended to associate with those who spoke English and were of a more conservative political orientation. In October, the Americans brought Syngman Rhee back to Korea from the United States even though there were divisions within the U.S. government whether or not Rhee was the best choice of a conciliatory leader based on his hard line anticommunist views. The KPG remained in China, even though Kim Ku, the KPG leader, expressed his desire to return to Korea and participate in the political process. In late November, Kim and several of his associates did return although they were not warmly welcomed by Hodge and others in the USAMGIK because of suspicions concerning their preferred policies and objectives. In December, Hodge became completely disillusioned with the KPR and banned this political organization. The outcome of these decisions was that by the end of 1945, the Americans had pretty much cast their lot with Syngman Rhee and to a lesser extent the KPG while leftist elements were largely marginalized.[16]

In the northern half of the peninsula, the Soviet Union also was attempting to establish political organizations through the formation of people's committees. These committees then set up the Five Provinces People's Committee in Pyongyang. The Soviets appointed Cho Man Sik to lead this administrative unit. Cho was a respected nationalist figure who had remained in Korea during the Japanese period. The USSR also relied heavily on the several thousand ethnic Koreans who had lived in Russia during World War II to provide administrative experience. Although Stalin was much more interested in Europe than Korea, he continued to base a sizeable military force in the northern zone to ensure that Soviet policies were implemented as intended.[17]

In December 1945, the foreign ministers of the United States, Great Britain, and Soviet Union met in Moscow in what became known as the Moscow Conference. Regarding Korea, the foreign ministers decided that a provisional Korean democratic government should be established as well as a Joint Commission composed of representatives of the American command in the south and the Soviet command in the north. The primary task of this commission was to work with the provisional Korean government and develop democratic institutions and prepare for independence. Most important, the Moscow Conference participants determined to establish a four power trusteeship that would serve as the government of Korea for a period of up to 5 years. This trusteeship would include the United States, Soviet Union, Great Britain, and China.[18]

As could be expected, most Koreans south of the 38th parallel found the trusteeship proposal to be a great disappointment because they viewed this agreement as just another example of great power interference in Korean affairs that would delay the independence process. For Koreans north of the 38th parallel, the situation was a little more complex because the Soviet Union supported the trusteeship concept and did not encourage dissent. As an example, Cho Man Sik refused to accept the trusteeship proposal, and the Soviets removed him from his position as head of the Five Provinces People's Committee in December 1945. He was not heard from again.[19]

As the Cold War intensified in 1946 and 1947, the Joint Commission proved to be ineffectual in creating a unified, democratic Korean government as called for at the Moscow Conference. After several inconclusive meetings, the Joint Commission met for the final time in August 1947. After this meeting, U.S. representatives referred the Korean issue to the United Nations for a solution. In a General Assembly resolution during November 1947, the United Nations formed the UNTCOK (United Nations Temporary Commission on Korea) to oversee the election of a Korean national assembly. The Soviet Union refused to participate in this commission and barred the members of UNTCOK from entering its zone. Consequently, the commission was only able to observe legislative elections in southern Korea that occurred in August 1948. This elected legislature then chose Syngman Rhee as president of the newly independent ROK on August 15. Koreans in northern Korea subsequently held elections under Soviet control, and the DPRK came into existence on September 9, 1948, under the leadership of Kim Il Sung. The Soviets removed their military forces except some advisers by the end of 1948, and the United States did the same from the ROK by the summer of 1949. Only a small advisory group remained in Seoul.

The Korean War, 1950–1953

The Korean War and who was responsible for its beginning still remains controversial for some people more than 50 years after the war's conclusion. There are those who believe that the Soviet Union directed Kim Il Sung to launch the attack on the ROK in June 1950.[20] Others take a more revisionist approach and argue that there were raids occurring across the 38th parallel frequently in 1949 and 1950, and that North Korea may have been responding to one of these raids when the war began.[21] However, more recent scholarship by experts who have had access to the Soviet Archives presents a more complex scenario in which Kim Il Sung bears most of the responsibility for convincing Stalin and Mao Zedong to support his plans to invade the ROK and reunify the peninsula under his control.[22]

Although Korea was important to Stalin, he was more concerned with Europe and Japan. As related earlier, Korea was not a major topic at either the Yalta or

Potsdam Conferences, and Stalin accepted the division of Korea at the 38th parallel. Apparently, he believed that the United States was intent on remaining in Korea and the risk was not worth it to Stalin to try to force the Americans to leave. After the formation of the DPRK in September 1948, the USSR continued to exercise major political and economic influence over Kim Il Sung whom the Soviets had placed in power.

In late March and April 1950, Kim traveled to Moscow to meet with Stalin. His primary mission was to convince the Soviet leader to support his planned attack on the ROK.[23] Initially, Stalin was not enthusiastic about this plan because of his concern over the likely American response to such an attack. Kim argued that the Truman administration was not predisposed to fight in Korea, and he based his position on two major premises. First, Kim believed his surprise attack would be successful and result in the collapse of the ROK within 3 days before the Americans could respond. Second, Kim predicted that thousands of communist sympathizers in South Korea would rise up and support the DPRK invasion. After his meetings with Stalin, Kim traveled to China and met with Mao who agreed to support the North Koreans. The Chinese decision may also have influenced Stalin in the larger context of Sino-Soviet relations. In any event, Stalin decided to approve the invasion and provided extensive planning expertise to North Korea prior to the attack on June 25, 1950.

Kim Il Sung also may have been influenced by a speech Secretary of State Dean Acheson gave to the National Press Club in Washington during January 1950. In this speech, Acheson referred to an American "defensive perimeter" in Asia that extended from the Aleutians Islands in the north through Japan to the Philippines. He did not mention Korea being within this defensive perimeter and went on to state that if an attack were to occur outside this defensive perimeter, it would be up to the country involved to provide for its defense with additional assistance coming from the United Nations. Although Acheson would later defend his speech as not reflecting a change in American policy or strategy in Asia, Kim may have interpreted this speech differently, particularly since the United States had withdrawn its combat forces from Korea in 1949. Another factor that may have played a role in the decision to invade South Korea occurred in the American Congress in early 1950. The Truman administration requested $150 million in assistance legislation to be provided to South Korea. The Senate passed this legislation, but it failed in the House by one vote. In a compromise, most of the funding was restored in February, but the delay may have been a further indicator to Kim, Stalin, and Mao that not only the executive branch, but the legislative branch too may have been wavering in its support for the ROK.[24]

Whatever his assumptions, Kim was wrong, and President Truman responded immediately to the North Korean invasion. According to one of his biographers, Truman was influenced by the Munich experience prior to World War II and feared that if the United States and other countries did not respond to this North

Korean aggression, it could lead to another world war. Also, Truman was concerned that if the United Nations did not oppose the North Koreans, it could lead to the demise of this institution much as the League of Nations had failed in the 1930s and 1940s. Another factor influencing Truman was his concern that American status and prestige would be significantly harmed if the United States did not respond to the attack on South Korea and could encourage additional communist aggression elsewhere.[25] Because the Soviet Union was boycotting the UN Security Council in the summer of 1950 over the question of which Chinese government should hold the China seat in the United Nations, the Security Council passed a resolution establishing the UNC (United Nations Command) with General Douglas MacArthur in charge. MacArthur's mission was defined as repelling the North Korean invasion. The Korean War lasted until July 1953 when an Armistice Agreement was signed.

Despite the initial DPRK victories including the capture of Seoul and most other ROK cities, the UNC counterattacked in September 1950. With the brilliant MacArthur amphibious landing at Inchon, the North Koreans retreated back across the 38th parallel. The Security Council, at American urging, passed a resolution in October calling for all necessary action to achieve "the establishment of a unified, independent democratic government in the sovereign state of Korea" and approved "all appropriate steps be taken to ensure conditions of stability throughout Korea."[26] With this authorization, President Truman ordered General MacArthur to cross the 38th parallel. MacArthur drove deep into North Korea and approached the Chinese border along the Yalu River. The Chinese responded by sending more than a million "volunteers" into the war. The Soviets also supported the North Koreans although primarily through the use of air power.

The Chinese intervention drove UN forces back across the 38th parallel and once again Seoul was captured. After regrouping, the UNC liberated Seoul and established defensive positions roughly along the 38th parallel by June 1951. Truce negotiations began and lasted for the next 2 years although extensive fighting continued. A major issue was the voluntary repatriation of prisoners of war that was very contentious for both sides. Finally in July 1953, representatives of the UNC (an American general), the Chinese volunteers, and the DPRK signed the Armistice Agreement. South Korea under President Rhee refused to sign this agreement. No formal peace treaty has been negotiated and the Armistice Agreement remains in effect.

The Korean War came close to destroying both Koreas. Estimates are that more than 4 million people were killed on both sides during the conflict with millions of refugees flowing across the 38th parallel, mostly from North Korea. Of the number of combatants killed and wounded, 900,000 were believed to be Chinese; 520,000 North Koreans; 400,000 from the UNC with the vast majority being South Koreans, and about 36,000 Americans. Property losses in the ROK were thought to be approximately $2 billion or about equal to its gross national product in 1949. North Korea's property losses were estimated at just slightly less than for South Korea.[27] Without the tenacity of the Korean people on both sides of the 38th parallel along with extensive foreign assistance largely from the United States and Soviet Union, recovery in the two Koreas would have taken even longer than it did.

NOTES

1. Donald S. Macdonald, *The Koreans: Contemporary Politics and Society* (Boulder: Westview Press, 1990), 1–2.

2. The information on natural resources is found in the *Central Intelligence Agency Factbook* at http://www.cia.gov/cia/publications/factbook.

3. Macdonald, *The Koreas,* 28–30 and Bruce Cumings, *Korea's Place in the Sun: A Modern History* (New York: W. W. Norton & Company, 1997), 26–34.

4. Cumings, *Korea's Place in the Sun,* 51–55. The reference to the number of Korean missions to China is found on page 90.

5. For a good history of this colonial period, see Claude A. Buss, "At the Beginning," in *Reflections on a Century of United States–Korean Relations,* a series of conference papers sponsored by the Academy of Korean Studies and the Wilson Center (Lanham: University Press of America, 1982). The Buss article is found on pages 43–64.

6. Gregory Henderson, *Korea: The Politics of the Vortex* (Cambridge: Harvard University Press, 1968), 74–75.

7. Ibid., 94–96 and Cumings, *Korea's Place in the Sun,* 177–79.

8. Ibid., 81–83 and Cumings, *Korea's Place in the Sun,* 155.

9. Ibid., 85–86 and Cumings, *Korea's Place in the Sun,* 159–60.

10. Cairo Conference Declaration 1943 released on December 1, 1943, can be found at http://www.yale.edu/lawweb/avalon/wwii/cairo.htm.

11. Yalta Conference Declaration, February 1945 found at http://www.yale.edu/lawweb/Avalon/wwii/yalta.htm.

12. The Potsdam Declaration can be found at http://www.yale.edu/lawweb/avalon/decade/decade17.htm.

13. Dean Rusk (as told to Richard Rusk), *As I Saw It* (Middlesex England: Penguin Books Ltd., 1991), 124.

14. Henderson, *Korea,* 125.

15. For a thorough analysis of the Korean People's Republic, see Bruce Cumings, *The Origins of Korean War: Liberation and the Emergence of Separate Regimes 1945–1947* (Princeton: Princeton University Press, 1981), 68–100.

16. Henderson, *Korea,* 125–30.

17. Macdonald, *The Koreans,* 45–46.

18. Soviet-Anglo-American Communiqué, Moscow Conference, December 1945 available at http://www.nautilus.org/DPRKBriefing Book/agreements/CanKor_VTK_1945_12_27_soviet anglo american communique.pdf.

19. Macdonald, *The Koreans,* 49.

20. For examples, see David Rees, *Korea: The Limited War* (Baltimore: Penguin Press, 1964), 19 and David Dallin, *Soviet Foreign Policy After Stalin* (Philadelphia: J.B. Lippincott, 1961), 60.

21. Bruce Cumings, *The Origins of the Korean War,* vol. II (Princeton: Princeton University Press, 1981), 445–48.

22. Kathryn Weathersby, "Soviet Aims in Korea and the Origins of the Korean War, 1945–1950: New Evidence from the Russian Archives," The Cold War International History Project, Woodrow Wilson International Center for Scholars, Washington, DC, November 1943.

23. Ibid., 27–32. The details of Kim's visit to Moscow and his discussions with Stalin are taken from these pages.

24. Dean Acheson, *Present At the Creation: My Years in the State Department* (New York: W. W. Norton & Company, 1969), 356–58. See also Robert L. Beisner, *Dean Acheson: A Life in the Cold War* (New York: The Oxford University Press, 2006), 329–31.

25. David McCullough, *Truman* (New York: Simon and Schuster, 1992), 776–79.

26. The Security Council resolution quotes are found in Gregory Henderson, Richard Ned Lebow, and John G. Stoessinger, *Divided Nations in a Divided World* (New York: David McKay Company Inc., 1974), 54–55.

27. For casualty figures, see Macdonald, *The Koreans,* 51–52 and footnote 35 on page 65. See also Don Oberdorfer, *The Two Koreas: A Contemporary History* (New York: Basic Books, 2001), 9–10.

CHAPTER 2

Political Development in South Korea

Since independence in 1948, the ROK has progressed through six republics. The first was during the presidency of Syngman Rhee from 1948 to 1960; the second under Prime Minister Chang Myon from 1960 to 1961; the third under President Park Chung Hee from 1961 to 1972; the fourth also under Park Chung Hee from 1972 to 1979; and the fifth was during the presidency of Chun Doo Hwan from 1980 to 1988. The sixth republic has included the presidencies of four men: Roh Tae Woo from 1988 to 1993; Kim Young Sam from 1993 to 1998; Kim Dae Jung from 1998 to 2003; and Roh Moo Hyun from 2003 to the present. The two major goals of this chapter are first to trace the democratization process in South Korea from the authoritarian governments of the initial 20 years of independence to the democratic governments of today and second, to review the evolution of the security relationship between the United States and the ROK.

THE FIRST AND SECOND REPUBLICS, 1948–1961

As referenced in chapter 1, there was some concern in the State Department about Syngman Rhee before he returned to Korea in late 1945. Rhee had spent many years in the United States during the Japanese occupation of Korea and was well known for his strong anticommunist beliefs and rather inflexible nature. Whether these qualities would allow him to be a conciliatory figure in Korea during these turbulent times was an issue. Nonetheless, return to Korea he did to become the ROK's first president in August 1948. The Korean people would reelect him in 1952, 1956, and 1960. However, his presidency was marked by increasing authoritarian policies including amending the 1948 Constitution in

1956 to allow him to run for a third term. There were also widespread allegations of corruption. By the time he ran for reelection in 1960, he was 85 years old.

During the March 1960 presidential election, the Rhee government resorted to strong-armed methods to influence the outcome. After the Rhee victory, demonstrators, led primarily by students, took to the streets of Seoul and other cities. Security forces fired on the demonstrators killing more than 200 of them. The United States, which had been largely tolerant of Rhee because of Cold War considerations, expressed concern over the violence. By the end of April, the demonstrations had become so widespread that Rhee resigned and left for the United States, where he remained until his death in 1965. An interim government under Huh Chung replaced Rhee and authored an amendment to the Constitution changing the form of government from a presidential to a parliamentary system. An election for the legislature occurred in July that in turn selected Chang Myon as prime minister and Yo Po Son as the figurehead president. Thus began the second republic. Despite new political freedoms under Prime Minister Chang and his government, infighting between the supporters of the prime minister and president contributed to ineffective governance. When Prime Minister Chang called for reunification talks with North Korea, the military intervened. On May 16, 1961, Major General Park Chung Hee led a coup against the government and seized control ending the second republic.[1]

The security relationship with the United States was very important during the Rhee presidency. The historical vulnerability experienced by Korea was partly responsible for how the Rhee government viewed the American connection, but this orientation was reinforced by the realities of the immediate post–Korean War period. In October 1953, United States and ROK officials signed the MDT (Mutual Defense Treaty).[2] Article III of this treaty provides that each country agrees an external attack in the Pacific on either of their territories "would be dangerous to its own peace and safety and declares that it would act to meet the common danger in accordance with its constitutional processes." Article IV stipulates that the ROK grants to the United States the right to station land, air, and naval forces in South Korea. When the U.S. Senate ratified the MDT, it added an "understanding" that stated an American response under Article III would apply only if an external armed attack is directed at South Korea. The Senate presumably intended to ensure through this stipulation that the MDT would not require a U.S. response if the ROK launches an attack against the DPRK. The two sides completed the ratification process in November 1954, and this treaty remains in effect.

The presence of American military forces in South Korea under the provisions of the MDT has always been very significant to the ROK government and public. The pledge to come to South Korea's defense "in accordance with its constitutional processes" serves as a deterrent to North Korea, but this clause implies that the Congress would need to declare war. The presence of American Army units along the most likely invasion routes contributes to a more robust deterrent effect on North Korean calculations. The "trip-wire" nature of how these forces are deployed ensures that the United States would become immediately involved in any attack from North Korea because American forces would be engaged from the beginning of such an attack. As the years have passed since the MDT went into effect, the presence of American military forces has been at the heart of any discussions between the two allies on security issues as will become evident later in this chapter.

In 1951, the Truman administration entered into security pacts with the Philippines, Japan, Australia, and New Zealand. The Eisenhower administration negotiated the MDT with South Korea and a similar treaty with Taiwan in December 1954. By the mid-1950s, these security relationships were at the center of the American containment policy designed to keep in check Soviet and Chinese military expansion in East Asia.

THE THIRD REPUBLIC, 1961–1972

Park Chung Hee was born in 1917 and came from a poor rural environment in southern Korea. After graduating from the Taegu Teacher's College in 1937, he taught for a few years. In 1940, Japanese occupation officials selected Park to attend the Manchukuo Academy in Manchuria for a 2-year training program. After successfully completing this program, the Japanese chose Park for admission to the Tokyo Military Academy where he studied from 1942 to 1944. This was a highly selective program and only a few Koreans were allowed to participate. Beginning in 1944, Park fought in the Japanese Army against Chinese guerrilla forces in Manchuria. At the end of World War II, he returned to Korea and entered the KMA (Korean Military Academy) graduating in 1946. He then joined the fledgling military in the southern part of Korea sponsored by the United States. During a highly controversial part of his military career, Park was arrested in 1948 for allegedly participating in the Yosu rebellion, a communist-led uprising. Subsequent to being arrested and tried by a military court, he provided information to the authorities regarding others involved in the alleged rebellion. After American intervention on his behalf, Park continued his military career, fought in the Korean War, and emerged as a brigadier general. By 1961, the ROK army had promoted him to major general.[3]

In the aftermath of the successful coup in May 1961, Park formed the Supreme Council for National Reconstruction and conducted major purges of civilians and military officers who opposed his programs. Through the Supreme Council, he amended the Constitution to revert to a presidential political system. Under these new provisions, Park held presidential elections in 1963, 1967, and 1971. He won each of these elections although in 1971, Kim Dae Jung ran against him and probably would have won if this election was a fair contest.

Based at least in part on the time he spent in Japan, Park was convinced that economic growth and development were key not only to his political legitimacy but also to the future of South Korea. Accordingly, Park's economic policies were sometimes referred to as "guided capitalism" or "Korea Inc." because the government played major roles. The Economic Planning Board, the Ministry of Trade and Industry, and the Ministry of Finance were dominant agencies in directing the economy. Park followed the Japanese export-led economic model and favored largely family owned businesses known as chaebol. His government provided these chaebol with low interest loans and other advantages in return for their support of his economic model.

In the late 1960s and early 1970s, President Park began the Heavy and Chemical Industries Plan that was designed to support six strategic industries: iron and steel, shipbuilding, chemicals, electronics, nonferrous metals, and machinery. Park had both economic and political reasons for initiating this plan. He believed that the ROK needed to become an industrially advanced country mainly to compete with the DPRK. From the political perspective, Park was concerned about the reliability of the United States and wanted to do all that he could to have South Korea become as self-reliant as possible. The ROK economy also received major boosts in the 1960s from the normalization of diplomatic relations with Japan and the Park decision to support the United States war in Vietnam. When Japan and South Korea normalized relations in 1965, Japan provided an assistance package worth more than $800 million. In 1966, revenues from the war in Vietnam provided approximately 40 percent of the ROK's foreign exchange earnings. Also very important to the South Korean economic recovery from the deprivations of the Korean War were substantial American economic and military assistance programs. From 1953 to the early 1970s, the United States sent more than $6 billion in economic support and more than $7 billion in military aid to South Korea. Further, ROK exports were given special access to the American market.[4]

Despite substantial economic growth and development during President Park's first 10 years in office, he also took several actions that limited political development. The 1963 Constitution provided for an executive-driven political system with only very minor powers for the legislative and judicial branches. Furthermore, Park created the KCIA (Korean Central Intelligence Agency) that exercised extensive control over public dissent. The military also played major roles in the politics of South Korea by supporting Park against the already marginalized opposition forces.

The security relationship with the United States during the third republic was influenced by the war in Vietnam. When Park staged his coup in 1961, the Kennedy administration was caught up in the Bay of Pigs fiasco in Cuba and did not respond very effectively to developing events in Korea. Similarly, during the Johnson administration, the American president was intent on expanding the number of countries supporting the United States in Vietnam, and South Korea responded by sending two divisions to Vietnam. President Park realized there could be economic rewards from his assistance to the Johnson administration, but Park also was concerned that the United States might reduce its military presence in his country to support the buildup in Vietnam. He hoped that his decision to send Korean divisions to Vietnam would eliminate any possible American reduction of forces in the ROK. During a 1966 visit to Seoul, Vice President Hubert Humphrey strongly endorsed the continuation of American force levels in South Korea. President Johnson affirmed this commitment during a summit meeting with President Park in April 1968.[5] In addition, the Park administration benefited politically through its support of the United States in Vietnam because the Johnson administration muted its criticisms of Park's increasingly authoritarian policies at home.

The South Korean leader was particularly anxious during the 1968 summit with Johnson because North Korean infiltrators had attempted to attack his residence in Seoul early in January of that year and then seized the USS *Pueblo*, an American spy ship, in international waters the same month. Two other significant events also occurred during the third republic that influenced the security relationship. In 1966 and 1967, the United States and ROK negotiated the SOFA (Status of Forces Agreement) providing legal protections for American military forces serving in South Korea. In 1968, the two sides established the SCM (Security Consultative Meeting) process that provided for annual discussions between the American secretary of defense and Korean minister of national defense and their staffs. The SCMs have become very important fora to address and resolve national security issues between the two allies.

Soon after Richard Nixon became president in early 1969, he announced what became known as the Nixon Doctrine during a brief visit to Guam that July. While noting that the United States would remain involved in East Asia, President Nixon stressed that American allies were capable of assuming more of the responsibilities for their own defense. Specifically, Nixon intended to reduce the American ground force presence in the region in the hope that the United States would not become involved in another war in Asia.[6] In 1971, President Nixon began to reduce the number of Army forces in the ROK. Prior to this time, there were two infantry divisions in South Korea, the 7th and the 2nd Divisions. Nixon decided to redeploy the 7th Division from the ROK, and this redeployment reduced the number of American ground forces from 60,000 to 40,000. More disturbing to President Park was the realization that President Nixon made this decision after little or no consultation with the Park government. Not coincidentally, it was during this general time period of the late 1960s and early 1970s that Park made his decision to begin the Heavy and Chemical Industries Plan both to enhance the ROK economy and to begin the process of providing more of the resources needed to develop South Korea's military capabilities. Perhaps more important, he began to consider the possibility of developing a nuclear weapons program.

THE FOURTH REPUBLIC, 1972–1979

In late October 1972, President Park took a series of actions that would dramatically change South Korean politics for the next several years. He rescinded the 1963 Constitution and replaced it with what became known as the Yushin Constitution. Yushin in the Korean language translates to restoration or revitalization. He also declared martial law, prorogued the National Assembly, and arrested several political opponents. To justify his actions, Park cited the threat from North Korea and a changing international environment. The DPRK had conducted some aggressive acts against the ROK in the late 1960s such as attacking the Blue House and seizing the USS *Pueblo* both in January 1968 as referenced earlier in this chapter. As far as the international environment was concerned, President Park was upset by the United States–China rapprochement highlighted by Nixon's visit to China in February 1972 and the beginning of the American withdrawal from Vietnam. Park became even more worried about the American commitment to South Korea based on these events.

However, equally important in explaining Park's decision to initiate the Yushin Constitution were domestic events, particularly the strong showing of Kim Dae Jung in the 1971 presidential election. The new Constitution provided even more powers to the executive branch than had the 1963 Constitution. Under Yushin, the president would serve a 6-year term with no limits on the number of terms that could be served. The Constitution designated the National Conference for Unification as an electoral college that would indirectly elect the president. Obviously, Park could easily control this conference to ensure that he would remain in power for an extended period of time. Finally, the new Constitution permitted the president to appoint a significant number of members of the National Assembly that guaranteed the legislature would remain largely a rubber stamp for the executive branch. Under this system, President Park would be reelected in 1972 and 1978 without opposition.[7]

One year later, in October 1973, the Park administration attempted to settle scores with Kim Dae Jung through violence. After the declaration of martial law and the drafting of the Yushin Constitution, Kim had become even more critical of the government even though he was forced to go abroad or be arrested. While in Tokyo during August 1973, KCIA agents kidnapped Kim and brought him back to the ROK by boat. There was significant negative reaction from the United States and Japan in particular because the kidnapping took place there. Under this pressure, the Park government released Kim for a short period and then placed him under house arrest. Without this external intervention on Kim's behalf, it is very unlikely that he would have survived the trip from Japan or his initial incarceration.[8] The kidnapping of Kim Dae Jung serves as a good indicator of how repressive the Park regime had become by the mid-1970s.

Another event that would contribute to Park's more hard-line positions occurred in August 1974 when Mun Se Kwang, a Korean living in Japan, attempted to assassinate the ROK president as he was making a speech in Seoul. Mun's shot missed Park but killed Yook Young Soo, Park's wife, who was sitting behind him on the stage. One of the effects of her death was that President Park became increasingly isolated without her moderating influence. Another consequence was that Park Keun Hye, the president's eldest daughter, took over some of her mother's responsibilities and would become an important political figure in her own right as a possible presidential candidate leading up to the 2007 election.

North Korea also contributed to growing tensions on the Korean peninsula in the mid-1970s. In late 1974, South Korean military units patrolling near the DMZ discovered a North Korean tunnel that had been dug deep beneath the DMZ into South Korean territory. In February 1975, ROK soldiers found a second tunnel amid speculation that there were probably several more. Another concern about the DPRK's intentions related to the defense budget that Kim Il Sung allocated to his military as well as the expanding size and technological capabilities of the KPA (Korean People's Army) by mid-decade. By 1974, North Korea was producing large quantities of field artillery, rocket launchers, armored personnel carriers, main battle tanks, and surface to air missiles. Further, Kim Il Sung proved himself to be very adept at playing the Soviets against the Chinese so that the two North Korean allies would compete to provide the DPRK with modern weapon systems. Finally, the KPA expanded to more than 400,000 soldiers which was the fourth largest army in the world at that time.

One of the most troubling DPRK actions took place in August 1976 when North Korean troops entered the DMZ and engaged a combined South Korean and American work detail involved with trimming a tree in the DMZ that was blocking an observation post. Two American officers were beaten to death by the North Koreans and several ROK military were injured. The Ford administration responded to what became known as the ax murders with a massive show of military force in and near the Korean peninsula. After a few days of extreme tension, the DPRK expressed some regret over the incident, and the tensions subsided somewhat.[9]

President Park responded to the challenges from the increased North Korean threat and from what he perceived as flagging support in the United States, particularly in the American Congress, in a number of ways. First, he attempted to influence Congress through buying the support of some influential members of the legislative branch. This vote buying scheme became known as the Koreagate Scandal in the mid-1970s.[10] Second, the ROK expanded its own military spending and weapons development. Between 1975 and 1979, President Park quadrupled the defense budget. In absolute terms, the ROK was spending more on defense by the end of the 1970s than was the DPRK although North Korea's defense share of its GNP was much higher than in South Korea. Third and most controversial was the South Korean initiative to develop nuclear weapons. The Nixon administration's policy to withdraw the 7th Infantry Division influenced Park's decision, and his government began working with France in 1972 to acquire a plutonium reprocessing plant. The United States was adamantly opposed to a South Korean nuclear weapons program primarily because of concerns over nuclear proliferation. The Ford administration placed increased pressure on both the ROK and France to terminate this program. Finally in December 1975, the United States threatened to end the bilateral security relationship if South Korea continued this initiative. Faced with this option, President Park complied with the American demand, and the crisis passed.[11]

The presidency of Park Chung Hee ended on October 26, 1979, when Kim Jae Kyu, the director of the KCIA, assassinated Park during a dinner on the grounds of the Blue House. In the months leading up to the assassination, President Park was under increasing pressure because there was more overt political opposition to his dictatorial style and policies. In addition, the economy was not performing as well as it had previously primarily because of the increasing oil prices caused by the Iranian revolution and its aftermath. Kim's motives for assassinating Park remain somewhat nebulous because he had been a close and trusted associate for many years. It is inconceivable that Park would have appointed him to such an important position if he did not have trust in Kim. At his trial, Kim indicated he killed the president because Park had become increasingly autocratic under the Yushin Constitution. Whatever his motives, Kim's act ended the 18-year reign of Park Chung Hee unexpectedly. Prime Minister Choi Kyu Ha became acting president upon Park's death although events were underway that would profoundly influence the political dynamics in South Korea.[12]

The security situation between the United States and ROK during the second half of the Park era was contentious basically because of the Park's abortive nuclear weapons aspirations and President Jimmy Carter's plans to remove most of the remaining American ground forces from South Korea. President Ford and Secretary of State Henry Kissinger had attempted to assuage Park's concerns about American credibility after President Nixon was forced to resign because of the Watergate scandal. In July 1976, Secretary Kissinger gave a speech in Seattle pledging that the United States would not withdraw unilaterally any additional forces from the ROK. The unification of Vietnam under North Vietnamese control despite American efforts to prevent this outcome caused major credibility issues, and the Ford administration did not want to make matters worse by any further troop reductions or withdrawals in Asia.[13]

During the Carter administration, relations between the ROK and United States sank to one of the lowest levels since the end of the Korean War because of fundamental differences about the importance of human rights and the proper level of American forces in the ROK. As a candidate in 1976, Jimmy Carter pledged to remove U.S. ground forces from South Korea, but because he was viewed as a long shot candidate, not many national security experts or members of the Park government paid much attention. That inattention changed after he won the 1976 election. Soon after taking office, President Carter announced his decision to remove the 2nd Infantry Division from the ROK over a 5-year period. He argued that South Korea had the necessary capabilities to meet the requirements for its own defense if the American withdrawal was spread over a few years. Carter intended to retain U.S. Air Force units in South Korea and stated that the MDT would remain in effect. In May 1977, the White House issued Presidential Directive 12 ordering the Departments of Defense and State to implement the Carter withdrawal plan. Although not publicly stated at the time, President Carter's strong stance in support of human rights influenced his troop decision and his overall relationship with President Park. Carter was not impressed by the human rights situation in South Korea under the Yushin Constitution and Park's autocratic policies. He decided to send a strong signal of his displeasure, and the withdrawal of military forces provided the opportunity to do so.

From the South Korean perspective, the Carter policy was very unpopular among many Koreans because of the deterrent value provided by American ground forces. Perhaps at least as important was the fact that President Carter made his decision unilaterally with no consultation with his Korean allies much as President Nixon had done in the early 1970s. For Park, this was just another incident reinforcing his concerns about the American commitment to defend South Korea.[14]

An American intelligence reassessment of the balance of forces on the Korean peninsula in 1979 cast doubts on the troop withdrawal plan. This reassessment emphasized that the DPRK's military capabilities were expanding rapidly and that Kim Il Sung continued to move many of his military units closer to the DMZ. Based on this reassessment plus strong domestic and international criticism of Carter's withdrawal plan, the president announced that he was holding his plan in abeyance until at least 1981. Carter visited Park in Seoul during the summer of 1979, and this meeting between the two leaders did not go well. In fact, one American diplomat present described it "as terrible a bilateral meeting between treaty allies as you can have."[15] When all was said and done, the 2nd Infantry Division remained in the ROK, but the relationship between the two allies suffered. In just a few months after the Carter–Park summit, President Park would be dead, and in little more than a year, President Carter would lose his bid for reelection.

Despite the problems in the security relationship during the 1970s, two developments occurred that were much more positive. First, in 1976, the United States and ROK conducted the first Team Spirit annual military exercise. Team Spirit was a large field exercise conducted in the ROK that enhanced the deterrent effect of the United States presence by proving that the Americans could reinforce their forces rapidly if necessary. Second, the two allies formed the CFC (Combined Forces Command) in November 1978. The primary mission of CFC remains to integrate the American and South Korean forces into an effective warfigthing command.

THE FIFTH REPUBLIC, 1980–1988

After the assassination of President Park Chung Hee in late October 1979, Prime Minister Choi Kyu Ha became acting president under the provisions of the Yushin Constitution. In early December, the National Conference for Unification elected him president. As stated previously, President Park expanded executive powers substantially over his 18 years in office. There was no question that he was the dominant political force in South Korea during his presidency. President Choi on the other hand was not a dominant political figure and had a weak political base of support. The ROK military had gained much political power and influence as a major pillar of Park's regime, and there were fundamental concerns among many South Koreans as to how the military would respond to the new president and the changed political conditions as 1979 drew to a close.

Elements of the ROK Army answered this question on December 12, in what became known as the "12/12 incident" or "the night of the generals." These events occurred under the leadership of Major General Chun Doo Hwan, who was the commanding general of the Defense Security Command. In this position, Chun was responsible for the investigation of the Park assassination. Perhaps more important, Chun's actions represented a struggle for control within the ROK Army because Chun's initial efforts confronted the Army leadership. General Chun and several of his associates were graduates of the KMA's eleventh class. They had graduated from the KMA in 1955 and were the first class to complete a 4-year course of instruction after the Korean War. Members of this class formed a secret organization named Hanahoe (one group in Korean) in the 1960s, and it was largely members of this group who launched the coup in December 1979.

General Chung Seung Hwa was the Army chief of staff at this time, and there was some speculation that he was about ready to remove Chun as part of the process of reassigning him to a less powerful position. In any event, Chun struck first and arrested General Chung and several other Army leaders. Roh Tae Woo, another member of the KMA eleventh class, assisted Chun in his efforts to remove Chung from his position. Chun then appointed Roh to head the Capital Security Command resulting in Chun and Roh consolidating their power in the two most important ROK Army commands. In early 1980, Chun Doo Hwan became acting director of the KCIA, a move that further strengthened his power base.[16] American reactions to the events in South Korea were somewhat muted partly because the Carter administration was focusing on the Iranian hostage crisis that began in November 1979. There is an interesting parallel here between the Kennedy administration's concentration on the Bay of Pigs crisis in Cuba when Park Chung Hee seized power in 1961 and the Carter administration's reaction to Chun's power grab in late 1979 and early 1980.

After the Park assassination, major demonstrations began across South Korea, especially in Seoul, demanding a more democratic political process and specifically the direct election of the president. Students took the lead in many of these demonstrations, but they were joined by labor and religious groups protesting not only political repression but problems with the South Korean economy too. These demonstrations became more widespread in April and May 1980 not only geographically but also in the breadth of those participating. In mid-May, the Choi government declared martial law, closed the National Assembly, and imposed strict press censorship.

The authorities also arrested the major opposition leaders including Kim Young Sam, Kim Jong Pil, and Kim Dae Jung, the famous "three Kims" in South Korean politics. Kim Dae Jung had just been released following the Park assassination from the house arrest imposed after his kidnapping in 1973. His arrest provided the impetus for increased demonstrations in the two Cholla provinces in the southwest part of the country, Kim's home territory. Kwangju is the largest city in this region and was the scene for one of the most controversial events in ROK history. In response to the antigovernment demonstrations, President Choi, under pressure from Chun Doo Hwan and the ROK Army who argued that North Korea was behind these demonstrations, sent in military forces to confront the demonstrators and restore order.

This response resulted in the deaths of 240 demonstrators according to official statistics, but the opposition has always maintained that the number killed was far higher. Whatever the actual casualty count, the "Kwangju massacre" as the event became known convinced many South Koreans that Chun Doo Hwan and his associates could not be trusted. The repression associated with this response also raised serious questions about American culpability in supporting the ROK government. The National Security Council met in Washington during the May demonstrations and urged the Choi government to use moderation, but it did not specifically rule out the use of force to end the demonstrations. For many ROK citizens, this American reaction was too timid and became the source of increasing anti-Americanism. As the political unrest continued through the summer of 1980, President Choi decided to resign his office in early August stating that he was taking responsibility for the military's actions in Kwangju. On August 27, the National Conference for Reunification elected Chun Doo Hwan as president.[17]

Shortly after Chun's "election," Ronald Reagan won the American presidential race in November 1980 defeating Jimmy Carter. Just before Reagan's election,

Kim Dae Jung was tried by a military court in Seoul with one of the charges against him including the plotting of the Kwangju uprising. The military court convicted him and sentenced Kim to death in September 1980. This conviction presented a problem for the new American administration. The solution involved an invitation to President Chun to visit Reagan in the White House. In return, Chun commuted Kim's sentence to life in prison, and he lifted martial law. In early February 1981, Chun traveled to Washington and received a warm welcome from Reagan. This visit and reception contributed to increased political legitimacy for Chun with his supporters, but also hardened the opposition to Chun among other South Koreans. It contributed to increased anti-American sentiment as well. In December 1982, the Korean government released Kim Dae Jung and allowed him to go into exile in the United States.[18]

Early in the Chun presidency, the ROK was confronted with two major crises. In September 1983, KAL (Korean Airlines) flight 007 disappeared while flying from New York to Seoul with a refueling stop in Alaska. For reasons that remain unclear, the crew on this flight flew into Soviet airspace after the refueling stop, and a Soviet fighter shot the plane down killing all 269 people onboard. Later in 1993, after the collapse of the Soviet Union, Russian officials released the official records that indicated KAL 007 had strayed 360 miles off course because of navigational errors. A Soviet air defense commander decided to shoot it down believing erroneously that the plane was conducting a spy mission. This event caused a further deterioration in United States–Soviet relations early in the Reagan administration, and also interrupted the very early stages of Soviet–ROK trade contacts.

In October 1983, the second event occurred and was even more devastating to the South Korean government. President Chun Doo Hwan accepted an invitation for a state visit to Rangoon, Burma and took with him some of his most senior cabinet officials and advisers. While waiting for a ceremony at Burma's Martyr's Mausoleum at the National Cemetery, three North Korean agents detonated a bomb planted in the roof of the mausoleum killing a total of seventeen Koreans including cabinet ministers, two presidential advisers, and the ROK ambassador to Burma. President Chun was delayed in Rangoon traffic that no doubt saved his life. Among those killed were Foreign Minister Lee Bum Suk, Presidential Secretary General Hahm Pyong Choon, and Presidential Secretary Kim Jae Ik, three of Chun's closest advisers. Burmese officials quickly arrested the North Koreans responsible for the attack, and one of them made a full confession.[19] President Chun was deprived of valued senior advisers, and the perceived ramifications of the KAL shoot down and the bombing in Burma convinced him to further circle the wagons at home by coming down even harder on political dissent.

During the first half of the Chun presidency to the middle of the 1980s, the Korean economy was not particularly strong. Part of the explanation for these problems involved corruption and what became known as crony capitalism. Chun and his close associates formed a number of foundations that basically were used to collect forced donations from the major chaebols. The Ilhae Foundation was one of the largest of these foundations, and the funds collected allowed the Chun government to spend money on a variety of projects with little or no oversight and to fatten their own bank accounts. Another economic problem was the increased ROK foreign debt that doubled between 1980 and 1984 as the government continued to spend large sums in support of the heavy industrial projects begun under Park Chung Hee. Finally, the South Korean currency, the won, was loosely pegged to the American dollar. As the dollar strengthened in the 1980s, particularly against the Japanese yen, Korean exports became more expensive, and this problem with export growth further reduced economic performance.

The economy received a major boost in September 1985 when what became known as the Plaza Accords, named after the hotel in New York where the negotiations occurred, came into effect. In this economic agreement among the five major economic powers, the parties agreed to depreciate the dollar to make U.S. exports more competitive. Since the won was tied to the dollar, ROK exports benefited too as evidenced most dramatically with automobiles, semiconductors, consumer electronics, ships, and steel leading the way. Between 1985 and 1988, Korean exports doubled providing a major stimulus to the ROK economy.[20]

As the economy began to improve, more South Koreans questioned why the political system remained so repressive. In 1981, the IOC (International Olympic Committee) made a decision that would have profound effects on political reforms in the ROK. During the presidency of Park Chung Hee, the ROK government determined to compete for the right to host the 1988 Summer Olympics. In September 1981, the IOC awarded the games to Seoul over Nagoya, Japan, the second place city. To win the competition to host the games was a tremendous achievement for South Korea made even sweeter because of winning against Japan. From the political perspective, the Olympics proved very significant because preparing to host the games focused international attention on South Korea, and the Chun government had to be cautious how it responded to domestic pressure for political liberalization. A repeat of the Kwangju incident would most likely have resulted in the IOC rescinding its decision for Seoul to host the 1988 Olympics.

Another important factor favoring democratization was that President Chun was well aware that he lacked political legitimacy with many of his countrymen because of how he had come to power. In an effort to mitigate this lack of legitimacy, he amended the Constitution when he came into office so that the president could only serve one 7-year term. By so doing, Chun indicated his intent to have a peaceful transfer of power when his term ended. Student-led demonstrations increased in number and frequency of occurrence in the spring of 1987. One of the major demands was that the indirect election of the president must be replaced by direct elections. Chun resisted these demands, and in June 1987, he announced that the ruling Democratic Justice Party had nominated Roh Tae Woo, his KMA classmate and longtime supporter, to run for president. Chun's decision infuriated the opposition, and the number and scope of demonstrations increased. This period of time became known as the "June resistance" in the ROK, and concerns increased that the military was likely to intervene as it had in 1961 and 1979.

In an effort to defuse the increasing tension, Roh Tae Woo appealed to the military not to become involved in the political process. In late June 1987, Roh announced an 8-point declaration that shocked his country. In this declaration, he accepted that the Constitution should be amended to provide for the direct election of the president. Roh also called for a more open political system to include press freedom, more latitude for educational institutions, the development of opposition political parties, and more regional autonomy. Finally, Roh argued that Kim Dae Jung should be given amnesty and have his civil rights restored so that he could return to South Korea and compete in the 1987 presidential election if he chose to do so. After his declaration became public, Roh met with Chun and convinced him to accept its provisions[21]

In the fall of 1987, the ROK National Assembly amended the Constitution. Article 41 now provides for the direct election of the National Assembly and Article 67 similarly mandates the direct election of the president with the president limited to one 5-year term in office. Article 128 stipulates that the Constitution can not be amended to allow the sitting president to serve another term.[22] These constitutional provisions went into effect by the time the December 1987 presidential election took place. Roh Tae Woo ran as the Democratic Justice Party's candidate. However, the two major opposition candidates, Kim Young Sam and Kim Dae Jung, were unable to reach a compromise on which of them should be the primary candidate running against Roh. Consequently, they both ran and split the opposition vote. The final outcome of the first direct presidential election since 1971 was that Roh Tae Woo was elected with 36 percent of the vote; Kim Young Sam received 28 percent, and Kim Dae Jung 27 percent.[23] The fifth republic had come to its end.

The national security relationship between the United States and the ROK improved significantly during the Chun–Reagan presidencies. As noted, President Chun was one of the first foreign leaders to visit the White House after Reagan became president. In early February 1981, Reagan and Chun released a joint communiqué that clearly stated the continuing importance of the 1954 MDT. Further, this communiqué stated that President Reagan assured President Chun that the United States had no plans to withdraw American ground combat forces from South Korea.[24] In 1983, Reagan visited Chun in Seoul and traveled to the Joint Security Area in the DMZ. He again reiterated that U.S. military forces would remain in the ROK. In the May 1985 SCM, the communiqué related that the ROK was "pivotal" to peace and stability in Northeast Asia and "vital" to the security of the United States.[25]

THE SIXTH REPUBLIC, 1988–PRESENT

Roh Tae Woo, 1988–1993

Roh Tae Woo focused much of his attention during his presidency on three major issues: the hosting of the 1988 Olympics; the establishment of diplomatic relations with several Eastern European countries, the Soviet Union, and China under his Nordpolitik program; and developing relations with North Korea. This section addresses the first two of these initiatives with ROK–DPRK relations considered in chapter 6. Winning the right to host the Olympics was a source of great pride for the people of South Korea. Much as the 1964 Olympics had showcased Japan's recovery from World War II, the 1988 Games provided South Korea with the opportunity to publicize its economic prowess and also to make some highly important national security initiatives. There is no question that the 1988 Olympics held in Seoul represented one of the most important accomplishments of modern Korean history.

The DPRK was not happy about the IOC's selection of the ROK to host the Olympics. After the decision was announced in 1981, North Korea began a series of efforts either to convince its allies not to attend the Games or to cohost the Olympics with South Korea. Since the Soviet Union had boycotted the 1984 Games in Los Angeles, there was no way that the USSR was not going to participate in 1988. Although there were some negotiations between the two Koreas and the IOC regarding sharing some of the events, no successful compromise was reached, and in August 1987, the IOC announced that all events would be held in the ROK.

The DPRK responded aggressively to this decision, and in November 1987 dispatched two of its agents to destroy a KAL aircraft in flight. On November 29, KAL flight 858 was flying from Baghdad to Seoul with a stop in Abu Dhabi. A powerful bomb destroyed this aircraft after leaving Abu Dhabi killing all 115 people onboard. The two North Korean agents were later arrested in Bahrain where the older of the two committed suicide. Bahrain officials prevented the younger agent, Kim Hyun Hui, from the same fate. She was extradited to South Korea and, after several days of interrogation, admitted to her part in the crime. Later, she received a presidential pardon and now lives in Seoul. The North Korean intent in destroying the KAL aircraft apparently was to convince those countries planning to attend the Olympics that it was too dangerous to do so. This effort failed, and athletes from 161 countries participated beginning in September 1988, the largest Olympic Games to that point. The Chinese, Soviets, and several countries from Eastern Europe sent teams which further infuriated the North Koreans. As a result of the destruction of the KAL airliner, the United States placed the DPRK on the State Department's list of state-sponsors of terrorists where it still remains.[26]

In July 1988, President Roh made a very important speech entitled "A Single National Community; Special Declaration in the Interest of National Self-Respect, Unification, and Prosperity."[27] Roh began this speech by addressing "my sixty million compatriots" a clear indication that he was speaking to Koreans on both sides of the 38th parallel. He continued by citing several changes that were occurring in the international environment in the late 1980s that provided opportunities for new policy initiatives. Specifically, he supported increased visits between North and South Koreans, the opening of trade relations between the two countries, and the establishment of trade contacts between the DPRK and several allies of South Korea. He closed his speech by clearly stating that his government was willing to cooperate with North Korea in establishing diplomatic relations with the United States and Japan. Similarly, Roh indicated that the ROK would seek to improve its relations with the Soviet Union, China, and other socialist countries.

The ROK actually began efforts to improve relations with the Soviets and Chinese during the presidency of Chun Doo Hwan and named this policy Nordpolitik after the West German policy of Ostpolitik. Both China and the USSR became more receptive to these efforts after Deng Xiaoping and Mikhail Gorbachev came to power respectively. Deng was intent on pursuing economic reforms, and Gorbachev was open to "new thinking" in foreign policy. The first South Korean successes with Nordpolitik occurred in Eastern Europe. In late 1984, Kim Woo Choong, the chairman of Daewoo Group, visited Budapest, Hungary to explore business options. By 1987, Hungary and the ROK established trade offices in each capital. As trade relations expanded, South Korea also became an important source of foreign aid and investment in Hungary. Just before the opening of the 1988 Olympics, the two countries announced plans to establish diplomatic relations and this occurred in February 1989.

Responding to another of Roh's Nordpolitik goals, relations between the United States and North Korea began to improve somewhat when the Reagan administration approved a policy allowing for more nonofficial travel between the two countries, the easing of financial regulations on Americans traveling to North Korea, and the commercial export of humanitarian goods such as food and medicines. Perhaps even more important, President Reagan gave permission for substantive discussions between North Korean and American officials to occur at neutral locations. In 1988, direct channels were established, and between December 1988 and September 1993, more than thirty meetings between American and North Korea diplomats took place.[28]

The primary incentive for the Soviet Union to improve relations with the ROK was financial. Gorbachev was fully aware that the Soviet economy was in deep trouble by the late 1980s, and he was looking for new sources of trade, aid, and investment. The Soviet participation in the 1988 Olympics was important in convincing Gorbachev that South Korea had something to offer. In January 1989, Chung Ju Yung, the chairman of Hyundai, visited the USSR much as Kim Woo Choong had done in Hungary a few years earlier. Chung and his Soviet counterparts reached an agreement on business cooperation. Shortly after this visit, the two countries agreed to establish unofficial trade offices in Moscow and Seoul. In May 1990, Anatoly Dobrynin, the former Soviet ambassador to the United States, visited South Korea as a Gorbachev emissary. He informed President Roh that Gorbachev was willing to meet Roh preferably in a neutral location. The George H. W. Bush administration assisted with the necessary arrangements, and in early June 1990, Gorbachev and Roh met in San Francisco. Formal diplomatic relations between the Soviet Union and South Korea were established on September 30, 1990. The ROK promised to provide $3 billion to the Soviets during negotiations that accompanied the establishment of relations. By the time the Soviet Union collapsed in December 1991, the ROK had provided about half of that amount.[29]

Trade between China and the ROK increased significantly in the late 1980s from $1.2 billion in 1985 to $3.2 billion in 1989, and in October 1990, the two countries set up trade offices. In addition to the expanding economic relationship, China also saw political advantages in that the ROK still maintained diplomatic relations with Taiwan. It was Chinese policy to force countries to make a choice between the mainland or Taiwan if diplomatic relations came to fruition. Chinese officials also decided to no longer object to both Koreas joining the United Nations. Previously, China had opposed such a move because of North Korean opposition. Consequently, in September 1991, both the ROK and DPRK became UN members and the UN then provided another venue for ROK–China diplomatic contacts. As Deng Xiaoping announced his intentions to open further China's economy during his travels in south China in early 1991, South Korea became even more attractive as a source of trade, aid, and investment. In August 1992, South Korea broke diplomatic relations with Taiwan and established relations with Beijing.[30] In a remarkably short period of time, Roh Tae Woo's Nordpolitik strategy had achieved almost unimaginable successes in establishing relations with the Soviet Union, China, and most of the Eastern European countries. These diplomatic gains were seen as major defeats for North Korea. How the DPRK responded to some of these events will be addressed in chapter 3.

Regarding the security relationship with the United States, there was continued progress between the Roh and Bush administrations. As the Cold War came to a close, the United States reevaluated its security policy in East Asia and other geographical regions. The Pentagon published a report entitled "A Strategic Framework for the Asia Pacific Rim: Looking Toward the 21st Century" in 1990.[31]

In addressing Korean issues, this document recommended a three-phased restructuring of American military forces totaling approximately 7,000 troops over several years. This report also established certain burden sharing requirements for both countries particularly involving base relocation costs. In September 1991, Secretary of Defense Dick Cheney attended the annual SCM in Seoul. During this meeting, Cheney announced that the proposed troop redeployment would be held in abeyance because of growing concerns that North Korea may be involved with a nuclear weapons program. On burden sharing, Cheney and his ROK counterpart agreed that the ROK would increase its host nation support from $150 million to $180 million in 1992.[32] Finally, President Bush announced in September 1991 that the United States was withdrawing all of its land- and sea-based tactical nuclear weapons worldwide. In the case of the ROK, it was speculated that there were about 100 American nuclear warheads there at that time.[33]

The major point here is that the ROK by the early 1990s was much more sanguine about changes in the security relationship with the United States than in previous eras because it was in a better position to provide for its own defense against North Korea. In addition, South Korean confidence was enhanced by the success of its Nordpolitik foreign policy in reducing the threat by establishing relations with North Korea's major allies. Finally, the Bush administration consulted with its ally so that when changes in policy were necessary, those changes occurred in a mutually acceptable manner as indicated by the agreement to rescind the troop reduction decision during Cheney's visit.

Kim Young Sam, 1993–1998

In January 1990, the ruling Democratic Justice Party joined with Kim Young Sam's Reunification Democratic Party and Kim Jong Pil's Democratic Republican Party to form the DLP (Democratic Liberal Party). This combined party was thus able to exercise majority control in the National Assembly during the last year of Roh Tae Woo's presidency. In May 1992, the DLP selected Kim Young Sam as its nominee for the presidential election scheduled for that December. In this election, the Korean people elected Kim with 42 percent of the popular vote. Kim Dae Jung came in second with 34 percent and Chung Ju Yung was a distant third with 16 percent. With these results, Kim Young Sam became the first truly civilian president since Park Chung Hee's coup in 1961. Kim was a veteran politician who had served nine terms in the National Assembly and had been a leading critic of the Park and Chun governments.

Once he became president, Kim set out to establish civilian control over the military. He removed many of the senior military officers who had been involved with the previous regimes and disbanded the Hanahoe organization. Kim restructured the Agency for National Security Planning, the former KCIA, so that it would be more accountable. President Kim also made fighting corruption one of his major domestic priorities. Early in his presidency, he authored a presidential decree banning the use of anonymous bank accounts and required that all accounts bear the true names of the owners. The main intent of this decree, which later became law, was to break the collusion between business and government and to address a major problem of tax evasion.[34]

In December 1995, the National Assembly enacted a special law permitting the prosecution of former presidents Chun and Roh as well as other military leaders for their involvement in the 1980 Kwangju massacre. The two presidents also were charged with establishing huge political slush funds and bribing/extorting leading business leaders to contribute to these funds. The trial of Chun and Roh occurred in the summer of 1996. The three judge court found them guilty of mutiny, treason, and corruption. Chun was sentenced to death and Roh to 22.5 years in prison. In late 1996, the Seoul High Court reduced Chun's sentence to life in prison and Roh's sentence to 17 years. As part of the Christmas pardon tradition in the ROK, President Kim pardoned Chun and Roh in December 1997 just before he left office.[35] Nonetheless, Kim's efforts to establish a true name banking system and hold government officials, including former presidents, accountable for their actions were viewed as important policies in the attempt to reign in corruption in South Korea.

The Asian financial crisis struck the ROK at the very end of Kim Young Sam's presidency. The South Korean won had begun to fall in comparison with the American dollar in October 1997, and the Korean Stock Exchange went into a downward spiral. Part of the reason for these difficulties was that during the 1990s, the Korean economy became more susceptible to external shocks. There were two primary contributing factors to this vulnerability. First was the short-term oriented foreign debt and a shortage of foreign exchange reserves. Once the won came under attack, the ROK did not have the reserves sufficient to protect its currency from further depreciation. Second was the ROK's highly leveraged corporate structure. The chaebols continued to expand their operations frequently into product lines where they did not enjoy comparative advantage. To finance many of these expansions, the chaebols became more dependent on debt financed growth as evidenced by increased borrowing from local banks. As the economic crisis in Korea deepened, a series of corporate bankruptcies occurred even among the major chaebols such as Hanbo, Kia, and Yuwon. These bankruptcies then rippled through the ROK financial sector as more and more banks were confronted with nonperforming loans.

In November 1997, President Kim sought assistance from the IMF (International Monetary Fund). The IMF responded in December with a $57 billion loan, the largest loan the IMF had ever given at that time. To have to apply to the IMF for a bailout loan was extremely embarrassing to the ROK government and the Korean people. The IMF attached conditions that South Korea had to accept included implementing a much more disciplined financial and monetary system, restructuring its financial institutions, establishing more control over its labor force, and opening up its markets to foreign competition. Finally, the chaebols had to accept more transparency and accountability in their policies.[36]

Security issues during the Kim presidency were dominated by the North Korean nuclear weapons program that will be addressed in chapter 4. However, there were other issues in play. In July 1993, President Bill Clinton introduced his Pacific Community concept in a speech before the National Assembly in Seoul. Among the priorities for this community, President Clinton included the continuation of the American military commitment to East Asia. Regarding the ROK specifically, he stated that "our troops will stay here as long as the Korean people want and need us here."[37] As the nuclear crisis became more threatening in 1993 and 1994, the United States and South Korea modified Operations Plan 5027. This war plan had been in effect for several years, but the changes introduced during this period of crisis provided for a massive counterattack on the DPRK if the Kim regime launched an invasion. The primary goals were to destroy Pyongyang and other North Korean cities and then invade the DPRK. The removal of the North Korean government and reunification of Korea would follow according to this plan.[38]

Another important decision occurred during the 1994 SCM held in Washington during early October. The two allies stated that the ROK was "assuming the lead role in the defense of the peninsula." Further, the defense officials announced that on December 1, 1994, operational control of ROK military forces during peacetime would switch to South Korean authorities from the CFC. Operational control of ROK forces in wartime would remain with the commander of CFC, an American general.[39] Finally, in 1998, the Pentagon published "The United States Security Strategy for the East Asia Pacific Region." In this document, the Department of Defense pledged to keep American military forces in East Asia at approximately the 100,000 level and to maintain its bilateral alliances including that with the ROK. The report identified the DPRK's conventional forces and WMD (weapons of mass destruction) as being major concerns and promised the CFC would be maintained as an effective deterrent against North Korea.[40]

Kim Dae Jung, 1998–2003

There is no question that Kim Dae Jung is one of the signature political survivors of the twentieth century. He ran for president on three separate occasions in 1971, 1987, and 1992 before his successful campaign in 1997. Perhaps more important, Kim was probably the most important opposition political leader in South Korea fighting for increased political liberalization during the Park and Chun administrations. He almost paid the ultimate price on two occasions for his efforts against these regimes. After his defeat by Kim Young Sam in 1992,

Kim Dae Jung "retired" from active politics. However, by 1995, he had changed his mind and formed a new political party named the NCNP (National Congress for New Politics) and was its presidential candidate in 1997. Also in 1995, President Kim Young Sam changed the name of the DLP to the New Korea Party. After the election for the National Assembly in 1996, the New Korea Party expanded to include more independents and opposition party members. With this expanded membership, the party leadership once again changed the party's name to the GNP (Grand National Party). In the December 1997 presidential election, the GNP's candidate was Lee Hoi Chang, but one of the party leaders, Rhee In Je, decided to run as a third candidate. With three major candidates in the race, Kim Dae Jung was elected with 40.3 percent of the vote while Lee Hoi Chang came in second place with 38.7 percent and Rhee In Je took third with 20 percent.[41]

On the domestic scene, President Kim confronted major problems associated with the Asian economic crisis. Kim Young Sam had begun to implement the essential reforms, but his administration ended soon after the crisis began. The IMF bailout of $57 billion came with some specific strings attached as mentioned previously. Many of these reforms were controversial, and President Kim had difficulties convincing the National Assembly to pass the necessary legislation because he did not have a majority in the legislature. In the April 2000 National Assembly elections, his party, now renamed the MDP (Millennium Democratic Party), received only 115 of the 273 seats while the GNP won 133 seats.[42] Despite these difficulties, the ROK made remarkable headway in correcting some of the most serious economic problems and was able to repay the IMF loan in 2001, earlier than required.

Kim Dae Jung's presidency is perhaps most noted for his Sunshine Policy toward North Korea and the related inter-Korean summit between President Kim and North Korean leader Kim Jong Il that occurred in Pyongyang during June 2000. The sunshine name came from an Aesop fable in which the wind and the sun competed to see which could be more effective in convincing a man to remove his coat. When the wind blew, the man pulled his coat tighter, but when the sun came out, the man removed his coat. For Kim Dae Jung, he intended his Sunshine Policy to result in improved relations between the two Koreas. In his February 1998 inaugural address, he outlined the major points that came to identify his policy. First, there would be no ROK toleration of North Korean armed provocations. Second, the ROK had no intentions to absorb the DPRK as had occurred earlier with German reunification. Third, South Korea would take active steps to promote reconciliation and cooperation between the two Koreas.[43] In essence, President Kim was implying that his administration would separate politics from economics regarding relations with the DPRK in that economic contacts would not be held hostage to political issues. It was also apparent the Kim Dae Jung had been influenced by

Roh Tae Woo's Nordpolitik policies with the Sunshine Policy representing an evolution of Roh's earlier initiatives. After President Kim's inaugural address, South Korean business leaders began to look for opportunities to invest in North Korea.

During March 2000, Kim Dae Jung visited several European countries. While in Berlin, he indicated his support for North–South Korean government to government talks. He related the ROK's willingness to support the DPRK's infrastructure development and to provide food assistance. Kim also promised to encourage South Korean business leaders to expand their investments in North Korea. North and South Korean emissaries met in Shanghai later in the spring to begin to work out details for a summit meeting between Kim Dae Jung and Kim Jong Il. In April, just days before the National Assembly elections, the two sides announced the summit would occur in Pyongyang during the middle of June. Kim Dae Jung sent Lim Dong Won, the director of the NIS (National Intelligence Service), on a secret mission to North Korea. Lim was one of Kim's closest confidants on North Korean issues, but it was unclear when he left Seoul whether Kim Jong Il would meet with him. He did and the two conferred for more than 4 hours. In his report to the South Korean president, Lim stated that Kim Jong Il was a decisive leader and showed a certain pragmatic sense along with an open mind. The way was now clear for the summit meeting.[44]

Kim Dae Jung and Kim Jong Il met for 3 days in Pyongyang from June 13 to 15, 2000. At the conclusion of the summit, the two leaders released a joint declaration. This declaration made clear that Korean reunification was a subject to be resolved by the Korean people "who are the masters of the country." It called on both countries to address humanitarian issues such as divided families through exchange visits and other contacts. Both countries pledged to enhance mutual trust by cooperating on economic projects along with other efforts in the civic, cultural, sports, health, and environmental fields. At the end of the declaration, Kim Dae Jung invited Kim Jong Il to visit Seoul, and Kim promised to do so "at an appropriate time."[45]

The summit meeting and the joint declaration remain extremely important in the development of inter-Korean relations, especially South Korean perceptions of North Korea. First, Kim Jong Il was no longer viewed as some sort of lunatic leader by many in the ROK, but rather as a more pragmatic and thoughtful figure. Kim Jong Il look alikes suddenly appeared all over the ROK. Second and perhaps more important, South Koreans began to see their compatriots north of the 38th parallel as poor cousins desperately in need of economic and food assistance. Threat perceptions started to change in that many ROK citizens became convinced that North Korea was not likely to invade the ROK again or use its military might to attack Seoul. This fundamental change in threat perceptions is not only important for effects on inter-Korean relations but also for the bilateral security ties between the ROK and United States as will be discussed in chapter 6. For his participation in the Korean summit as well as his long years campaigning for democracy in the ROK, Kim Dae Jung won the Nobel Peace Prize in 2000. North Korea was busy on the diplomatic front too and established diplomatic relations with Italy, Australia, the Philippines, Great Britain, Holland, Belgium, Canada, Spain, and Germany. Although the Sunshine Policy remains controversial in South Korea, primarily over questions of North Korean reciprocity (e.g., Kim Jong Il has not visited the ROK as he promised), there can be no question of the importance of the summit meeting held in Pyongyang during the summer of 2000.

The national security relationship with the United States during the Kim presidency went through two distinct phases. For the first 2 years during the end of the Clinton administration, the relationship was favorable in that the American president supported Kim's Sunshine Policy. In late October 2000, Secretary of State Madeleine Albright traveled to North Korea and conducted a series of meetings with Kim Jong Il. This harmonious security relationship between the ROK and United States would change with the election of George W. Bush who took office in January 2001.

Early in the Bush first term, Kim Dae Jung pressed hard for a visit to Washington. Foreign affairs had not been a major focus of the 2000 presidential election, but candidate George Bush had been critical of the Clinton administration's policies involving North Korea. He had been particularly negative about the 1994 Agreed Framework between the DPRK and United States, and after becoming president, Bush ordered a policy review of the DPRK–United States relationship. This review was still underway when Kim came to Washington in March 2001. In the joint statement issued at the conclusion of their meeting, President Bush expressed his support for President Kim's "policy of engagement" with North Korea and acknowledged Kim's "leading role" in addressing inter-Korean issues. The two presidents also reaffirmed their commitment to the 1994 Agreed Framework.[46] At the subsequent press conference, President Bush was a little more negative in expressing "skepticism about the leader of North Korea." He also emphasized the need for effective verification of any agreement with the DPRK because of its secretive nature.[47] While these public statements were largely cordial, some experts have reported that the actual talks between Bush and Kim were strained primarily because Bush was less than enthusiastic about Kim's policy of engagement with North Korea.[48]

President Bush announced the results of his administration's policy review in June 2001. He directed his national security team to conduct "serious negotiations" with the DPRK, but he expanded the agenda for new negotiations beyond nuclear weapons to include limitations on North Korea's missile programs and a ban on missile exports. Further, the review added the DPRK's large conventional military forces and its human rights record as topics for any future negotiations.

In his concluding remarks announcing the policy review results, President Bush stated that if the DPRK responded affirmatively to these demands, the United States would expand its efforts to assist the North Korean people by easing sanctions and taking some other nonspecific steps to improve relations.[49] The results of this policy review were not received particularly well on either side of the 38th parallel because of perceptions that the new American administration had raised the bar substantially for any successful negotiations with North Korea.

In 2002, the Bush administration published two documents that influenced the relationship with North Korea. The first was the Nuclear Posture Review released to the public in January, and the second was the National Security Strategy of the United States made available in September. The Nuclear Posture Review outlined plans to develop conventional and nuclear weapons that would be able to attack underground bunkers and specifically mentioned the DPRK as one of the seven countries against whom these weapons might be targeted.[50] The National Security Strategy was more specific concerning the DPRK. This document identified the very real danger that the United States and other countries confronted from terrorist organizations that have global reach and receive support from nation states possessing WMD. It also described the current threats to be more "complex and dangerous" than those faced during the Cold War because of rogue states and their possible support for terrorist groups. In this context, the National Security Strategy specifically mentioned North Korea as "one of the world's principal purveyors of ballistic missiles" and also as a country "developing its own WMD arsenal." Since traditional forms of deterrence would not be effective according to this analysis, the United States would incorporate preemptive attacks as the most effective means to deal with these threats.[51]

President Bush made his position even more clear in his State of the Union address in January 2002 when he identified North Korea as a member of "the axis of evil" along with Iran and Iraq.[52] In an August 2002 interview with Bob Woodward, Bush went further when he expressed his visceral hatred for Kim Jong Il because of Kim's mistreatment of his own people through starvation, prison camps, and torture.[53] In February 2002, President Bush visited Kim Dae Jung in Seoul. This would be the last meeting between the two leaders before Kim left office in February 2003. In remarks made before the press corps after their official session, Bush expressed his support for the ROK's Sunshine Policy. However, he again stated that he was "troubled" by the North Korean regime because of its lack of transparency and the minimal freedoms available to its people. In response to a question about the axis of evil speech, Bush defended his use of this term by referencing Ronald Reagan's characterization of the Soviet Union as an evil empire. Bush's argument was that despite the use of this term, Reagan and Gorbachev were able to negotiate with each other. The implication was that the same could happen between the United States and North Korea.[54]

Roh Moo Hyun, 2003–2008

Roh Moo Hyun was born after World War II in 1946 and represents a new era of South Korean political leaders. After graduating from high school, he served his mandatory 2 years military commitment. He never went to college but studied law on his own and passed the bar exam in 1975. Roh practiced labor and human rights law for a number of years and won a seat in the National Assembly in 1988. He joined Kim Dae Jung's MDP, and Kim appointed him to be Minister of Maritime Affairs and Fisheries in 2000. The MDP selected Roh as its presidential candidate in 2002. In the presidential election that December, he won with 48.9 percent of the vote defeating the GNP's Lee Hoi Chang who finished a close second with 46.6 percent of the votes cast. In 2003, several members of the MDP left the party and formed the Uri Party. Roh also withdrew from the MDP but did not immediately join the new party. However, in the campaign for the National Assembly elections in 2004, he urged the Korean people to vote for Uri candidates. Since his support for the Uri Party violated election laws that require the president to remain neutral, GNP and MDP members of the legislature brought three articles of impeachment against Roh before the National Assembly. The legislature passed these bills of impeachment by a vote of 193-2 in March 2004 since the Uri Party legislators did not vote. President Roh stepped aside and allowed Prime Minister Goh Kun to serve as acting president, while Roh appealed the impeachment decision.[55]

The Korean public reacted negatively to the Roh impeachment, and this reaction was reflected in the outcome of the National Assembly elections in April. The Uri Party won a slight majority taking 152 of the 299 seats (the number of seats in the National Assembly had been expanded from 273 to 299 before this election). The GNP won 121 seats, and the MDP was the big loser winning only 9 seats. In May, the Constitutional Court overturned the impeachment verdict, and Roh Moo Hyun once again was president. He joined the Uri Party later that month. Since that time, he has been plagued by defections within his party in the National Assembly that have cost him the majority won in 2004. By early 2007, the Uri Party only had 110 seats in the National Assembly as a result of these defections and losses in several by-elections. The GNP has gained 6 seats to become the largest party with 127 seats.[56] The loss of his majority in the legislature has made life even more difficult for the president to pass legislation to support his agenda.

As an indication of his frustration, President Roh announced that he intended to submit a constitutional amendment to the National Assembly that would allow a future president to serve two 4-year terms rather than the one 5-year term at present. His argument was that a president under the current arrangement becomes basically a lame duck by the middle of his term which limits the president's effectiveness. In April 2007, Roh decided to suspend his constitutional amendment until the new National Assembly is elected in April 2008. Despite this delay, it is likely that a major revision of the presidential term will be considered after the next legislative election.[57]

By late 2006, President Roh's public support had declined to 11 percent primarily because of domestic economic problems. It was not that the economy did not continue to grow, but more that the disparities between the very rich and the rest of the South Korean population were increasing. In addition, rising household costs, educational expenses, and soaring real estate prices were causing major concerns among the population and contributing directly to Roh's problems.[58] Finally, President Roh has had only limited success confronting corruption. During his presidential campaign, he tried to distance himself from some of the problems Kim Dae Jung experienced with corruption, particularly what became known as the "cash for summit scandal" related to a $500 million payoff to North Korea to agree to the 2000 leadership summit in Pyongyang. Despite these good intentions, Roh has had problems with combating corruption and difficulties with implementing governmental reform.[59]

The security relationship with the United States during the Roh presidency has progressed through some difficult periods but remains relatively sound. In the summer of 2002, an incident occurred in the ROK involving two American soldiers and two young Korean school girls. The soldiers were driving a heavy vehicle north of Seoul when they inadvertently struck the two girls killing both. The issue then became which country under the SOFA would exercise jurisdiction. In the end, the United States retained jurisdiction since this incident involved official duty on the part of the soldiers. Public reaction in South Korea opposed this decision arguing that the soldiers should be tried in Korean courts.[60] The two soldiers were tried by military court martial in November 2002 and acquitted of the charges. This verdict resulted in major demonstrations in the ROK and strained the bilateral ties. As the presidential election in December approached, Roh Moo Hyun tapped into some of this anti-American sentiment to enhance his campaign chances. After his victory, there was concern in the United States that his presidency might be problematic because of these recent issues and also because he had called for a reduction in the American military presence earlier in his career while serving in the National Assembly.[61] Some Bush administration officials also were worried because Roh announced he would continue Kim Dae Jung's engagement policy toward North Korea although he changed the name to the Peace and Prosperity Policy in the effort to indicate to the Korean people that his policy would result in more reciprocity from the DPRK and other benefits to his country.[62]

President Roh came to Washington in May 2003 to meet with President Bush. In the joint statement issued after their meeting, the two leaders agreed to support the redeployment of some American forces in the ROK out of major urban areas. Although not stated specifically, this plan addressed Korean concerns about accidents such as had occurred the previous year. Roh and Bush also agreed that they would "not tolerate" nuclear weapons in North Korea, and Bush pledged his support for Roh's Peace and Prosperity Policy.[63] During another meeting between the two presidents at the Asia Pacific Economic Cooperation annual summit in Bangkok, President Roh promised to increase the ROK military presence in Iraq to 3,000 personnel making it the fourth largest foreign contingent serving there.[64]

In late 2002 and early 2003, the United States and South Korea established what came to be known as the FOTA (Future of the Alliance Policy Initiative). The primary intent was to study contentious issues such as force redeployments and draw downs so that the interests of both sides were considered. It was through this process that the allies agreed to move the American military headquarters from Yongsan Garrison in Seoul to an area south of the Han River near Pyongtaek although the timing for this move remains under discussion. Progress occurred with the SCMs too in 2004, 2005, and 2006. At the 36th SCM held in Washington in October 2004, the defense officials agreed on the relocation of certain U.S. forces from areas along the DMZ and to a gradual reduction of 12,500 from the current American force level of 37,000 troops by the end of 2008. This redeployment was part of the American proposal that the forces in the ROK have greater "strategic flexibility" regarding other possible contingencies in East Asia. One of the hallmarks of former Secretary of Defense Donald Rumsfeld was the Integrated Global Presence and Basing Study, more commonly referred to as the GPR (Global Posture Review). Rumsfeld's idea regarding the American forces in the ROK was not only to continue their primary responsibility for deterring North Korea, but also to have these forces available for other missions in the region. It is a testament to the increased capabilities of ROK forces plus the continuation of the American nuclear umbrella under the MDT that the two sides could agree to this proposal with relatively little debate. Most recently in October 2006, ROK and American defense leaders agreed that wartime operational control of South Korean forces would be transferred to the ROK Ministry of National Defense sometime during the period of October 15, 2009 and March 15, 2012.[65]

CONCLUSION

The ROK can take great credit for the economic and political progress that has occurred from 1948. The ROK economy is now the world's 11th largest and democratization has firmly taken hold. There are still some political issues that need to be resolved such as improved and enhanced institutionalization, particularly more effective political parties that are not just based on regions or individuals, and reduced corruption among public officials. The art of political compromise also needs some work as evidenced in the 2004 impeachment of Roh Moo Hyun for a relatively minor transgression. These are manageable problems that South Koreans will work to resolve. Similarly, the security relationship has matured nicely over the more than 50 years since the MDT was negotiated. At times, the ROK experiences some of the pangs associated with being the junior partner in this relationship with concerns being expressed about either abandonment or entanglement on the part of the United States. Most recently, the discussions over reducing the American presence and moving some of the remaining forces to new locations away from the DMZ provided examples of both concerns. Some Koreans were worried the removal of the "tripwire" forces represented just the first step in the United States withdrawal of its forces from the ROK. Others were concerned that the "strategic flexibility" espoused by Rumsfeld and others would lead to South Korean involvement in conflicts not of their interest such as between China and Taiwan. In the final analysis, the two allies have adjusted to changing threat perceptions regarding North Korea in an effective manner, but challenges remain for the future.

NOTES

1. Mark L. Clifford, *Troubled Tiger: Businessmen, Bureaucrats, and Generals in South Korea*, (Armonk: M.E. Sharpe, 1994), 30 and McDonald, *The Koreans: Contemporary Politics and Society*, 52–53.

2. "Mutual Defense Treaty Between the United States of America and the Republic of Korea; October 1, 1953," can be found at www.yale.edu/lawweb/avalon/diplomacy/Korea/Kor001.htm.

3. Clifford, *Troubled Tiger*, 35–36 and Oberdorfer, *The Two Koreas: A Contemporary History*, 31–32.

4. Ibid., 37–52; Oberdorfer, *The Two Koreas: A Contemporary History*, 33–37; and MacDonald, *The Koreans: Contemporary Politics and Society*, 195–96.

5. Han Sunjoo, "South Korea's Participation in the Vietnam Conflict: An Analysis of the U.S.–Korean Alliance," *Orbis* (Winter 1978): 893–908.

6. A copy of the Nixon Doctrine can be found at http://www.mrs.umn.edu/~joos/class/usfp_s/reading/nixon.

7. Oberdorfer, *The Two Koreas: A Contemporary History*, 37–46.

8. Clifford, *Troubled Tiger*, 85–86.

9. Oberdorfer, *The Two Koreas*, 59–64 for the North Korean military buildup and pages 74–83 for the ax murders in the DMZ.

10. Clifford, *Troubled Tiger*, 86–90.

11. Oberdorfer, *The Two Koreas*, 67–68. For the ROK's nuclear weapons program and the U.S. response, see pages 86–90.

12. Ibid., 111–16.

13. A copy of Kissinger's July 1976 speech entitled "America and Asia" can be found in *Department of State Bulletin* 75, no. 1938, August 16, 1976, 217–26.

14. "U.S. Troop Withdrawal from the Republic of Korea," A Report to the Committee on Foreign Relations, U.S. Senate, 95th Congress, 2nd Session, January 9, 1978 by Senators Hubert H. Humphrey and John Glenn. See page 1 for background on the Carter decision and pages 20–23 for the South Korean response.

15. Oberdorfer, *The Two Koreas,* 106. The American diplomat was Richard Holbrooke who at that time was assistant secretary of state for East Asia and the Pacific.

16. For good coverage of the events after the Park assassination and the Chun coup, see Oberdorfer, *The Two Koreas: A Contemporary History,* 111–24 and Clifford, *Troubled Tiger: Businessmen, Bureaucrats, and Generals,* 144–49.

17. For a comprehensive overview and analysis of these critical events leading the Chun election including interviews with Chun and Roh Tae Woo, see Oberdorfer, *The Two Koreas: A Contemporary History,* 124–33.

18. Oberdorfer, *The Two Koreas,* 133–38.

19. Ibid., 139–44 provides details on both the KAL shoot down and the Rangoon bombing.

20. Clifford, *Troubled Tiger,* 208–40.

21. Roh Tae Woo's June 29, 1987, Declaration can be found in Robert E. Bedeski, *The Transformation of South Korea: Reform and Reconstruction in the Sixth Republic Under Roh Tae Woo, 1987–1992* (New York: Routledge, 1994), 169–70.

22. The Constitution as amended in 1987 can be found at http://www.odfre.unibc.ch/law/icl/ks00000_html.

23. Oberdorfer, *The Two Koreas,* 172–78.

24. "The Joint Communiqué Following Discussions with President Chun Doo Hwan of the Republic of Korea" dated February 2, 1981, can be found at http://www.reagan.utexas.edu/archives/speeches/1981/20281d.htm.

25. The 1985 Security Consultative Meeting Communiqué was included in "Wireless File," USIS-Embassy Seoul, May 8, 1985, 4–7. See especially paragraph 5.

26. Oberdorfer, *The Two Koreas,* 180–86 provides good coverage of the 1988 Olympics.

27. A copy of Roh's July 8, 1988 speech is found in *Korea Under Roh Tae Woo: Democratization, Northern Policy, and Inter-Korean Relations,* ed. James Cotton (Canberra: Allen and Unwin Publishers, 1993), 328–30.

28. Oberdorfer, *The Two Koreas,* 186–96.

29. Ibid., 204–28.

30. Kim Hak Joon, "The Republic of Korea's Northern Policy: Origin, Development, and Prospects", in *Korean Under Roh Tae Woo: Democratization, North Policy, and Inter-Korean Relations,* ed. Cotton (Canberra: Allen and Unwin Publishers), 260–66 and Oberdorfer, *The Two Koreas: A Contemporary History,* 229–48.

31. "A Strategic Framework for the Asia-Pacific Rim: Looking Toward the 21st Century" is available at http://www.shaps.hawaii.edu/security/report-92.html.

32. For details of the Cheney visit to the ROK, see "Seoul to Pay more for U.S. Troops", *International Herald Tribune,* September 28–29, 1991, 2.

33. Oberdorfer, *The Two Koreas,* 258–59.

34. Doh C. Shin, *Mass Politics in Democratizing Korea,* (Cambridge: Cambridge University Press, 1991), 6–7.

35. Shin, *Mass Politics and Culture in Democratizing Korea,* 201–03 and Oberdorfer, *The Two Koreas: A Contemporary History,* 376–82.

36. Chae-Jin Lee, *A Troubled Peace: U.S. Policy and the Two Koreas,* (Baltimore: Johns Hopkins University Press, 2006), 193. See also Gifford Combs, "The Role of International Finance in the Korean Economic Reconstruction and Reunification," *NBR Analysis* vol. 10, no. 5, December 1999, The National Bureau of Asian Research, 5–22 and Charles S. Lee, "Aftershocks Rumble," *Far East Economic Review,* February 26, 1998, 56–58.

37. "Remarks by the President in an Address to the National Assembly of the Republic of Korea", July 10, 1993 available at http://www.fas.org/spp/starwars/offdocs/w930710.htm. The specific reference to U.S. troops in Korea is on page 3.

38. Oberdorfer, *The Two Koreas,* 312.

39. "The 27th ROK–U.S. SCM and 17th MCM Joint Communiqué," October 7, 1994. The reference to operational control in peacetime is on page 2. See http://www.shaps.hawaii.edu/security/korea/militref1.html.

40. "The United States Security Strategy for the East Asia–Pacific Region," 1998, 22–26. See http://www.dod.mil/pubs/easr98.

41. See a good review of the 1997 presidential election in "Economic Country Briefing" available at http://www.economist.com/countries/SouthKorea/profiles.cfm.

42. Ha Young Chol, "South Korea in 2000: A Summit and Search for New Institutional Identity," *Asian Survey,* 41, no. 1(January 2001): 30–39.

43. Norman D. Levin and Han Yong Sup, *Sunshine in Korea: The South Korean Debate Over Policies Toward North Korea* (Santa Monica: Rand Corporation, 2002), 24–25.

44. Oberdorfer, *The Two Koreas,* 423–31 provides an excellent summary of the events leading to the June 2000 summit.

45. "The South–North Joint Declaration, Pyongyang, June 15, 2000" is available at http://www.usip.org/library/pa/n_skorea/n_skorea06152000.html.

46. "Joint Statement Between the United States and the Republic of Korea, March 7, 2001" at http://www.whitehouse.gov/news/releases/2001/03/print/20010307-2.html.

47. "Remarks by President Bush and President Kim Dae Jung of South Korea," March 7, 2001 at http://www.whitehouse.gov/news/releases/2001/03/print/20010307-6.html.

48. Jonathan D. Pollack, "The United States, North Korea, and the End of the Agreed Framework," *Naval War College Review,* LVI, no. 3 (Summer 2003): 25–26.

49. "Statement of the President," June 13, 2001 at http://www.whitehouse.gov/news/releases/2001/06/print/20010611-4.html.

50. The Nuclear Posture Review can be found at http://www.globalsecurity.org/wmd/library/policy/dod/npr.htm. See page 4 for references to North Korea. For more on the Nuclear Posture Review, see Morton I. Abramowitz and James T. Laney, "Meeting the North Korean Nuclear Challenge," Report of the Independent Task Force Sponsored by the Council of Foreign Relations, June 2003, 12.

51. The National Security Strategy of the United States of America, September 2002, 6–15.

52. For good reactions to Bush's axis of evil speech in Seoul and Pyongyang, see John Larkin, "Axis of Uncertainty," *Far Eastern Economic Review* (February 14, 2002): 12–15.

53. Bob Woodward, *Bush At War* (New York: Simon and Shuster, 2002) 340.

54. "President Bush and President Kim Dae Jung Meeting in Seoul," February 20, 2002 at http://www.whitehouse.gov/news/releases/2002/02/print/20020220-1.html.

55. Lee Sook Jong, "The Transformation of South Korean Politics: Implications for U.S.–Korean Relations" (Washington, DC: The Brookings Institute, September 2004), 3–4.

56. "Mass Defections Turns Uri Party Into a Minority," JoongAng Daily, February 7, 2007 available at http://joongangdaily.joins.com/article/print.asp.

57. "Roh Plans Amendment for 2-Term Presidency," JoongAng Daily, January 10, 2007 available at http://joongangdaily.joins.com/article/print.asp. For the decision to delay the constitutional amendment, see Ryu Jin, "Parties Pledge to Revise Constitution," The *Korea Times,* April 14, 2007 available at http://times.hankooki.com.

58. Norimitsu Onishi, "South Korea's President Sags in Opinion Polls," *New York Times* (November 7, 2006): 6. For a current review of the ROK economic performance, see "Republic of Korea," in *Asian Development Outlook 2007,* Asian Development Bank, March 2007, 144–48.

59. Young Whan Kihl, "The Past as Prologue: President Kim Dae Jung's Legacy and President Roh Moo Hyun's Policy Issues and Future Challenges," in *A Turning Point: Democratic Consolidation in the ROK and Strategic Readjustment in the ROK Alliance,* ed. Alexander Y. Mansourov (Honolulu: Asia-Pacific Center for Security Studies, 2005), 8–14.

60. For the Korean reaction to this incident, see "Rising Anti-Americanism" an editorial in *The Korean Herald,* an English language daily, August 8, 2002 available at http://www.koreaherald.co.kr.

61. For some good newspaper accounts of these events in late 2002, see Howard French, "Candidates in South Korea Differ Sharply on the North," *New York Times* (December 4, 2002): 13; Howard French and Don Kirk, "Under Fire in South Korea: U.S. Policies and Presence," *New York Times* (December 8, 2002): 10; and Doug Struck, "Resentment Toward U.S. Troops Is Boiling Over," *Washington Post* (December 9, 2002): 17.

62. For more specifics about Roh's Peace and Prosperity Policy, see Jong-Chul Park, "The Policy of Peace and Prosperity: Its Characteristics and Challenges," *The Korean Quarterly,* 4, no. 1 (July 2006): 26–31.

63. "Joint Statement Between the United States of America and the Republic of Korea," May 14, 2003 at http://www.whitehouse.gov/news/releases/2003/05/print/20030514-17.html.

64. "President Bush Meets With President Roh Moo Hyun," October 20, 2003 at http://www.whitehouse.gov/news/releases/2003/10/print/20031020-2.html.

65. See "Joint Communiqué: Thirty-Sixth Annual U.S.–ROK Security Consultative Meeting, October 22, 2004" and "The 38th Security Consultative Meeting Joint Communiqué, October 20, 2006." For more on the GPR and its application to the Korean peninsula, see Bruce Vaughn, "U.S. Strategic and Defense Relationships in the Asia-Pacific Region," CRS Report to the Congress, January 22, 2007, 12–13.

CHAPTER 3

Kim Dynasty in North Korea

The DPRK is one of the most closed societies in existence which makes any analysis of its political and economic systems difficult. Two leading American experts on the DPRK have referred to this country as "a combination of a Confucian kingdom and a twentieth-century totalitarian socialist state" where the political leadership lives in a "reality sealed off from the outside."[1] Despite these analytical difficulties, this chapter will examine the development of the Kim Dynasty in North Korea beginning with the rule of Kim Il Sung from 1948 to his death in 1994 and the succession process to his son Kim Jong Il. The important roles that the Juche ideology and the Kim cult of personality have played and continue to play in providing for the regime's legitimacy will be included. This chapter will then address some of the tools the Kims have employed to ensure regime survival and the economic policies initiated that have resulted in the almost total collapse of the country's ability to feed its people. The concluding part of the chapter will focus on the DPRK's foreign policies with China, Russia, and Japan.

KIM IL SUNG

Kim Il Sung was born Kim Song Ju on April 15, 1912 near Pyongyang during the Japanese occupation of Korea. In 1920, Kim and his family moved to the Chinese city of Jilin in Manchuria where several hundred thousand ethnic Koreans had moved mainly to escape Japanese repression in Korea or to find better ways to make a living. Kim became involved with the Korean Youth League in Manchuria and then joined anti-Japanese groups after Japan attacked parts of China beginning in 1931. Eventually, he joined the anti-Japanese United Army under the direction of the Chinese Communist Party. It was during this period of time as an anti-Japanese fighter that Kim took the name of Kim Il Sung, a well-known Korean resistance leader. From this time onward, Kim's reputation as a Korean leader of the anti-Japanese forces became established, and this reputation would be very important in contributing to his political legitimacy once he returned to Korea.

In 1941, the Japanese forces in China proved very effective in combating both Chinese and Korean resistance in Manchuria. As a result of this increasing Japanese pressure, Kim and other Koreans were forced to flee across the Soviet border where Kim established a camp near Khabarovsk. The Soviets provided military training to the Koreans in their territory, and Kim Il Sung became a captain in the Soviet Red Army's Eighty Eighth Rifle Brigade. He served with the Soviet military until the end of World War II in August 1945. It was during this period of time living in the Soviet Union that Kim married Kim Jong Suk. On February 16, 1942, their first son, Kim Jong Il, was born. Because of his service in the Soviet military, Kim Il Sung was well known to the Russians as the war drew to its conclusion.

In September 1945, after the division of the Korean peninsula, the USSR brought Kim back to Korea and promoted him to the rank of general. Despite Kim's favor with the Russians, he was not selected as the initial political leader in the northern part of Korea. That honor went to Cho Man Sik, a nationalist who had remained in Korea during the Japanese occupation. However, Cho refused to accept the trusteeship proposal for Korea outlined in the December 1945 Moscow Conference. He pressed for Korean independence, and the Soviets forced him out. With Soviet backing, Kim Il Sung became premier of the DPRK when North Korea came into existence in August 1948 and general secretary of the KWP (Korean Worker's Party) in 1949.[2] In 1972, the DPRK's Constitution was amended and Kim Il Sung became president, the position he held until his death in 1994. In 1998, North Korean officials amended the Constitution again. In the Preface, Kim Il Sung is designated as the "eternal President" of the DPRK.[3]

As related in chapter 1, Kim Il Sung was largely responsible for convincing Joseph Stalin and Mao Zedong to support his efforts to unify the Korean peninsula by force in June 1950. The basis of his argument was that the United States would not oppose this attack, at least not militarily, and that the war would only last a few days before the South Korean government collapsed. Kim was proved wrong on both of these arguments, and the KPA was routed after the Inchon amphibious landing later in 1950. When the Korean War ended, Kim began a series of brutal purges to rid the DPRK of his political opponents and others who raised questions about his leadership abilities. These purges continued through the 1950s and early 1960s until the Kim Dynasty was firmly established.[4] By the 1970s, Kim Il Sung had decided to arrange for his succession.

He was concerned about what he had seen happen in the Soviet Union after the death of Stalin and in China after Mao's death. In order to prevent attacks on his legacy and his policies, Kim selected Kim Jong Il as his successor and began an organized campaign to ensure this hereditary succession would be accomplished as planned.

THE SUCCESSION PROCESS OF KIM JONG IL

After his birth in Khabarovsk, Kim Jong Il remained in the Soviet Union until late 1945 when he and his mother returned to Korea and rejoined Kim Il Sung. In the USSR, he was known as Yuri Irsenovich Kim with the nickname of Yura. His brother, Kim Pyong Il, known by the Russian nickname of Shura, was born in 1943 but died in a swimming accident in 1948. Kim Jong Il's mother also died accidentally during childbirth. Kim Il Sung remarried in the early 1960s and had another son also named Kim Pyong Il. In 1964, Kim Jong Il graduated from Kim Il Sung University after majoring in political economy. By the early 1970s, Kim Il Sung was actively involved with efforts to designate his elder son as his successor.

In 1973, Kim Jong Il became a member of the KWP Politburo and was appointed the director of the party's Organization and Guidance Department, one of the most powerful positions in the KWP. The North Korean press also began to refer to Kim Jong Il as the "party center," another indication that he was his father's designated heir. As part of his effort to consolidate his power and eliminate any opposition to his succession, Kim Jong Il purged many KWP members and replaced them with younger people who would be responsible to Kim for the jobs they held. His position as director of the Organization and Guidance Department allowed Kim to remove and promote KWP cadre at his discretion. Kim also solicited the support of the KPA because, in contrast to his father, Kim Jong Il had no military experience. Finally, after the KWP's Sixth Party Conference in October 1980, Kim Jong Il was listed as second on the KWP Secretariat, fourth of the five members on the Politburo Standing Committee, and third of ten on the National Defense Commission. The only other person to hold positions on each of these groups was Kim Il Sung.[5]

During the 1980s and the early 1990s, Kim Jong Il began to assume more of the day-to-day functions of running North Korea although much of his power was exercised behind the scenes. Nevertheless, by the early 1990s, Kim Jong Il had become a marshal in the KPA and the supreme commander of all DPRK military forces. Shortly thereafter in 1993, he was named chairman of the National Defense Commission providing him with tremendous power over the state apparatus. Although Kim Il Sung appeared to be in relatively good health for man 82 years old, he suffered a fatal heart attack on July 8, 1994. Kim Jong Il took over for his father assisted by the fact that he had been very active in running the country before his father's death. After 3 years of mourning, Kim assumed the general secretary's position as leader of the KWP in 1997. Despite speculation at the time of Kim Il Sung's death that his designated heir might be vulnerable, Kim Jong Il has consolidated his power and appears to be in unchallenged control through his leadership positions in the party, military, and state.[6] The only position of power that Kim Jong Il does not hold is president which the Constitution now reserves for his father.

Kim Jong Il's reputation prior to becoming the North Korean leader was of a playboy and heavy drinker. There was speculation that he would not be able to succeed his father for long. He also was directly implicated in supporting terrorist activities such as the 1983 Rangoon bombing of the South Korean cabinet and the 1987 downing of the KAL aircraft prior to the Olympics. However, over the past several years, Kim has established himself as a capable leader if still unpredictable and callous to his own people's needs. The 2000 summit meeting with Kim Dae Jung certainly burnished his image in South Korea. Similarly, when he met with Secretary of State Madeleine Albright in late 2000, she found him to be well informed on the issues they discussed.[7] The practical reality is that in his more than 12 years as North Korea's preeminent leader, he is well established in power. In his mid-60s and in relatively good health, he does not appear to have a serious challenger to his continued rule. Hwang Jang Yop, the highest ranking North Korean official to defect to South Korea and someone who was close to Kim Jong Il for many years, has stated unequivocally that Kim is the only leader in the DPRK who exercises "real power."[8] Possible succession scenarios to Kim Jong Il will be addressed later in this chapter.

JUCHE IDEOLOGY AND THE CULT OF PERSONALITY

Article 3 of the DPRK Constitution states that the country "is guided in its activities by the Juche idea, a world outlook centered on people, a revolutionary ideology for achieving independence of the masses of people." This statement is somewhat nebulous, but so is the whole Juche concept. Nonetheless, Juche remains a core principle in understanding how the Kim Dynasty has become such a dominant force in North Korean society and provides some clues as to what the future may hold for the country. Kim Il Sung introduced the Juche idea in a speech to the KWP during December 1955. Over the years, Juche has developed into a combination of Korean nationalism and a strong sense of national self-reliance. For Kim Il Sung and later for Kim Jong Il, Juche represents an effort to adapt Marxist–Leninist principles to North Korean conditions. The economic implications of Juche will be discussed later in this chapter.

Juche has also proved useful in comparisons between the two Koreas because from Pyongyang's perspective, North Korea represents true Korean independence since the ROK remains dependent on the United States for its security, particularly the presence of American military forces. One author has described this interpretation of Juche as "militant nationalism" in that North Korea rails against foreign dominance and promotes all things Korean.[9] After the collapse of the Soviet Union and several socialist governments in Eastern Europe, Juche took on a more defensive tone when the two Kims used this principle to differentiate between North Korean socialism and, from their perspectives, the inferior offshoots in the Soviet Union and Eastern Europe. The Kims have made similar criticisms against China and the market reforms introduced by Deng Xiaoping and others.[10]

The Juche ideology has played important roles in the succession process from Kim Il Sung to Kim Jong Il too. Since the younger Kim had very few viable credentials qualifying him to lead the country, he needed something that would enhance his political credibility and legitimacy. One of the reasons he was appointed director of the KWP's Organization and Guidance Department was to facilitate his becoming the primary spokesman for the implementation of the Juche ideology. He is credited with writing more than 400 articles interpreting Juche and encouraging its acceptance by the North Korean people.[11] One of the problems that has developed with Kim Jong Il's dependence on Juche for his legitimacy is that it has made it very difficult for him to initiate or support necessary economic reforms because to do so challenges the very basis of his political support. This dilemma will become more apparent later in this chapter in the discussion of the North Korean economy.

There are elements of traditional Korean Confucian values involved with the development of the Kim Dynasty's cult of personality. True to Confucian principles, the virtuous society is to be ruled by a wise, benevolent leader to whom the people give unquestioned obedience and loyalty. In the case of Kim Il Sung, he began to develop his cult of personality soon after coming to power in 1948 modeled on Stalin's example. The thousands of statues of the Kims throughout the DPRK, the photographs in public buildings and homes as well as the ubiquitous lapel pins are all examples of the Kims' personality cults. But these cults go far beyond just political legitimization in that both Kim Il Sung and Kim Jong Il have become figures of worship. As such, they are considered to be above reproach and cannot be held responsible for their actions and policies.

This belief in the infallibility of the leader is another reason why economic reforms have been so difficult in the DPRK. The cult of personality has contributed to Kim Jong Il's political legitimacy by tying him directly to his father, the original benevolent leader. It has also reduced the likelihood of direct criticism of the younger Kim's disastrous policies. As Kongdan Oh and Ralph Hassig have argued, a regime based on the Juche ideology and the cult of personality is a regime built on lies. Once the North Korean people become aware of these lies, assuming they eventually do, then the Kim Dynasty will have to revert to even more extreme coercive means to maintain its powers.[12]

THE KPA AND OTHER ELEMENTS OF DPRK COERCIVE CONTROL

One of the most striking attributes of the KPA is its shear size in relation to the population as a whole. With a North Korean population of approximately 23 million, the KPA has more than 1,106,000 members on active duty or just about 5 percent of the population. By contrast, the ROK with a population more than twice as large as the DPRK has an active military force of about 687,000. In the North Korean military, the Army is the dominant service with 950,000; the Air Force has 110,000; and the Navy 46,000. Paramilitary forces total an additional 189,000. As a separate entity, there are more than 4,700,000 North Koreans in the Reserves. Of particular concern to the United States and South Korea are the unconventional forces in the KPA known as special purpose forces. These forces are organized into twenty-two brigades and seven separate battalions and are highly trained soldiers. Estimates of the number of special purpose forces range from 88,000 to 120,000 troops. Among the missions assigned to them are: seizure or destruction of South Korean command, control, and communication assets; interdiction of strategic targets such as air bases, port facilities, and nuclear plants in the ROK; establishing intelligence gathering networks in South Korea; and providing target information for conventional weapons and WMD.[13]

Since the DPRK has a conscription system, the terms of service for the Army are from 5 to 12 years; 5 to 10 years for the Navy; and 3 to 4 years for the Air Force. These active duty requirements are followed by compulsory part-time service to 40 years of age and then service in the Worker/Peasant Red Guard until age 60.[14] The numbers and length of service of those involved with the military provides the North Korean government with the opportunity extensively to indoctrinate a sizeable percentage of the population during their military commitment.

The estimates for the DPRK military budget range from 15.5 percent of GNP (gross national product) from North Korean sources to more than 30 percent of GNP from South Korean Ministry of National Defense statistics. Since 1998, the DPRK has adopted the "military first" policy whereby the KPA has surpassed the KWP as the primary institution in the policy-making process. During Kim Il Sung's rule, he relied more on the KWP as his major source of support. For Kim Jong Il, he has favored the KPA. Part of the explanation for this reversal is that Kim Jong Il had no military experience in comparison with his father, and he may well see the "military first" policy as an effective means to keep the military loyal to him by providing the military with the resources demanded. Furthermore, the younger Kim has forced the retirement of many of the older officers who were appointed by his father and replaced them with more than 1,200 general officers who owe their positions to Kim Jong Il.[15] As stated previously, Kim Jong Il is the supreme commander of the KPA and the chairman of the National Defense Commission. These positions provide him with unchallenged control over the KPA.

The KPA performs several important functions within the society, but among the most critical are the following. First, the KPA is responsible for national security, and that is very significant because of the threat environment confronting North Korea. Article 60 of the Constitution reinforces the Juche principle of self-reliance by stating that "the state shall implement the line of self-reliant defense, the import of which is to arm the entire people, fortify the country, train the army into a cadre army on the basis of equipping the army and people politically and ideologically." There is somewhat of a paradox here in which North Korea wants to maintain its self-reliance through the "military first" policy of the KPA, but the country also has depended on China and the Soviet Union/ Russia to support its national security requirements for much of its history as will be documented later in this chapter. The second major KPA function is to contribute to domestic peace and stability. The primary tasks associated with this mission include assisting with internal security, providing intelligence on possible dissident groups, conducting foreign infiltration and espionage, supplementing border security, and serving as labor support for industry and agriculture. Third, the KPA is held up as a political role model for the society through its reported willingness to suffer hardships without complaining.[16]

The domestic intelligence functions of the KPA are directly supportive of what can only be described as the North Korean gulag and provide the KPA with a major role in the social control mechanism of the state. Under the Kim Dynasty, the North Korean people have been classified as belonging to one of three broad categories: loyal, wavering, or hostile. To handle those certainly in the third category but also some in the second, the DPRK has established two major prison systems. The first of these are known as political penal-labor colonies and primarily contain political prisoners as well as those inmates alleged to have committed common crimes. It is estimated there are between 150,000 to 200,000 prisoners from these two categories. The vast majority of those confined in these facilities have no legal right nor have they participated in any judicial process. They simply have been arrested and incarcerated. What is even more astounding is that up to three generations of the prisoner's family are also subject to be imprisoned in these facilities as part of collective punishment or guilt by association. Those imprisoned are forced to perform slave labor working in mining, forestry, or agriculture. Food rations are minimal so that many of these prisoners and their families are confronted with basic death sentences and there are no reeducation possibilities. In earlier times under Kim Il Sung's regime, many of those jailed were potential rivals purged by Kim and his supporters. Later, Kim Jong Il followed this same practice to remove those who might challenge his power. More recently, North Korean students or diplomats who were in Eastern Europe or the Soviet Union when those governments collapsed have been classified as political prisoners because of what they saw or experienced.[17]

The second example of the prison system functioning under the North Korean gulag are the detention facilities for those North Koreans who have been forcibly repatriated from China. The estimates are that between 200,000 and 300,000 North Koreans have crossed into China since the late 1990s to scavenge for food or to find employment in order to send money back to the DPRK to support their families. As the North Korean economy collapsed, the numbers of refugees increased dramatically. In the summer of 2004, 468 North Koreans made their way through China and entered Vietnam where they were then repatriated to South Korea. This large number of North Koreans escaping to the ROK infuriated DPRK authorities, and they announced more stringent policies to prevent recurrences. In addition, China, under DPRK pressure, classifies refugees from the DPRK as economic migrants rather than political refugees. This classification allows China to send the North Koreans back to the DPRK rather than protecting them under international law as would be required if they were considered political refugees. Further, China is concerned about the bad publicity associated with North Koreans seeking political asylum at foreign embassies or consulates in Beijing or elsewhere in China especially as the 2008 Olympics hosted by China approach.

All of these factors have contributed to the increasing numbers of North Koreans imprisoned in DPRK detention centers. Those treated particularly harshly are detainees who have had some contact with South Koreans while in China. North Korean women impregnated by Chinese men are frequently forced to have abortions and infanticide is also common if these children come to full term.[18] The breadth and scope of the North Korean gulag almost defies description, but these prisons have achieved a level of effectiveness in maintaining social control over the North Korea population.

Two other means to achieve social control involve the education system and efforts to limit the flow of information to the North Korean people. Education in the DPRK is still based largely on Kim Il Sung's 1977 Thesis on Socialist Education which is heavy on class consciousness, the establishment of the Juche ideology, revolutionary practices, and the government's responsibility for overseeing the educational system. Political studies make up a significant part of the curriculum and reinforce the Kim Dynasty's cults of personality. Study sessions continue for adults throughout their lives. Information control has been very effective until recent times since the vast majority of North Koreans did not have access to foreign newspapers, radio, or television.[19]

It is becoming much more difficult to control information in contemporary times particularly with the availability of cell phones, fax machines, and the Internet. Nonetheless, the DPRK remains one of the most closed societies on earth. The effects of implementing the Juche ideology, the Kim Dynasty's cults of personality, and the coercive methods employed by the state, especially the gulags, have been relatively effective in maintaining control over the North Korean people. However, the deprivations that so many of the people now confront caused mainly by the collapse of the economic system will represent a major challenge to the Kim government if and when the people become more aware of their failed economy, particularly in comparison with that of the ROK.

THE COLLAPSE OF THE NORTH KOREAN ECONOMY

In the 1960s, many economists predicted that the DPRK would develop the more dynamic economy in competition with South Korea. Because of North Korea's natural resources and electricity generation along with its industrial facilities provided by the Japanese during the occupation, the DPRK responded reasonably well to Kim Il Sung's plans to follow Stalin's industrial model. By the mid-1950s, Kim had collectivized agriculture and nationalized all industries. At the end of this decade, the remaining Chinese soldiers who had been in North Korea since the end of the Korean War returned to China. Since many of these soldiers had been involved with providing labor in agriculture and industries after the war, their loss of productivity caused problems for North Korea. Kim Il Sung attempted to make up for these losses through espousing and implementing Juche principles of self-sufficiency and the mobilization of remaining resources. The Three Revolutions Campaign featuring emphases on technology, ideology, and culture was introduced and the people were encouraged to believe that by just working harder, they could overcome all obstacles.[20]

By the 1970s, serious problems were confronting the DPRK's economy. Major reasons for these difficulties included the deleterious effects of the nationalization of industries and collectivization of agriculture; the inefficiencies association with a command economy; and the inability to continue mass mobilization campaigns over long periods of time. DPRK products became more and more inferior and much less competitive on the international market. In addition, the economic ramifications of the oil shocks resulting from the crises in the Middle East during the early to mid-1970s also hurt the North Korean economy. The international economic slowdown that resulted reduced the prices that the DPRK mineral exports received.

Beginning in 1974, North Korea was unable to repay its international debts, and these defaults resulted in greatly reduced foreign direct investments and technology transfers to the Kim Il Sung regime. In the mid-1980s, the DPRK's foreign debt had reached $5.2 billion, and many foreign banks filed suit to try to get at least some of their money returned. Foreign debt would continue to grow to more than $12 billion in 1997. While there was little chance that North Korea would be willing or able to repay its loans, additional sources of capital were no longer available through traditional banking arrangements. In the late 1990s, the economy had collapsed. The national budget for 1999 was 50 percent less than the comparable budget for 1994, and the GNP for 1998 was $12.6 billion whereas the GNP in 1990 had been $23.1 billion.[21]

As bad as these statistics were as a reflection of a failed economic model, the conditions for the North Korean people were worse. In 1999, Andrew Natsios, who had been a senior official in the U.S. Agency for International Development, wrote a special report for the United States Institute for Peace entitled "The Politics of Famine in North Korea." In this report, Natsios related that as the economic crisis worsened by the mid-1990s, North Korean authorities reduced the annual grain ration for farm families from 167 kg per person to 107 kg. As a result of this dramatic reduction in food rations, he pointed out three severe consequences that further compounded the food shortage throughout the country. First, the social contract between the farmers and the rest of society was ruptured. In previous times, farmers would produce food to support the urban centers in return for the industrial products they needed to bring in their harvests. As pesticides, fertilizers, and herbicides were no longer available to the farmers and their rations reduced, the incentives to produce food for the cities declined or even disappeared.

The second outcome Natsios identified was that as the situation in the rural areas deteriorated further, farmers became more involved with preharvesting or building up the family stocks of food to prevent the starvation of their families rather than meeting their quotas for state production. Third, farmers spent much of their time and efforts cultivating secret plots of land outside the control of the collective farms. In several instances, soldiers had to be employed to take the place of the absent farmers to till the fields and bring in the crops. All of these factors contributed to massive food shortages so that between 1994 and 1998, the estimates are that as many as 3 million North Koreans died because of malnutrition and starvation.[22]

Natsios also pointed out another major consequence of the massive starvation that occurred in the mid-1990s. In previous times, the DPRK government had used what was known as the PDS (Public Distribution System) as a central component of its food rationing program. North Koreans were issued ration cards that they would use to obtain food. In many instances, the ration cards were distributed through the work place, and this process amounted to another form of social control in that the individual was forced to remain close to the work place. As the famine worsened, North Koreans were on the move to scavenge for food either in the countryside or by leaving for China. Kim Jong Il and others in his regime further emasculated the PDS by reallocating food to select members of their regime, and this only compounded the problems with distributing food. Natsios found that so many North Koreans were crossing into China to look for food, that the DPRK government set up additional camps to confine those found outside their villages or urban areas without the proper travel documents. These camps supplemented the detention centers already described as part of the gulag.

Disaffection also occurred in the Korea People's Army. Although many KPA units benefited from Kim's reallocation of food rations as an example of the "military first" policy, several individual soldiers were influenced by the hardships that affected their extended families as food became even scarcer. The additional duties that many KPA soldiers were forced to perform in the countryside to harvest food caused discontent too. In some instances, soldiers became known as "corn guards" because they were sent to prevent farmers from hoarding food. This was not exactly the duty that many of them had signed up to perform. Kim Jong Il apparently became concerned enough that he launched a series of purges of high ranking officers in 1996 and 1997 so that he could install new military leaders in whom he had more confidence of their loyalty.[23]

In the industrial sector, limited foreign competition, a small domestic market, a lack of technological innovation, and poor labor discipline all had contributed to poor productivity and a lack of foreign investment. The debt defaults of earlier years compounded the problems with foreign investment and technology transfers. As indicated, the agricultural sector was woefully inadequate to meet the basic minimum food requirements. One expert on the DPRK's economy has written that the combination of lack of food, fuel, and foreign exchange earnings meant that North Korea did not have the economic growth and development essential to replace/build needed infrastructure or to procure the technologies that would contribute to increased productivity.[24]

In analyzing this economic collapse, it is possible to identify three broad areas of contributing causes. The first of these were the economic policies that Kim Il Sung and Kim Jong Il devised and implemented during the Kim Dynasty. The second cause involved fundamental changes in the international political system in the last decade of the twentieth century, and the third cause were acts of nature that affected the agricultural sector in particular. The government policy failures were many, but the focus here will be on the basic Juche ideology and the "military first" policies. The autarkic nature of the Juche ideology basically violated the economic principle of comparative advantage and resulted in import substitution policies in the extreme. North Korea simply did not have the natural resources, the technology, or the market to give this policy option any long-term chance of success. As an example, the Soviet Union offered the DPRK the opportunity to join COMECON, a Soviet trading block, that would have provided access to a guaranteed export market and technological innovation. The primary reason for declining this offer was that it would have violated the Juche principle.[25]

The "military first" policy resulting in inordinate percentages of the GNP being allocated to the KPA may make some sense from the perspective of ensuring the military's loyalty. However, it makes very little economic sense in a country where vital investments in agricultural and industrial productivity are necessary. In this instance, efforts designed to ensure regime survival through the support of the military may have the unintended consequence of contributing eventually to regime collapse because of the failure of the economy to meet the basic needs of the North Korean population.

The change in the international political system that most affected the DPRK's economy was the collapse of the Soviet Union in late 1991. Over the years, Kim Il Sung had been very skillful in playing the USSR off against China to the benefit of North Korea. When Roh Tae Woo first began to attract the attention of both the Soviets and Chinese with his Nordpolitik initiatives, the Kims became very concerned. Later when both DPRK allies established diplomatic relations with South Korea, it became clear that fundamental changes were in store for the DPRK. Even before the USSR disintegrated in December 1991, Mikhail Gorbachev had begun to rescind the "friendship prices" that the Soviets had extended to North Korea for many years, and China followed suit. Since North Korea was so strapped for foreign currencies, it became almost impossible to purchase the necessary imports to sustain the economy.

The final factor that adversely influenced North Korean economic performance was a series of natural disasters in the 1990s—most specifically the occurrences of floods followed by droughts. Although the Kims could not control these natural disasters, their policies in place tended to exacerbate the consequences. For example, in order to increase agricultural productivity and self-reliance, North Korea introduced terraces to grow more rice. This required cutting down trees and vegetation to put more land into cultivation. When the rains then began, the resultant flooding was more severe because of the lack of vegetation on the hillsides. Silting also occurred in major rivers that contributed to the flooding problems. As the economic conditions became more dire, the government was forced to begin to consider possible policy options that they had largely resisted when North Korea was in a stronger bargaining position.

In 1984, even before the most serious economic problems developed, the Supreme People's Assembly passed the Joint Venture Law with the twin goals of increasing technological innovation and providing for the introduction of much needed foreign investments. However, because of the continuing poor credit rating of the country based on loan repayment defaults, only minimal successes occurred. In 1991, North Korea established the Rajin-Sonbong SAR (Special Administrative Region) in the northeast part of the country near the Tumen River Basin and not far from the borders with China and the Soviet Union. This SAR was loosely based on the Chinese special economic zones that had been so important to China's economic boom under Deng Xiaoping. The major problem with this SAR was that its location was not conducive to foreign investment, particularly from the ROK.

The location of the Rajin-Sonbong SAR is instructive, however, because it illustrates the fundamental dilemmas Kim Il Sung and Kim Jong Il confronted and still confront with economic reforms. On the one hand, they desired the technology and foreign exchange that may be gained, but they were concerned about the foreign influences that almost always come with these projects. As a result of the Kims' paranoia regarding foreign influence, Rajin-Sonbong was located in an isolated area with poor infrastructure available, and, consequently never has developed into a successful economic venture.[26]

The Sinuiju SAR represented at least a more viable economic venture when it was proposed in 2002. Sinuiju is a North Korean city located along the Yalu River just across from Dandong, China. This Chinese city has a well-developed economic infrastructure in place, and the initial hope was that this infrastructure would be useful for the new SAR. Kim Jong Il selected Yang Bin, a Chinese–Dutch national and one of the wealthiest men in China, to be the first governor of this Sinuiju SAR. Unfortunately, the Chinese government subsequently arrested Yang on charges of fraud and bribery and sentenced him to 18 years in prison. Speculation at the time of his arrest was that China was not happy with the Kim government because of a lack of coordination with China before the Sinuiju SAR was announced. It may also be true that Kim Jong Il and other DPRK officials became concerned that officials in the SAR would exercise too many powers including making monetary policy and controlling currency transfers within the SAR. At least initially, Yang had indicated that South Koreans would be welcome in the Sinuiju SAR.[27] The problems associated with the Sinuiju SAR and the subsequent lack of economic success there is but another example of North Korean paranoia related to meaningful economic reforms.

There has been more success in establishing two mainly inter-Korean economic cooperative efforts in recent years. These are the Mt. Kumgang Tourism Project and the KIC (Kaesong Industrial Complex). In 1998, Chung Ju Yung, the founder of Hyundai and born in northern Korea during the Japanese occupation, decided to take advantage of Kim Dae Jung's Sunshine Policy and attempt to establish a tourism business venture in North Korea, not far from his birth place. In October of that year, he met with Kim Jong Il in Pyongyang and received the North Korea leader's approval for the Mt. Kumgang project. Mt. Kumgang, also known as Diamond Mountain, is a famous tourism attraction for Koreans in both countries, and Chung saw this venture as a good business opportunity as well as a chance to improve relations between the two Koreas.

Hyundai promised to pay the DPRK $942 million over a period of 75 months for the rights to bring tourists to Mt. Kumgang. In addition, Hyundai was able to obtain exclusive long-term rights for seven other projects related to Mt. Kumgang. This latter initiative became controversial in South Korea because Hyundai paid the North Korean government $500 million at the time of the summit meeting between Kim Jong Il and Kim Dae Jung in June 2000. Several South Koreans view this payment as nothing more than a bribe for Kim Jong Il to participate in the summit.[28]

Hyundai's timing for the Mt. Kumgang project was not opportune since it began right in the middle of the Asian economic crisis. In fact, Hyundai had difficulties meeting its payment schedule for the $942 million and was forced to seek assistance from the ROK government. Nonetheless, the North Koreans have been willing to provide certain concessions to assist in making this cooperative effort successful. For example, during the first several years of this project, ROK visitors to Mt. Kumgang had to travel by expensive cruise ships because land routes across the DMZ were not available. Beginning in 2005, the DPRK agreed to allow a land route connection which not only has resulted in more tourists participating, but also has reduced Hyundai's costs. The number of tourists to Mt. Kumgang increased from 57,879 in 2001 to 298,247 in 2005. This increased participation has contributed directly to Hyundai making a profit for the first time beginning in 2005. Despite these improvements, the North Korean authorities have attempted to control the visitors to Mt. Kumgang, particularly opportunities to meet local people, to the maximum extent possible. Hyundai anticipates that casino operations in the Mt. Kumgang resort area will eventually attract many foreign visitors especially Chinese and if this increase in visitors happens, it may make the North Korean government even more concerned about foreign influence.

The KIC is a more extensive economic project between the two Koreas. Construction began in 2003, and the first companies were up and running in 2004. By the end of 2006, fifteen South Korean companies were operating in the KIC employing approximately 10,000 North Korean workers. When the complex is completed in 2012, the estimates are there will be more that 2,000 companies in operation employing perhaps 300,000 workers.[29] From the South Korean perspective, the KIC is very attractive because it combines the cheap land and labor available in North Korea with the ROK's technology, investment capital, and impressive infrastructure. The complex is just 6 miles north of the DMZ and within approximately 40 miles of Seoul. The KIC is also close to the new international airport at Inchon and the harbor there. Kaesong should provide a major boost to South Korea as it attempts to remain competitive with China and attract foreign investment.

In the longer term, South Koreans see the KIC benefiting the DPRK's economy and, hopefully, reducing the eventual costs of reunification. There remain some issues to be resolved. For example in the recently negotiated Free Trade Agreement between the United States and ROK, the two sides could not reach a compromise on whether items produced in the KIC would be included in this agreement. The specifics of this dispute will be covered in chapter 6. For North Korea, the cost-benefit analysis involving the KIC is more difficult to evaluate. The economic advantages are evident in technology access, foreign investment, and employment. However, the political issues cause concern because there is no question that perhaps hundreds of thousands of North Koreans are going to come into daily contact with their South Korean cousins. It will be interesting to see how these interactions play out over time and whether the North Korean authorities will be able to control their population as effectively as in the past.

The opening of the SARs as evidenced by Rajin-Sonbong, Sinuiju, Mt. Kumgang, and Kaesong represents one aspect of North Korean economic reforms in an effort to try to move the country out of the near total economic collapse in the late 1990s. In July 2002, the DPRK announced another series of reforms that have affected the economy although in fits and starts. These economic reforms included the following. First, the government ended the food rationing system, relaxed price controls, and allowed wages to increase. Second, the won was allowed to depreciate from 2.2 won to the U.S. dollar to 150 won to the dollar. The purpose here was both to attract foreign investment and to increase North Korean exports to gain foreign currency. Third, the authorities began to decentralize economic decision-making from the central government to local officials. The government encouraged the formation of farmers markets and required industrial enterprises to assume responsibilities to meet their own costs as subsidies were reduced. Fourth, the government went on record as supporting SARs as a means to increase productivity and foreign investment.[30]

As North Korea has attempted to implement these reforms, major questions remain about what the eventual effects will be on the economy. The depreciation of the won and the increases in wages resulted in hyperinflationary pressures across the country. One authoritative source reported that the price of rice increased by 550 percent after the reforms were implemented, but wages for laborers only increased by 18 percent and 20 percent for managers. The end result was that many North Koreans were worse off after the reforms that before.[31] It is not clear whether these reforms have improved either industrial or agricultural productivity. North Korea remains largely dependent on humanitarian relief agencies such as the United Nations' WFP (World Food Program) and massive food assistance from South Korea, China, and even the United States to supplement its domestic shortfalls. In 2005, the government reduced the geographic access that some humanitarian groups such as the WFP had in distributing food to all regions of the country. In addition, the Kim Jong Il regime attempted to restart the PDS of food rationing.

The government may have been influenced by the relatively good harvest in 2005, but the more likely rationale is that the government wanted to reduce the access agencies such as the WFP had to common North Koreans. As indicated previously, the PDS served as a source of social control, and to have that means of control no longer available was an outcome that Kim was not willing to countenance any longer. In April 2007, the WFP country director for North Korea announced that a WFP survey team had been allowed into the country for the first time since 2004. The results of this survey indicated the DPRK will be short more than 1 million tons of food in 2007. This survey certainly suggests that the economic reforms initiated so far in North Korea have not met with success, and the North Korean people remain at grave risk.[32]

NORTH KOREAN FOREIGN RELATIONS: CHINA, RUSSIA, AND JAPAN

In reviewing North Korea's foreign relations, two observations are apparent. First, the DPRK is influenced by Korea's long history of living in a dangerous neighborhood surrounded by more powerful countries. Second, the Juche ideology affects foreign policy just as it does domestic issues and tends to reinforce self-reliance. As is obvious, these two factors sometimes work at cross purposes in forging a coherent foreign policy approach. Because China and the Soviet Union/Russia have been linked during most of the DPRK's history, they are considered together in this analysis. North Korea's relations with South Korea and the United States will be the subject of chapter 6.

A common phrase used to describe North Korean and Chinese relations is "as close as lips and teeth." The derivation of this phrase usually comes from the significant assistance that China provided during the Korean War when hundreds of thousands of Chinese volunteers entered North Korea. Without this intervention, Kim Il Sung and his forces would have been defeated and the Korean peninsula reunified in the early 1950s. Elements of the Chinese People's Liberation Army remained in the DPRK until 1959 providing important benefits to the North's economy by supplementing its labor force as industrialization began. Although not as publicized as Chinese support during the Korean War, the Soviet Union also was involved, particularly Soviet pilots who engaged U.S. and UN forces over the skies north of the 38th parallel. The USSR provided necessary support to the industrial efforts in the DPRK during the 1950s too.[33]

By the early 1960s, evidence of the Sino-Soviet split was becoming apparent to Kim Il Sung, and he started to exploit these differences for his own purposes. In 1961, both the USSR and China signed individual security treaties with the DPRK, both known as the Treaty of Friendship, Cooperation, and Mutual Assistance. However, prior to the signing of this treaty with the USSR, the DPRK's relationship with Moscow developed strains. After Stalin's death in 1953, Nikita Khrushchev became the Soviet leader. At the 20th Party Congress in 1956, he was highly critical of Stalin's cult of personality and challenged some of Stalin's policies. Since Kim Il Sung was in the process of trying to establish his own cult at this time in North Korea, Kim was not pleased.

Later in October 1962 when the Cuban missile crisis occurred between the United States and USSR, Kim viewed what he considered to be Khrushchev's capitulation with disgust. As the DPRK became more aggressive toward the ROK in the late 1960s as evidenced by the attempt to assassinate Park Chung Hee in the Blue House and the seizure of the USS *Pueblo*, Soviet leaders became worried that their North Korean ally could drag them into a direct confrontation with the United States. Finally, the Soviets had clearly developed what became known as a two Korea position by the early 1970s in that it was evident the

ROK was becoming stronger politically, economically, and militarily and that there were in fact two countries on the Korean peninsula. The Soviets believed that to think otherwise was unrealistic, but Kim Il Sung viewed this change of policy on the part of his ally as a betrayal.[34]

The North Korean tilt toward China lasted until the onset of the Great Proletarian Cultural Revolution in China from the mid-1960s until the mid-1970s. Mao Zedong's Red Guards were particularly critical of Kim Il Sung for his bourgeois ways and squandering Chinese assistance during and after the Korean War. Kim also was less that impressed when Richard Nixon visited China in 1972 and met with Mao and other Chinese leaders. Kim viewed this rapprochement between the United States and China to be contrary to the DPRK's interests. In 1984, Kim Il Sung made his first visit to Moscow since 1962. As a result of this visit and improving relations with the Soviets, the DPRK received Soviet fighter aircraft, surface-to-air missiles, and Scud missiles that would become the backbone of the North Korean missile program. In return for this military equipment, North Korea permitted the Soviets over flight rights and access to certain ports. It was during this period too when the Soviet Union stepped up its support for the nascent DPRK nuclear program by offering to transfer certain technology to the North Koreans.[35]

With new political leadership under first Deng Xiaoping in China and Mikhail Gorbachev in the Soviet Union, the relationships between these two countries and North Korea began to change dramatically, at least from the North Korean perspective. These changes were complemented by Roh Tae Woo's Nordpolitik policies and Seoul's hosting of the 1988 Olympics. By the early 1990s, the ROK had established diplomatic relations with both the Soviet Union and China. At the end of 1991, the Soviet Union ceased to exist, and Russia was confronted with profound problems that basically removed events on the Korean peninsula from its radar screen for several years. Under Boris Yeltsin, the relationship deteriorated to the extent that in 1996, the security treaty with North Korea in effect since 1961 was allowed to expire. For China, North Korea had become even more of an economic drag during the 1990s as the DPRK's economy collapsed. China was no longer willing to extend "friendship prices" for the goods it provided to North Korea, and this policy only made the economic situation worse in the DPRK.

When Vladimir Putin replaced Yeltsin as the Russian leader, the bilateral relationship with North Korea began to improve. In 2000, the security treaty was renegotiated although with less stringent Russian requirements and went into effect. Further, Putin visited Kim Jong Il in July 2000, and Kim reciprocated by traveling to Moscow on a 24-day train trip in August 2001. One year later, Kim again met with Putin in the Russian Far East.[36] Despite these and other diplomatic exchanges, Russia remains limited as to how much influence it can exert on Korean issues. The six-party negotiations that have occurred since 2003 to address the North Korean nuclear weapons issue have allowed Russia to become more engaged. In the February 2007 negotiations, the countries involved selected Russia to chair one of the five WGs (working groups) established to implement the provisions agreed to in Beijing. This WG specifically will address Northeast Asia peace and security mechanisms that may eventually result in a regional security organization.[37] Involvements such as this may provide Russia with more opportunities to once again become a major player in Korean issues.

For both Russia and China, their political leaders see important national security reasons for remaining engaged with North Korea. Although there are historical and ideological factors at play, for both countries, maintaining regional peace and stability is of preeminent importance. China and Russia are engaged in major efforts to grow and develop their economies which requires a peaceful Northeast Asia. Neither country wants to see regime collapse in the DPRK because of the massive refugee flows across borders that this collapse would likely precipitate. In addition, South Korea has become a major source of foreign investment in both countries, and if North Korea collapsed, that investment would be redirected to economic recovery in a unified Korea. Russia and China also do not want to see a North Korea with nuclear weapons for fear that this development could result in regional nuclear proliferation and thereby increased regional instability. For China in particular, there is concern that if the DPRK collapses, reunification would result in American military forces remaining in Korea perhaps near the Chinese border, and this could cause major national security issues in Beijing.[38]

Because of China's interests in providing for regime survival in North Korea, China has played essential roles in fostering multilateral negotiations to resolve the DPRK's nuclear weapons program. It also has taken on the responsibility of providing Pyongyang with very important food and fuel shipments without which the Kim regime would be even in even worse shape. Since 2003, China has hosted a series of multilateral negotiations first involving North Korea, the United States, and China. Later in 2003, these negotiations expanded to include South Korea, Japan, and Russia. Although the substantive results of these negotiations have sometimes not met expectations, they remain the best option to eventually resolve the nuclear weapons problem. Similarly, China provides approximately 70 percent of North Korea's food supplies and between 70 and 80 percent of its petroleum products. China also is the DPRK's largest trading partner with its trade and investments totaling more than $2 billion in 2005.[39]

From North Korea's perspective, its long relationship with China and the Soviet Union/Russia has resulted in both positive and negative outcomes. Kim Il Sung and to a lesser extent Kim Jong Il have played off their two major allies over the years particularly during the height of the Sino-Soviet dispute. The assistance provided by the Chinese and Russians have been essential to North Korea. On the other hand, both Kims have chafed under the influence of their allies and have had to attempt to balance this dependence with the Juche principle of self-reliance, often a difficult challenge and one that has the potential to threaten regime survival. The Russian and Chinese decisions to establish diplomatic relations with South Korea were devastating blows to North Korea, and its economy has never recovered.

Two events that occurred in 2006 provide good examples of North Korean efforts to establish its independence of action from Russia and China. In early July, North Korea conducted a series of missile tests even though China and Russia warned Kim Jong Il not to do so. More importantly, in October, the DPRK tested its first nuclear weapon despite strenuous objections from its two allies. In both instances, the United Nations Security Council passed resolutions imposing sanctions on the DPRK for these tests. China and Russia voted in support of both resolutions disregarding the North Korean argument that these tests were within its legal rights as a sovereign nation state.[40] As a result of the UN sanctions, North Korea has become even more isolated internationally and more estranged from its two primary allies. Additional missile and/or nuclear tests only will result in more serious problems for the DPRK and its population.

Japanese–North Korean relations suffer from some of the same problems as do Japan's relations with South Korea. Foremost among these are the historical legacies from the 35 years of the Japanese occupation of Korea between 1910 and 1945. Although Japan and the ROK established normal diplomatic relations in 1965, normalization between the DPRK and Japan has not occurred. When the ROK and Japan normalized relations, Japan provided South Korea with $800 million as reparations or compensation for the colonial years of occupation. North Korea continues to demand between $5 to $10 billion from Japan during more recent negotiations in part because the DPRK claims the compensation should not only include the period from 1910 to 1945 but also from 1945 to the present. The Japanese do not accept this argument related to the period after the occupation ended, and until this issue is resolved, normalization remains doubtful.[41]

Another issue affecting the bilateral relationship involves North Korea's missile programs and its nuclear weapons development. In August 1998, the DPRK launched without warning a Taepodong 1 long-range missile that over flew the Japanese island of Honshu before crashing into the sea. The Japanese were outraged by this event, and Japan has significantly increased its cooperation with the United States on missile defense programs over the years since this launch. The North Korea missile tests in July 2006 and the nuclear weapon detonation in October have only increased Japan's suspicions about Kim Jong Il's ultimate intentions and have impeded any movement toward establishing diplomatic relations. It is no accident that of all the countries involved in the six-party negotiations, Japan has taken the hardest line against the DPRK by withholding economic assistance programs and being a very strong advocate of punitive sanctions through the United Nations.[42]

Perhaps the most serious contemporary bilateral issue, at least among Japan's public, involves the North Korean abductions of Japanese citizens during the late 1970s and early 1980s. In September 2002, then Prime Minister Junichiro Koizumi traveled to Pyongyang and met with Kim Jong Il to discuss the abduction problem. To the surprise of almost everyone, Kim admitted to Koizumi that North Korean agents had kidnapped thirteen Japanese in order to train North Korean spies in the Japanese language and customs. Kim denied any personal knowledge of these kidnappings and blamed them on overzealous officials. He did apologize for the kidnappings and assured Koizumi that such incidents would not recur. Subsequent negotiations between the two countries revealed that of the thirteen Japanese seized, only five remained alive with the other eight dying during their captivity.[43] North Korea eventually allowed the five survivors to visit Japan, but their family members had to remain in the DPRK.

Prime Minister Koizumi returned to Pyongyang in May 2004 to negotiate the return of the remaining family members and the remains of the deceased. Although the five survivors had only been given permission to visit Japan, none of them returned to North Korea. Eventually, the DPRK permitted the families to leave, and the surviving abductees and their families remain in Japan. In November 2004, North Korea sent the cremated remains of two of the eight deceased abductees to Japan, but questions have arisen from forensic testing as to whether or not these remains are those of the Japanese.[44] The abductions and subsequent events have struck a raw nerve among many Japanese and have become a major political issue in Japan. Evidence of the deterioration in Japanese–North Korean relations is apparent in the trade statistics between the two countries. In 2001, Japan was North Korea's second largest trading partner behind China with almost $1.3 billion in trade. By 2006, bilateral trade had declined to just over $120 million.[45] Until the DPRK is more forthcoming on the circumstances of the deaths of those who died in captivity, it is unlikely that the bilateral relationship will improve.

In summary, North Korea's foreign policy involving China, Russia, and Japan has been a mixed bag. The relationships with China and Russia are not nearly as strong at the beginning of the twenty-first century as they were earlier. Nonetheless, both countries do not want to see North Korea collapse because of their own security interests. As long as China and Russia provide the support that they do, particularly China's food and fuel assistance, North Korea probably will continue to muddle through. Japan, however, which could be a major source of financial assistance if normalization occurs, remains estranged from the leadership in North Korea and opposed to any improvement in relations until North Korea makes fundamental changes in its policies.

AFTER KIM JONG IL, WHO?

Kim Il Sung began the preparations for the succession to his son Kim Jong Il in the mid-1970s. By the time of the 6th Party Congress in 1980, he had officially designated his son as heir and went about placing Kim Jong Il in increasingly important party, KPA, and state positions. When Kim Il Sung died unexpectedly in July 1994, Kim Jong Il was well established and able to accomplish the succession much more easily than many Korean experts thought likely. The succession process from Kim Jong Il to the next political leader in North Korea appears far less certain.

Kim Jong Il has at least three sons: Kim Jong Nam (born in 1968); Kim Jong Chol (born in 1981); and Kim Jong Un (born in 1983). For several years, speculation was that Kim Jong Nam as the eldest son in a Confucian society would likely succeed his father. To support this possibility, Kim Jong Il appointed Kim Jong Nam a general in the KPA in 1995 even though the younger Kim had no military experience. This appointment seemed to be laying the ground work for the succession.[46] Unfortunately, for Kim Jong Nam, in May 2001, Japanese authorities detained him as he attempted to visit Disneyland in Tokyo. Kim was traveling under a false passport, but after several days in detention, Japan sent him back to the DPRK.[47]

The younger Kim's indiscretion was an extreme embarrassment to his father and seems to have removed him from succession consideration. Since Kim Jong Nam's fall from grace, Kim Jong Chol appears to be the front runner and in March 2006, a KWP publication began to refer to him as the "party's nerve center," somewhat similar to the reference to Kim Jong Il as the "party center" many years ago. However, there do not appear to be any further indications that Kim Jong Chol is taking on other positions that would prepare him for supreme leadership in North Korea.

If there is not a designated heir, then what other succession scenarios might apply? Perhaps the most likely is some sort of power struggle between those in North Korea who support economic reforms (reformers) and those who want to protect their privileged positions (hardliners). The reformers would probably look more toward the Chinese economic model and try to introduce certain market reforms in order to make the economy more competitive and able to meet the basic needs of the population. This orientation would entail jettisoning many of the basic tenets of the Juche ideology. The hardliners would include those within the KPA and KWP who already benefit from initiatives such as the "military first" policy. It is unlikely they would willingly give up these perks unless forced to do so.

Major questions over the succession process are just part of the puzzle that surrounds the future of North Korea. The collapse of the economy and the deepening isolation of the country internationally based on the nuclear weapons program all cast doubts on the long-term survivability of the DPRK. However, North Korea has faced difficult times in the past and survived. The North Korean people have one of the highest pain tolerance levels of any population. While the problems are daunting, the Kim Dynasty may yet find a way to preserve its power at least over the next few years.

NOTES

1. Kongdam Oh and Ralph C. Hassig, *North Korea Through the Looking Glass* (Washington: The Brookings Institution, 2000), 9–12.

2. Bradley K. Martin, *Under the Loving Care of the Fatherly Leader: North Korea and the Kim Dynasty* (New York: St. Martins Press, 2004), 51–56.

3. The Socialist Constitution of the Democratic People's Republic of Korea is available at http://www.novexcom.com/dprk_constitution_98.html.

4. Oh and Hassig, *North Korea Through the Looking Glass,* 83–85. See also Jasper Becker, *Rogue Regime: Kim Jong Il and the Looming Threat of North Korea* (New York: Oxford University Press, 2005), 59–63.

5. Ibid., 85–89

6. Park Haksoon, "Changing Dynamics of the North Korean System," in *Joint U.S.–Korea Academic Studies,* vol. 16 (Washington, DC: Korea Economic Institute, 2006), 126–27.

7. For an account of the Kim-Albright meetings, see Jane Perlez, "Visit Revises Image of North Korean," *New York Times* (October 26, 2000): 12. See also Martin, *Under the Loving Care of the Fatherly Leader: North Korea and the Kim Dynasty,* 658–59.

8. Oh and Hassig, *North Korea Through the Looking Glass,* 91.

9. Han S. Park, "The Nature and Evolution of Juche Ideology" in *North Korea: Ideology, Politics, and Economy,* ed. Han S. Park (Athens: University of Georgia Press, 1996), 10–12.

10. Oh and Hassig, *North Korea Through the Looking Glass,* 27–29.

11. Ibid., 21 and Martin, *Under the Loving Care of the Fatherly Leader,* 355.

12. Ibid., 100.

13. Andrew Scobell and John M. Sanford, *North Korea's Military Threat: Pyongyang's Conventional Forces, Weapons of Mass Destruction, and Ballistic Missiles* (Carlisle Barracks: Strategic Studies Institute, Army War College, 2007), 39–47 and Brian P. Duplessis, "The Democratic Peoples Republic of Korea: Conventional or Hybrid Military Threat?" *Policy Forum Online 07-36A* (May 8 2007): 1–8.

14. "The Military Balance 2007," published by the International Institute for Strategic Studies, London, 357–59.

15. Ken E. Gause, *North Korean Civil–Military Trends: Military First Politics to a Point* (Carlisle, PA: Strategic Studies Institute, U.S. Army War College, September 2006), 2–17. For the GNP statistics, see page 10. The promotion and retirement statistics are on page 13.

16. Oh and Hassig, *North Korea Through the Looking Glass,* 105–18.

17. David Hawk, "The Hidden Gulag: Exposing North Korea's Prison Camps," U.S. Committee for Human Rights in North Korea, April 2003 available at http://hrnk.org/hiddengulag/toc.html.

18. "North Korea: Harsher Penalties Against Border-Crossers," Human Rights Watch, Backgrounders, no. 1, March 2007, 1–5. This report is available at http://www.hrw.org/backgrounder/asia/northkorea0307.

19. Oh and Hassig, *North Korea Through the Looking Glass,* 140–43.

20. Han S. Park, "The Nature and Evolution of Juche Ideology," in *North Korea: Ideology, Politics, and Economy,* ed. Park (Athens: University of Georgia Press, 1996), 12–13.

21. Oh and Hassig, *North Korea Through the Looking Glass,* 42–57.

22. Andrew Natsios, "The Politics of Famine in North Korea," Special Report No. 51, August 2, 1999, United States Institute for Peace, 1–14. This report is available at http://www.usip.org/pubs/specialreports/sr990802html.

23. Ibid., 3–9.

24. Bradley O. Babson, "Economic Perspectives on Future Directions for Engagement With the DPRK in a Post-Test World," Policy Analysis Brief, December 2006, The Stanley Foundation, 1–15.

25. Becker, *Rogue Regime: Kim Jong Il and the Looming Threat of North Korea,* 108.

26. Eliot Syunghyun Jung, Youngsoo Kim, and Takayuki Kobayashi, "North Korea's Special Economic Zones: Obstacles and Opportunities," The Korea Economic Institute Ad Hoc Publication Series 2003, 48–49 available at http://www.keia.org/2-Publications/2-4-Adhoc/AdHoc2003/4YSKim.pdf.

27. Howard French, "North Korea to Let Capitalism Loose in Investment Zone," *New York Times* (September 25, 2002): 3.

28. Wonhyuk Lim, *Inter-Korean Economic Cooperation at a Crossroads* (Washington, DC: Korean Economic Institute, December 2006), 17–19.

29. The statistics for visitors to Mt. Kumgang and the employment in the KIC are found in Lim, "Inter-Korean Economic Cooperation at a Crossroads," 16–18.

30. Testimony of Victor D. Cha, "North Korea's Economic Reforms and Security Implications," Committee on Foreign Relations, U.S. Senate, March 2, 2004 available at http://www.senate.gov/~foreign/testimony/2004/Cha Testimony/040302.pdf.

31. Dick K. Nanto and Emma Chanlett-Avery, "The North Korean Economy: Overview and Policy Analysis," Congressional Research Service Report for Congress (RL 32493), Updated April 18, 2007, 9–10.

32. Bernhard Seliger, "North Korea's Economy at a Crossroads," *Korea's Economy 2006,* vol. 22 (Washington, DC: The Korea Economic Institute, April 2006), 62–71. The statement by Jean-Pierre Margerie from the WFP is found in "No Let-Up in Rice for North Korea, Despite Nukes," JoongAng Daily (Internet ed.), April 6, 2007, at http://joongangdaily.joins.com/article/print.asp.

33. Alexander Vorontsov, *Current Russia–North Korea Relations: Challenges and Achievements* (Washington, DC: The Brookings Institute Center for Northeast Asian Policy Studies, February 2007), 5.

34. Oh and Hassig, *North Korea Through the Looking Glass,* 153–54. For the effects of the Cuban missile crisis on Soviet–North Korean relations, see Martin, *Under the Loving Care of the Fatherly Leader: North Korea and the Kim Dynasty,* 124–25.

35. Becker, *Rogue Regime: Kim Jong Il and the Looming Threat of North Korea* (New York: Oxford University Press, 2005), 118–23.

36. Vorontsov, *Current Russia–North Korea Relations: Challenges and Achievements,* 9–12.

37. "North Korea-Denuclearization Action Plan" dated February 13, 2007, located at http://www.state.gov/r/pa/prs/ps/2007/february/80479.html.

38. David Shambaugh, "China and the Korean Peninsula: Playing for the Long Term," *Washington Quarterly,* 26, no. 2 (Spring 2003): 46–48 and John S. Park, "Inside Multilateralism: The Six-Party Talks," *Washington Quarterly,* 28, no. 4 (Autumn 2005): 81–85.

39. Richard Weitz, "The Korean Pivot: Challenges and Opportunities from Evolving Chinese–Russian and U.S.–Japanese Security Ties," *Korea Economic Institute Academic Papers Series,* 1, no. 3 (March 2007): 5–8.

40. United Nations Security Council Condemns Democratic People's Republic of Korea's Missile Launches, Resolution 1695, July 15, 2006, and UN Security Council Resolution on North Korea 1718, October 14, 2006.

41. Oh and Hassig, *North Korea Through the Looking Glass,* 160–65.

42. Weitz, "The Korean Pivot," 9.

43. Howard French, "North Koreans Sign Agreement With Japanese," *New York Times* (September 18, 2002): 1, and Howard French "Needing Each Other," *New York Times* (September 19, 2002): 8.

44. James Brooke, "Koizumi's Visit Gets Lukewarm Reviews," *New York Times* (May 24, 2004): 6.

45. Nando and Chanlett-Avery, "The North Korean Economy: Overview and Policy Analysis," 33–35

46. Martin, *Under the Loving Care of the Fatherly Leader: North Korea and the Kim Dynasty* (New York: St. Martins Press, 2004), 694–95.

47. Howard French, "Japan Detains Man Said to be North Korean Leader's Son," *New York Times* (May 4, 2001): 3.

CHAPTER 4

North Korean Nuclear
Weapon Programs

This chapter will address the North Korean WMD programs (nuclear, chemical, and biological) as well as the DPRK's ballistic missile development. The first part of the chapter attempts to answer the basic question of why Kim Il Sung and Kim Jong Il decided to spend scarce resources to develop these weapons and delivery systems almost from the very beginning of North Korea's history. The rest of the chapter traces the WMD programs as they have evolved until the time of the first detonation of a nuclear device in October 2006 and then looks to the future in an effort to determine where Kim Jong Il and those who follow him may choose to go with these programs.

NORTH KOREAN MOTIVATIONS FOR DEVELOPING NUCLEAR WEAPONS AND MISSILE SYSTEMS

It is important to reiterate that North Korea is one of the most closed and secretive nation states in existence. Therefore, any effort to determine why the DPRK would choose to develop nuclear weapons and ballistic missiles is at best an educated guess, and the analysis that follows should be viewed in this light. Nonetheless, there are clues that allow us to enter into such speculation.

The first reason for developing nuclear weapons is that by so doing, the Kim dynasty has attempted to provide for regime survival against both internal and external challenges as Kim Il Sung and Kim Jong Il have perceived these challenges. From the internal perspective, the institution that is of most concern is the KPA. Since 1998, Kim Jong Il has employed the "military first" policy whereby the KPA has received preferential treatment in budgetary allotments with as much as 20–25 percent of the country's gross national product supporting the military. Even though the KPA is the fourth largest military in existence, much of its equipment has become obsolete and in need of replacement. There is no question that the conventional military balance on the Korean peninsula has shifted over the past 20–30 years clearly to favor South Korea. Based on these realities, it may make more sense for Kim Jong Il to provide the KPA with nuclear weapons both to offset the ROK's conventional advantages and to keep the military satisfied. There may also be a cost benefit in that nuclear weapons can be less expensive than many conventional systems.

The external challenges of most worry to Kim Jong Il are primarily the United States and to a lesser extent South Korea. From the North Korean perspective, every American administration from Harry Truman to George W. Bush has been intent on destroying the DPRK, and if the United States had not intervened in the Korean War, Kim Il Sung always believed he would have achieved his goal of Korean reunification under the control of North Korea. Kim never forgot this lesson and neither has his son. Since the end of the war, the MDT and the American military presence in the ROK have continued to stymie the Kim dynasty's reunification aspirations. There is no way that Kim Jong Il would hope to match American nuclear weapons, but the presence of a few nuclear devices and the means to deliver them may chip away at the credibility of the extended deterrence, frequently called the nuclear umbrella, the United States provides to the ROK, Japan, and other friends/allies in East Asia.

This interpretation supports the basic concept that nuclear weapons provide an enhanced deterrent value over conventional weapons and could influence both American and South Korean responses to North Korean coercive actions. Two experts on North Korea have suggested that Kim Jong Il may have learned an important lesson from the 2003 American invasion of Iraq in that Kim perhaps believes that the United States might not repeat such an invasion if the DPRK has demonstrably established that it has nuclear weapons and thereby a credible deterrent.[1]

Finally, if North Korea still holds out the prospect of conducting some type of military action against the ROK that would result in a North Korean victory, it may be that nuclear weapons are seen as essential to this end. In a recent speech to the National Press Club in Washington, Park Geun Hye, the daughter of Park Chung Hee and a leading opposition political leader in South Korea in her own right, related that many South Koreans have changed their minds regarding the military balance after the North Korea tested a nuclear device in October 2006. In her speech, Park clearly stated that this nuclear test had fundamentally disrupted the military balance on the Korean peninsula and could lead to an arms race in Northeast Asia. She went on to state that the peaceful Korean reunification that her country had been working to achieve was now very much in jeopardy since North Korea had become a nuclear weapons country.[2]

A second possible motivation for developing nuclear weapons and missiles is to use them as bargaining chips so that the United States and other countries will treat North Korea as a serious negotiating partner. The argument here is that in return for guarantees of its sovereignty and security along with other political and economic rewards, the DPRK would agree to terminate its nuclear and missile programs.[3] There is some justification that North Korea is willing to follow this course of action. During the Clinton administration, the DPRK and United States entered into the Agreed Framework in October 1994. This agreement provided that in return for North Korea closing its nuclear facilities at Yongbyon and Taechon, the Americans would make available LWRs (light water reactors) and other rewards. Later, in 1999, North Korea agreed to a self-imposed missile test moratorium in return for U.S. movement toward establishing more normal economic and diplomatic relations. Both the Agreed Framework and the missile moratorium will be addressed in much more detail in chapter 5. The point here is that there is some precedent to support the argument that the DPRK is willing to negotiate if the incentives are perceived to be sufficient.

A third conceivable motivation is what is referred to as the hedging strategy or what Victor Cha has coined as the North Korean "cake and eat it too" approach.[4] Support for this argument is based on the belief that the DPRK wants both better relations with the United States *and* nuclear weapons. In case the improved relations do not eventuate, then North Korea will have the nuclear weapon threat to force the United States to take it seriously and compel negotiations. A variant of this argument is that North Korea is intent on cheating regardless of any agreement it enters into and will pursue nuclear weapons no matter what. The only reason the DPRK will agree to limit its programs is to buy time so that these programs can go forward. As we will see in the next chapter, several members of the Bush administration made this argument in criticizing the 1994 Agreed Framework. Another related argument is that there are divisions within the North Korean government between more pragmatic leaders who believe in negotiations and those who are more ideological and argue that nuclear weapons are essential for North Korean security. The policy varies from time to time based on which of these factions has the ear of Kim Jong Il.[5]

Fourth, having nuclear weapons reinforces, the North Korean Juche principle of self-reliance since these weapons provided Kim Il Sung and now Kim Jong Il with a certain amount of freedom of action from both China and the Soviet Union/Russia. As mentioned in chapter 3, the Kims have been very effective playing the USSR/Russia off against the Chinese, and there is clear evidence of this effectiveness with the nuclear weapons program as will become evident later in this chapter.[6] North Korean nuclear weapons also affect the relations between the two Koreas. South Korea once had aspirations to develop a nuclear weapons program during the presidency of Park Chung Hee, but was forced to give up this program under American pressure. Now, North Korea can claim it possesses the only Korean nuclear weapons program, and this claim allows it to play upon Korean nationalism very effectively. Similarly, having a nuclear weapons program was important to the succession process from Kim Il Sung to Kim Jong Il particularly because the younger Kim could take credit for supporting this program which he did even before his father died. This role in the development of the nuclear weapons program provides Kim Jong Il with additional credibility with the KPA.

Finally, the North Korean missile program in particular has become a crucial source of foreign exchange as the DPRK's economy has continued to decline with fewer and fewer products competitive on the international market. As will become evident, North Korea became an exporter of missiles and missile technology in the mid-1990s, and continues with these exports today to the extent that the international community permits. Nuclear weapons and missiles also are important to the DPRK because they provide certain status that would not be available if North Korea did not have these weapons. Korean nationalism is very important in the competition between the two Koreas, and the DPRK attempts to use its status to its advantage every time possible.

This list of possible motivations for North Korea to build nuclear weapons and missiles is not meant to be all inclusive, but only to suggest some of the advantages the Kims may have seen to spending so much of their scarce resources on these programs. Now we will turn to the evolution of the nuclear weapons program from the earliest days of North Korea's history.

THE NORTH KOREAN NUCLEAR WEAPONS PROGRAMS

Kim Il Sung was impressed by the prospect of nuclear weapons from the time he heard of the atomic bombs being dropped on the Japanese cities of Hiroshima and Nagasaki primarily because their use contributed directly to the Japanese surrender in World War II. Later, during the Korean War when the Eisenhower administration threatened the use of atomic bombs if the war did not come to an end, Kim was further impressed.[7] In 1956, North Korea entered into two agreements with the Soviet Union whereby the Soviets began to provide assistance for the DPRK's nuclear research. By the end of the 1950s, the North Koreans had negotiated similar agreements with China, another example of Kim Il Sung playing one of his allies off against the other. The cooperation with the Soviets expanded by the mid-1960s so that Russian scientists had set up a nuclear research facility at Yongbyon, approximately 60 miles north of Pyongyang. In 1965, a major milestone occurred when the Soviets supplied a small research reactor and a nuclear research lab. This research reactor was fueled by uranium which favored North Korea because it has large natural uranium deposits. The best estimate is that this research reactor began operation by 1967, and in 1974, the DPRK joined the IAEA (International Atomic Energy Agency).[8]

In the early 1980s, the DPRK began a serious program to expand its reactor capabilities. This program required the construction of three gas-cooled, graphite-moderated reactors: a small 5 MW reactor at Yongbyon; a 50 MW prototype power reactor also at Yongbyon; and a 200 MW power reactor at Taechon. Each of these reactors would use uranium produced at a fuel fabrication facility located at Yongbyon as the primary fuel rather than HEU (highly enriched uranium). This is important because North Korea does not have to import fuel to be used in its reactors. More important for achieving North Korea's overall nuclear goals was that in the early 1980s, the DPRK constructed an industrial scale reprocessing plant at Yongbyon. When completed, this facility provided the capability to separate weapons grade plutonium from the spent fuel that would be taken from the 5 MW reactor. This reactor came online in 1994 and is capable of producing approximately 6–7 kg of plutonium or roughly one Hiroshima-sized nuclear weapon per year. The two larger reactors could produce approximately 60 and 240 kg of plutonium respectively once they are completed. By the mid-1990s, the DPRK had mastered the full nuclear fuel cycle process from producing the uranium necessary to run its reactors to developing the facilities to reprocess plutonium from the spent fuel.[9]

In December 1985, North Korea signed the nuclear NPT (Non-Proliferation Treaty) largely because of pressure from the Soviet Union. However, after becoming a NPT signatory, the DPRK refused to sign the IAEA full-scope safeguards agreement that it was required to accomplish within an 18-month period. This refusal to sign the IAEA safeguards agreement meant that IAEA inspectors were not permitted to visit North Korean sites at Yongbyon and elsewhere. As the construction of the additional larger reactors progressed, international concern increased. This concern was exacerbated after the conclusion of the Gulf War in 1991 when it became apparent that Iraq was much further along with its nuclear weapons program than the IAEA and other intelligence sources had predicted. The fear was that the same may well be true for North Korea.[10]

Under increasing international pressure, North Korea eventually signed the IAEA full-scope safeguards agreement and then ratified it in April 1992. Between May 1992 and July 1993, the IAEA conducted a series of inspections at the Yongbyon location. Its inspectors became more suspicious because of apparent discrepancies in the amount of plutonium the DPRK had extracted. The United States and North Korea entered into long and complicated negotiations during the summer of 1993 until October 1994 when the Agreed Framework came into existence and reduced tensions on the Korean peninsula. The specifics of these negotiations will be addressed in the following chapter. For our purposes now, the Agreed Framework resulted in the shutting down of North Korea's plutonium production facilities at Yongbyon and elsewhere along with the DPRK remaining in the NPT and IAEA. North Korea had threatened to withdraw from both as the disputes with the United States and the IAEA became more acute.

In return, the United States pledged to provide two LWRs and 500,000 tons of HFO (heavy fuel oil) per year to North Korea. From the implementation of the Agreed Framework in 1994 until the end of the Clinton administration in January 2001, the North Korean plutonium-based nuclear weapons program remained frozen.

During the first almost 2 years of the George W. Bush administration, there was little contact between the United States and North Korea. This changed in October 2002 when President Bush dispatched James Kelly, the assistant secretary of state for East Asia and Pacific affairs, to Pyongyang. Kelly's specific mission was to confront the North Koreans with evidence obtained from intelligence sources indicating that the DPRK was involved with a HEU program. Such a program would be a violation of the 1994 Agreed Framework and a bilateral denuclearization agreement between the two Koreas that had been in effect since 1992. To the surprise of the visiting American delegation, the North Korean representatives admitted they were developing a HEU program after an initial denial. Subsequently, these representatives would reverse themselves again and argued that the DPRK did not actually have such a program, but only the sovereign right to develop one. Hwang Jang Yop , the highest ranking North Korean official to defect, has since provided information suggesting that North Korea entered into an agreement with the A. Q. Khan network in Pakistan during the summer of 1996 to trade DPRK ballistic missile expertise for HEU technology, particularly involving centrifuges.[11]

In November 2002, the board of the KEDO (Korea Peninsula Energy Development Organization) that had been established to oversee the building of the LWRs and the delivery of the HFO to North Korea voted to terminate both programs.[12] In response, the DPRK took a series of steps that caused even more concern in the United States and the international community. In December 2002, North Korean officials announced that they considered the Agreed Framework to be null and void based on the cancellation of the LWR project and HFO deliveries. Further, they stated that the DPRK would restart the 5 MW reactor as well as the reprocessing plant at Yongbyon and resume construction of the 50 and 200 MW reactors. The 8,000 irradiated fuel rods taken from the 5 MW reactor and stored in the cooling pond at Yongbyon as stipulated in the Agreed Framework would be retrieved for possible reprocessing. Finally, in January 2003, the DPRK declared its intention to withdraw from the NPT and IAEA safeguards agreement and to expel the IAEA inspectors from the country. The withdrawal from the NPT became effective in April 2003, and IAEA inspectors have not been present in North Korea since late in 2002.[13]

After the DPRK withdrawal from the NPT and IAEA, the nuclear weapons crisis on the Korean peninsula has only gotten worse. In February 2005, the North Korean Foreign Ministry issued a very important statement. In this statement, the spokesman referred specifically to the January 2005 confirmation testimony of secretary of state designate Condoleezza Rice in which she referred to North Korea as "an outpost of tyranny." From the DPRK's perspective, if there was to be an improvement in its relationship with the United States at the beginning of the second Bush term, this comment was interpreted as making such improvement impossible.[14] Later in the statement, the Foreign Ministry stipulated explicitly that North Korea was a nuclear weapons nation state but that its nuclear weapons were strictly for defensive purposes to serve as a deterrent against possible American military actions threatening the country.[15] In the past, North Korea had always been at least somewhat ambiguous as to whether or not it had nuclear weapons, but that ambiguity appeared to be put to rest by this statement. Also important was the defensive nature of the justification for having nuclear weapons and the deterrent value that the Foreign Ministry indicated as a critical advantages gained from having nuclear weapons.

One of North Korea's most provocative actions regarding its nuclear weapons program occurred in October 2006. The Foreign Ministry issued another statement in early October indicating that a nuclear test was imminent. This statement was extremely important from the perspective of trying to determine most clearly what the DPRK's motives were in developing nuclear weapons and then testing one of them. The ministry stressed that the country "stands at the crossroads of life and death" based largely on its perspectives of the hostile policies of the Bush administration and "North Korea's needs to bolster its war deterrence for self defense." Based on these circumstances, the statement went on to declare that North Korea was going to test a nuclear weapon under conditions where "safety is firmly guaranteed." The DPRK also pledged that it would not be the first to use nuclear weapons on the Korean peninsula and would not transfer nuclear weapons to others. In this part of the statement, the Foreign Ministry made it clear that a country without a "reliable war deterrent" was "bound to meet a tragic death and the sovereignty of the country is bound to be wantonly infringed upon." Although the statement did not mention Iraq specifically in this context, the meaning is clear. Finally, this statement indicated that since North Korea had stated in February 2005 that it possessed nuclear weapons, it was only natural to test these weapons. The statement concluded by assuring the world that North Korea would be a "responsible nuclear weapons state" and continued to support nuclear disarmament on the Korean peninsula as well as the prospect of improved relations with the United States.[16]

The international response to North Korea's statement that a nuclear weapons test was about to occur was overwhelmingly negative. Nonetheless, on October 9, 2006, the DPRK did in fact conduct an underground nuclear detonation in the northeast part of the country. This detonation measured less than 1 kton (the atomic bombs dropped on Hiroshima and Nagasaki were approximately 20 kton for comparative purposes). Just a few hours prior to the detonation, the North Koreans advised the Chinese and Russian embassies in Pyongyang that the test would occur. This notification indicated that the explosion would be about 4 kton which suggests that the actual detonation was less successful than the DPRK had anticipated. However, seismic and scientific evidence after the fact substantiated that North Korea did in fact test a nuclear device.[17]

After the nuclear detonation, the KCNA (Korean Central News Agency), the official voice of the North Korean government, issued a very brief announcement. In this announcement, the KCNA stressed the safety features of the test emphasizing that no "radioactive emission" took place. More important, the announcement made very clear that the test "was conducted with indigenous wisdom and technology 100%." It concluded by relating that the test "greatly encouraged and pleased the KPA and people that have wished to have a powerful and self-reliant defense capability" and would contribute to "defending the peace and stability on the Korean peninsula and the area around it."[18] The international reaction to the North Korean nuclear test, including a United Nations Security Council resolution, will be addressed in the next chapter.

There are some important conclusions that can be reached from an analysis of the official DPRK government statements made before and after the nuclear test relating to the motives behind this test. First, it is apparent that regime survival both from perceived internal and external sources was a major factor. The emphasis on the "hostile policies" of the Bush administration signaled that North Korea very much needed to develop and test a nuclear weapon. There were several specific references to a "war deterrent" and for the need to have a self-defense capability in these statements. The reference to the KPA being "pleased" by the nuclear test also was significant as evidence of the continuation of support for the military first policy and the government's efforts to keep the KPA satisfied. Second, the Juche principle of self-reliance was supported in the statement issued after the test praising the DPRK's "powerful self-reliant defense capability." Also evident was the North Korea's willingness to ignore the demands of the Chinese and Russians not to conduct the test. Third, although the government statements referred to hostile Bush administration policies as being major factors in the decision to test this weapon, it was also clear that North Korea did not want to completely end any possibility of improved relations with Washington. This desire to keep the channels of communication with the United States open may be another example of North Korea's concerns about the credibility of the support from China and Russia.

In addition to the plutonium-based fission nuclear program described above, the Bush administration charged in October 2002 that North Korea also was developing a HEU capability. Pakistani President Pervez Musharraf in a memoir written in 2006 seemed to support this charge when he alleged that North Korean agents began meeting with representatives of the A.Q. Khan network in 1999. Khan is generally considered to be the father of the Pakistani nuclear weapons program and established a rogue network to supply nuclear technology and equipment to other countries including North Korea apparently if the price was right. Musharraf wrote that the DPRK was particularly interested in centrifuge technology critical to the enrichment of uranium and essential to development of HEU as a bomb material. In his book, he speculated that North Korea may have been successful in obtaining the second generation P-2 centrifuges that are more efficient and faster in the enrichment process than the older P-1 centrifuges.[19] This account would seem to support the case made by Assistant Secretary of State Kelly in his October 2002 confrontation with North Korean officials.

Other experts with knowledge of HEU facilities and equipment are not so sure about the DPRK's program. David Albright, president of the Institute for Science and International Security, traveled to Pyongyang early in 2007 and met with senior North Korean officials. Although they denied a HEU capability, Albright is of the opinion that North Korea probably does have a small-scale gas centrifuge program involving perhaps a few dozen centrifuges derived through purchases made from the Khan network. However, he questions whether the DPRK has been able to develop a much larger number of centrifuges that would be needed to enrich enough uranium for a viable nuclear program, at least to this point. Albright is particularly suspicious of some of the American intelligence reports concerning the supposed North Korean purchase of thousands of the 6,000 series aluminum tubes from Germany and Russia in the early 2000s. His suspicions are fueled by the mistaken analysis of similar aluminum tubes procured by Iraq that turned out not to be involved with nuclear weapons.[20]

In conclusion concerning the North Korean nuclear weapons programs as of May 2007, the plutonium program is well established and a nuclear devise has now been tested, although the test did not go as well as planned. While there may also be a HEU program, it is not nearly as well developed, and serious questions exist as to what the North Koreans hope to accomplish with this program. At the end of this chapter, we will address the amount of plutonium that the DPRK is likely to have available in its inventory for nuclear weapon construction as well as some of the steps the country will need to take if it wants to carry this weapon program forward to a more advanced level.

NORTH KOREA'S CHEMICAL AND BIOLOGICAL WEAPONS PROGRAMS

Less is known about North Korea's chemical and biological weapons programs than about its nuclear weapons. Regarding chemical weapons first, it appears that Kim Il Sung had decided at least by the early 1960s, if not before, to develop chemical weapons. In 1961, he issued his "Declaration for Chemicalization" that outlined his plans for chemical weapons production. At about this same time, Kim established the Nuclear and Chemical Defense Bureau to oversee this program. By the mid-1960s, it appears that Kim turned more to the Soviet Union for assistance with chemical weapons primarily through obtaining training manuals and possibly small amounts of nerve and mustard agents.[21] The Defense Intelligence Agency in 1979 estimated that the DPRK had only a defensive chemical weapon capability, but by the end of the 1980s, intelligence estimates had changed to indicate that North Korea had developed the capability to produce large quantities of chemical weapons. It may be that Kim Il Sung was impressed with the use of chemical weapons during the Iran–Iraq war and decided to expand his stocks.[22]

At present, the best estimates by the Nuclear Threat Initiative organization are that North Korea has between 2,500 and 5,000 tons of chemical agents. Among these chemicals are blister (mustard), nerve (sarin), choking (phosgene), and blood (hydrogen cyanide) agents. According to this source, there are approximately twelve facilities in North Korea that produce these chemicals, precursors, and agents. One of the biggest challenges that the DPRK reportedly confronts with building and stockpiling chemical weapons has to do with the lack of indigenously produced precursors. There have been instances when ethnic Koreans have been apprehended in Japan with sodium fluoride that they were trying to bring to North Korea. This chemical is a known precursor for sarin gas, and the suspicion was that these individuals intended to bring this chemical into the country to serve as the precursor.

There is no such problem with a scarcity of delivery systems for chemical weapons, and North Korea has mastered the technology of developing warheads that can carry these weapons. The DPRK has extensive multiple rocket launchers, long-range artillery, and short-range missiles that could deliver devastating chemical attacks on Seoul and other cities throughout South Korea. Two experts on North Korean WMD have described chemical weapons as an "operational force multiplier" because they would be used as a "weapon of first resort" in any North Korean attack on the ROK.[23] Lastly, North Korea has not signed the Chemical Weapons Convention even though there has been pressure from South Korea, the United States, and several other countries to do so. Apparently in an internal debate in Pyongyang during the early 1990s, the Foreign Ministry argued in support of joining this convention, but the KPA and the Ministry of the People's Armed Forces opposed. Kim Jong Il sided with the military.

North Korea's biological weapons program appears to be less developed than that of either nuclear or chemical weapons. As he did with chemical weapons, Kim Il Sung expressed interest in biological agents in the early 1960s. By the 1980s, there were reports that North Korea had been able to develop cultures in as many as ten military and civilian research institutes to produce anthrax, smallpox, botulism, and plague agents.[24] However, there are at least three problems confronting North Korea with its biological program. First, it appears that the DPRK has had more problems weaponizing its biological agents than it has with its chemical agents. It is not clear that Pyongyang has been able to arm warheads with biological weapons although the evidence is not definitive on this point. Second, there is a basic question as to the utility of biological weapons on the Korean peninsula because of wind patterns and other climatic issues. An attempt to use these weapons against South Korea by using artillery or missiles could result in the toxins being blown back over North Korea. Third, to the extent it is relative, in 1987, North Korea became a signatory of the 1972 Biological Toxin and Weapons Convention whereas it never signed the Chemical Weapons Convention and has withdrawn from the NPT.

NORTH KOREA'S MISSILE PROGRAMS

Kim Il Sung became serious about developing a ballistic missile capability at least by the mid-1960s when he established the Hamhung Military Academy in 1965. This academy was charged with the responsibility of providing training to North Koreans so that they would be capable of participating in an indigenous missile program. Initially, much of the external support for the missile program came from the Soviet Union, but in 1971, China and the DPRK entered into an agreement that provided Chinese expertise on surface to air and cruise missiles. By the mid to late 1970s, North Korea was relatively well along in the creation of its SRBMs (short-range ballistic missiles) primarily through the transfer of Scud-B missiles and technology from the USSR and possibly from Egypt. North Korea was able to reverse engineer these missiles and renamed the Scud-B the Hwasong-5. This missile has a range of approximately 300 km and a payload of just under 1,000 kg.[25]

In 1987, North Korea entered into a commercial deal with Iran to supply possibly as many as 100 Hwasong-5 missiles for an estimated $500 million. Iran then used these missiles in the latter stages of its war against Iraq. Because the Hwasong-5 does not have the range to strike all areas of South Korea, the KPA requested a longer range missile that would have this capability. By the end of the 1980s, North Korean technicians developed the Hwasong-6 SRBM that has a range of 500 km although a slightly smaller payload of 770 kg. This missile is capable of reaching any part of the ROK. The total number of SRBMs in the North Korean inventory is estimated to be approximately 600 with all of them being liquid fueled to this point. Among those countries believed to have purchased SRBMs from North Korea in addition to Iran are Egypt, Libya, Syria, and possibly Pakistan.[26]

After the relative success of the SRBMs, the DPRK began an intermediate range ballistic missile program between 1987 and 1989. The Nodong missile has a range of approximately 1,000 km and a payload of 700 kg. The best estimates are that North Korea has between 175 and 200 Nodong missiles in its inventory. A couple of the major advantages of this missile are that it can be fired from mobile launchers that may reduce the preparation time for a launch and make targeting against it more difficult. The Nodong has the range to reach targets in Japan meaning that American forces there would be within range of this missile. The DPRK first tested the Nodong missile in 1990, but this test may have failed. In a subsequent series of tests, the Nodong was successfully tested in 1993 at a range in the northeast part of the country. Once again, North Korea has entered into commercial deals to sell this missile to Libya and Iran with possible additional sales to Syria and Pakistan. Reports have circulated that Iran has also flight tested one or more of the missiles purchased from the DPRK, and it is possible that Iran has shared data concerning these tests with the DPRK. To date, the Nodong missile is liquid fueled.[27]

In the early 1990s, North Korean missile specialists began to develop the Taepodong long-range ballistic missile. The Taepodong 1 was designed to have a range between 1,500 and 2,500 km and a payload between 1,000 and 1,500 kg. The more advanced Taepodong 2 missile reportedly has expanded capabilities that can deliver a similar warhead to a range of 4,000–8,000 km. It appears that North Korean technicians have used the Nodong missile as one of the two or three stages in the Taepodong missile. In August 1998, North Korea launched a Taepodong 1 missile over the main Japanese island of Honshu that caused a major incident. The United States, Japan, and several other countries brought pressure to bear against the DPRK, and in 1999, Kim Jong Il agreed to enter into a self-imposed missile testing moratorium as long as the United States would continue to engage in serious negotiations with North Korea. The specific negotiations between the United States and North Korea after the 1998 missile test will be discussed in the next chapter, but suffice it to say, Kim Jong Il learned an important lesson from this experience as far as how to get the attention of the Americans. The bilateral relationship between the United States and DPRK improved to the point that by the end of the Clinton administration, Secretary of State Madeleine Albright had visited Kim in Pyongyang, and there was even some speculation that President Clinton might visit North Korea.

During the Bush administration, the relationship clearly deteriorated through the actions of each side. However, by 2006, Kim apparently had become convinced that another missile test was necessary to focus American attention on his country and convince the American administration to negotiate. On July 4, in the United States (it was July 5 in the DPRK), North Korea launched seven ballistic missiles over and into the Sea of Japan from facilities located in the northeast of the DPRK. One of these missiles was the Taepodong 2 model on its first test. It is liquid fueled and capable of launching either a satellite or warhead although it is not certain that North Korea has developed a warhead that will fit on this missile. The Taepodong involved in this test only flew for less than a minute before crashing into the sea. Therefore, this launch is viewed largely as a failure although it is possible that the DPRK missile experts learned something during the short flight that might be useful for future tests. Three of the other missiles were Nodongs, and the other three shorter range models of the Scud variety. All of these missile launches were more successful than that of the Taepodong.[28]

North Korea made no attempt to keep these launches secret in the period of time leading up to the tests. In fact, satellites and other national technical means of intelligence gathering had detected the Taepodong missile in particular on a launch pad for weeks before the actual test firing. President Bush and Japanese Prime Minister Koizumi among other world leaders had issued public statements warning Kim Jong Il not to conduct the tests and promising that pressure would be brought to bear if North Korea went forward.[29] Despite these warnings, Kim ignored them, and this action raises questions as to what his motivations might have been. Two experts have suggested that he simply was following the model that had worked in the late 1990s after the test of the Taepodong 1 missile and wanted to force the United States to take North Korea seriously and negotiate.[30]

Others have suggested that the KPA very much wanted to conduct the tests to substantiate its capabilities and to prove to the North Korean elite that the money spent on the "military first policy" was worth it. Under this scenario, Kim Jong Il simply acceded to the military's wishes. Another possibility is that the continued viability of the North Korean missile program from the perspective of future international sales required testing since there had not been a long-range launch in almost 8 years. While the partial failure of the Taepodong 2 test would not enhance North Korea's reputation, the Nodong missiles performed much better. The Nodong may have more of a deterrent effect on the United States and other countries in the region because as an intermediate range missile, it is looked upon with some concern because Japan and American forces in Japan are well within its range. This missile also is believed to be capable of carrying conventional as well as chemical and perhaps nuclear warheads. In addition, the DPRK has more than likely learned valuable lessons from the Nodong missile tests that other countries such as Iran have conducted over the past few years and then shared with North Korea.[31]

Whatever North Korea's motivations for conducting the missile tests, the international reaction to these tests was remarkably fast and forceful. Although China and Russia had initially expressed some reservations concerning sanctions against North Korea, the United States, and Japan among other countries pressed hard for a United Nations Security Council resolution condemning the DPRK for its actions.[32] On July 15, 2006, the Security Council unanimously passed Resolution 1695 that among other demands required all UN member countries "to prevent missile and missile-related items, materials, goods, and technology" from being provided to North Korea or of procuring these items from the DPRK.[33] The fact that China and Russia agreed to support this resolution rather than veto it or at least abstain must have come as a particular disappointment to Kim Jong Il and reinforced his suspicions about two of his most important allies.

CONCLUSION

The concluding section of this chapter will examine three issues: the plutonium that North Korea likely has available based on reprocessing spent fuel from its 5 MW reactor at Yongbyon, its chemical weapons capability, and the missiles that could possibly deliver these WMD. The last section will then explore some steps the DPRK may take that could provide good indicators of the direction North Korea intends to take in the next several years regarding its WMD programs. In 1994 when the Agreed Framework went into effect resulting in the shutdown of North Korea's plutonium program, the estimates were that the DPRK perhaps had 5–10 kg of plutonium available reprocessed from the 5 MW reactor. That amount of plutonium could have produced not more than one or two nuclear weapons of the size used against Japan in 1945. But there also were 8,000 spent fuel rods that remained in cooling ponds at Yongbyon under the surveillance of IAEA inspectors.

After the collapse of the Agreed Framework in late 2002 and early 2003, experts believe that the DPRK reprocessed the 8,000 spent fuel rods resulting in the addition of between 27 and 29 kg of plutonium. Between April and June 2005, satellite imagery suggested that the 5 MW reactor was shut down. The informed speculation then was that the main purpose of this stoppage was to remove additional spent fuel rods from the reactor, and that between 13.5 and 17.1 kg of plutonium were reprocessed. Once the reactor began operations again in June 2005 until February 2007, the current estimate is that another 10–13 kg of plutonium has been produced, although there is no evidence this plutonium has been removed from the reactor.

Based on the best estimates possible from unclassified sources, some of the American nuclear weapons specialists who have visited North Korea are of the opinion that the DPRK has reprocessed between 46 and 64 kg of plutonium of which about 28–50 kg may be in separated and usable form to build nuclear weapons. If this estimate is accurate and it requires between 5 and 8 kg of plutonium to produce one rather crude nuclear weapon, North Korea may have between 5 and 12 nuclear weapons in its inventory. Another expert who has visited North Korea's nuclear facilities at Yongbyon has estimated the DPRK has between 40 and 50 kg of plutonium or enough for six to eight nuclear devices.[34] While it seems likely that North Korea is developing a HEU program, the evidence does not suggest that the DPRK program has matured to the extent necessary to make a major contribution to the nuclear weapons program. That situation certainly can change over the next few years if Kim Jong Il decides to continue allocating resources to the HEU effort.

What then are some clues that we can look for that will give us indications as to the direction North Korea intends to go in the next few years with its WMD programs? One option is that Kim Jong Il will be willing to negotiate away his WMDs if the right political and economic incentives are presented. This option will be evaluated fully in chapter 5. Once a country has developed a nuclear weapons capability, the possibility exists that the country can reconstitute that program at a later date even after arms control agreements have been negotiated. The other option is that Kim will move forward with efforts to more completely operationalize his WMDs to enhance his deterrent capabilities.[35] In order to do so, there are some obvious steps that North Korea will have to take. First, we know that the nuclear weapons test in October 2006 was only a partial success at best. Therefore, North Korea will have to use some of its stored plutonium to conduct at least one and perhaps a few more nuclear weapons tests to ensure that its nuclear weapons do in fact work. If the DPRK decides to detonate additional nuclear weapons to establish the viability of its capability, it will be evident to the international community.

Second, North Korea has been working on its missile program for several years and has conducted a number of launches. The DPRK has also benefited from the tests that other countries have conducted with missiles purchased from the North Koreans. However, the Taepodong 2 test in July 2006 raises more questions than it answers regarding the reliability of the long-range multistage ballistic missiles. Whether the Nodong missile can be an effective component of the longer range missile remains an important question. Third, North Korea must develop the capability to miniaturize warheads so that nuclear weapons can be fitted on its ballistic missiles. Again, there is insufficient evidence that the DPRK has mastered this technology. If missiles cannot be developed to be the necessary delivery system for WMD, then what other options such as aircraft or perhaps ships are available? This is less of a concern for chemical weapons, and most military experts believe that North Korea already could deliver these weapons using various artillery systems. Fourth, the 5 MW reactor at Yongbyon is only capable of producing 5 to 7 kg of plutonium per year basically enough for one nuclear weapon. To increase the plutonium supply appreciably, North Korea will have to resume construction of the 50 MW and/or 200 MW reactors. At present, there is no evidence that construction has been restarted, but it will not be possible to conceal such construction if it begins.[36]

The bottom line is that if North Korea does decide to go forward with operationalizing its WMD programs and delivery systems, there should be ample evidence of these efforts. Then it will be up to the international community to determine how to respond to these North Korean initiatives. A comparison of how the Clinton and Bush administrations have attempted to negotiate with North Korea since the early 1990s and to involve the international community should provide us with some guidance as to the effectiveness of negotiations with North Korea.

North Korean Nuclear Weapon Programs   87

NOTES

1. Andrew Scobell and John M. Sanford, *North Korea's Military Threat: Pyongyang's Conventional Forces, Weapons of Mass Destruction, and Ballistic Missiles* (Carlisle Barracks: Strategic Studies Institute, Army War College, April 2007), 81–82.

2. Park Geun Hye, "The North Korean Nuclear Issue and a New Vision for the Korean–U.S. Alliance," a speech delivered at the National Press Club on February 14, 2007. This speech is available at http://www.keia.org. For a broader view on the possible effects of the North Korean nuclear weapons test in the region, see Christopher W. Hughes, "North Korea's Nuclear Weapons: Implications for the Nuclear Ambitions of Japan, South Korea, and Taiwan," National Bureau of Asian Research, *Asia Policy,* no. 3 (January 2007):75–104.

3. Phillip C. Saunders, "Confronting Ambiguity: How to Handle North Korea's Nuclear Program," *Arms Control Today,* 33, no. 2 (March 2003):13.

4. Author's interview with Dr. Victor C. Cha, Associate Professor of Government, Georgetown University, Washington, DC, July 15, 2003. Later Cha would become a member of the National Security Council during the Bush administration before returning to Georgetown in 2007.

5. Saunders, "Confronting Ambiguity: How to Handle North Korea's Nuclear Program," 13–14.

6. Michael J. Mazarr, *North Korea and the Bomb: A Case Study in Nonproliferation* (London: Macmillan Press, Ltd, 1995), 18–19.

7. Scobell and Sanford, *North Korea's Military Threat,* 98.

8. Mazarr, *North Korea and the Bomb,* 24–25.

9. Siegried S. Hecker and William Liou, "Dangerous Dealings: North Korea's Nuclear Capabilities and the Threat to Export to Iran," *Arms Control Today,* 37, no. 2 (March 2007): 6–8.

10. Mazarr, *North Korea and the Bomb,* 62–63.

11. Larry A. Niksch, "North Korea's Nuclear Weapons Development and Diplomacy," Congressional Research Service, CRS Report of Congress, January 3, 2007, 17.

12. KEDO Executive Board Meeting Notes, November 14, 2002 available at http://www.kedo.org.

13. "North Korea: A Phased Negotiating Strategy," The International Crisis Group Asia Report No. 61, August 1, 2003, 13.

14. For a journal account of the DPRK's reaction to the Rice comments, see Anthony Falola, "High Stakes Gamble," in The *Washington Post National Weekly Edition,* (February 14–20, 2005):14. For Rice's "outpost of tyranny" reference to North Korea, see Opening Remarks by secretary of state-Designate Dr. Condoleezza Rice before the Senate Foreign Relations Committee, January 18, 2005 available at http://www.state.gov/secretary/rm/2005/40991.htm.

15. "DPRK FM on Its Stand to Suspend Its Participation in the Six-Party Talks for an Indefinite Period," Korean Central News Agency, February 11, 2005 available at http://www.kcna.co.jp/item/2005/200502/news02/11.htm.

16. "DPRK Foreign Ministry Clarifies Stand on New Measure to Bolster War Deterrent," Korean Central News Agency, October 4, 2006 available at http://www.kcna.co.jp/item/2006/200610/news10/04.htm.

17. Richard L. Garwin and Frank von Hippel, "A Technical Analysis: Deconstructing North Korea's October 9 Nuclear Test," *Arms Control Today,* 36, no. 9, November 2006 available at http://www.armscontrol.org/act/2006_11/tech.asp?print.

18. "DPRK Successfully Conducts Underground Nuclear Test," Korean Central News Agency, October 10, 2006 available at http://www.kcna.co.jp/item2006/200610/news10htm.

19. David E. Sanger, "In Book, Musharraf Expands on the North Korean Nuclear Link," *New York Times* (September 26, 2006):10. See also Siegfried S. Hecker, "Report on the North Korean Nuclear Program," Policy Forum Online 06-97A, November 15, 2006, Nautilus Institute available at http://www.nautilus.org/fora/security/0697Hecker.html.

20. David Albright, "North Korea's Alleged Large-Scale Enrichment Plant: Yet Another Questionable Extrapolation Based on Aluminum Tubes," Policy Forum Online 07-018A, February 27, 2007, Nautilus Institute available at http://www.nautilus.org/fora/security/07018 Albright.html. For an account of the Albright visit to North Korea, see Jim Yardley, "Nuclear Talks on North Korea Set to Resume In Beijing," *New York Times* (February 7, 2007): 6.

21. For a good overview of the North Korean chemical weapons program, see "North Korea Profile: Chemical Weapons," Nuclear Threat Initiative, updated in 2006 and available at http://www.nti.org/e_research/profiles/NK/index_1549.html. Unless otherwise cited, the technical details on the North Korean chemical weapons program are from this source.

22. Scobell and Sanford, *North Korea's Military Threat,* 103.

23. Ibid., 105–6.

24. For a good review of the North Korean biological weapons program, see "North Korea Profile: Biological Weapons," Nuclear Threat Initiative, updated in 2006 and available at http://www.nti.org/e_research/profiles/NK/Biological/Index.html.

25. "North Korea Profile: Missiles," Nuclear Threat Initiative, updated February 2006 and available at http://www.nti.org/e_research/profiles/NK/index_1667.html.

26. Scobell and Sanford, *North Korea's Military Threat,* 116–19

27. "North Korea Profile: Missiles," Nuclear Threat Initiative, updated February 2006 and available at http://www.nti.org/e_research/profiles/NK/index_1667.html.

28. Normitsu Onishi and David E. Sanger, "6 Missiles Fired by North Korea; Tests Protested," *New York Times* (July 5, 2006): 1. This article made it clear that more than six missiles may have been fired and that some uncertainty existed from initial observations. For the specific capabilities of the Taepodong 2, see Helene Cooper and Warren Hoge, "U.S. Seeks Strong Measures To Warn the North Koreans," *New York Times* (July 6, 2006): 10.

29. Sheryl Gay Stolberg, "Koizumi Joins Bush in Warning North Korea Not to Fire Missile," *New York Times* (June 30, 2006): 6.

30. Bruce Cumings and Meredith Jung-En Woo, "What Does North Korea Want?" *New York Times* (July 7, 2006): 21.

31. Scobell and Sanford, *North Korea's Military Threat,* 121–23 and Niksch, "North Korea's Nuclear Weapons Development and Diplomacy," 19.

32. For initial Chinese and Russian reluctance on sanctions, see Normitsu Onishi and Joseph Kahn, "North Korea's Neighbors Condemn Missile Tests, But Differ on What to Do," *New York Times* (July 6, 2006): 10 and Warren Hoge and Norimitsu Onishi, "China Fights Sanctions To Punish North Korea," *New York Times* (July 8, 2006): 5. For North Korea's objections to sanctions, see Normitsu Onishi, "North Korea Flatly Rejects Protests on Missile Firings," *New York Times* (July 7, 2006): 12.

33. "United Nations Security Council Condemns Democratic People's Republic of Korea's Missile Launches," UN Security Council Resolution 1695, July 15, 2006 available at http://www.state.gov/p/eap/rls/prs/69022.htm.

34. David Albright and Paul Brannan, "Korean Plutonium Stock, February 2007," Institute for Science and International Security (ISIS), February 20, 2007, 1–6. For a similar estimate up

to 2004, see "North Korea's Weapons Programmes: A Net Assessment," Press Statement of Dr. John Chapman, International Institute for Strategic Studies (IISS), January 21, 2004, 1–3. The last estimate of 40–50 kg of plutonium and six to eight nuclear devices comes from Siegfried S. Hecker, "Report on North Korean Nuclear Program," Policy Forum Online 06-97A, Nautilus Institute, November 15, 2006, 3 available at http://www.nautilus.org/fora/security/0697 Hecker.html.

35. For some similar arguments, see Jonathan D. Pollack, "North Korea's Nuclear Weapons Program to 2015: Three Scenarios," National Bureau of Asian Research, *Asia Policy,* no. 3 (January 2007): 107–13.

36. For current overhead surveillance photos of the 5, 50, and 200 MW reactors, see Albright and Brannan, "Korean Plutonium Stock, February 2007," 11–13.

CHAPTER 5

U.S. Responses to the North Korean Programs

North Korea joined the IAEA in 1974 and signed the nuclear NPT in December 1985 primarily because of Soviet pressure. In exchange for these Korean initiatives, Soviet assistance for the DPRK's nuclear power program continued.[1] In the mid-1980s, this program consisted of one 5 MW reactor located at the Yongbyon site approximately 60 miles north of Pyongyang. However, after becoming a NPT signatory, the DPRK refused to sign the IAEA full scope safeguards agreement that it was obliged to do within 18 months under provisions of the NPT. Although there were some administrative problems that contributed to the North Korean delay in the signing of the safeguards agreement (the IAEA sent the wrong forms initially), the more substantive reasons involved North Korea's sensitivities or even paranoia that foreign inspectors working in the country would be a challenge to the DPRK's national security.

Concern over the North Korean refusal to sign the IAEA safeguards agreement and delays in permitting IAEA inspections of its nuclear facilities increased in 1989 when U.S. intelligence reports indicated the DPRK was building what appeared to be additional reactors and possibly a nuclear fuel reprocessing plant at its Yongbyon site. The reactors under construction were thought to be a 50 MW model at Yongbyon and a 200 MW model at Taechon, both graphite reactors that would use uranium fuel.[2] At the end of the Gulf War in 1991, the United States and other countries became even more concerned about the DPRK's nuclear weapons capabilities because Iraq's programs turned out to be far more advanced than intelligence sources had detected before the war. A North Korean defector informed officials in South Korea in 1991 that the DPRK had no intention of signing the IAEA safeguards agreement and was only using the offer to buy more time to develop its nuclear weapons program.[3]

Tensions eased in late 1991 and early 1992 in large part because the two Koreas signed an agreement entitled the Joint Declaration on the Denuclearization of the Korean Peninsula (see Appendix B, Document 1). Representatives of the two countries signed this agreement on January 20, 1992.[4] In this document, the parties agreed "not to test, manufacture, produce, receive, possess, store, deploy, or use nuclear weapons" or to "possess nuclear reprocessing and uranium enrichment facilities." This agreement called for the establishment of a South–North Joint Nuclear Control Commission and for inspections of suspected facilities on both sides. Also in January 1992, North Korea signed the promised agreement with the IAEA that provided international inspections of its nuclear facilities. The DPRK legislature ratified this agreement in April meaning that in accordance with IAEA regulations, inspections could begin within 90 days of ratification. Subsequently, North Korea provided the IAEA with detailed information about its nuclear power facilities including those at Yongbyon. Between May 1992 and July 1993, the IAEA conducted seven ad hoc inspections at DPRK nuclear facilities with each inspection lasting between 1 and 2 weeks.[5]

After the first ad hoc inspection in May 1992, Hans Blix, then the IAEA director general, held a press conference. He related that he and his inspectors had been allowed to visit all the sites they requested, including the operational 5 MW reactor and the 50 and 200 MW reactors under construction. Of perhaps more significance, the inspectors had access to the facility that the United States believed may be a nuclear reprocessing plant, a facility that the North Koreans referred to as a "radiochemical laboratory." The Korean authorities admitted to Blix that they constructed this laboratory to experiment with plutonium extraction in the event they ever desired to build a breeder reactor that uses plutonium as fuel. Additionally, the North Koreans confirmed they had extracted some plutonium, but they claimed this extraction only amounted to a few grams and was strictly for experimental purposes.[6]

During some of the subsequent inspections between May and November 1992, the inspectors became more suspicious due to some apparent discrepancies in the amount of plutonium the North Koreans may have extracted. These discrepancies involved North Korean claims that the plutonium extracted only occurred on one occasion, and the IAEA's collective opinion that fuel had been reprocessed perhaps as many as three times. If true, this observation could mean that the DPRK had stored more weapons-grade plutonium than the few grams its officials admitted. In late 1992, IAEA inspectors requested that they be given access to two additional sites that the agency suspected of being storage sites for nuclear waste. North Korean officials denied these two facilities were waste sites and claimed instead that they were military warehouses, and, therefore, not subject to IAEA inspections. By the end of 1992, North Korea had also broken off discussions with South Korea concerning the bilateral inspections provided for in the denuclearization agreement.[7] This was the situation on the Korean peninsula when the Clinton administration came into office in January 1993. The major purpose of this chapter is to compare and contrast the efforts of the Clinton and Bush administrations to resolve the challenges presented by the DPRK with the development of its nuclear weapons programs.

THE CLINTON ADMINISTRATION AND THE NORTH KOREAN NUCLEAR WEAPONS PROGRAMS

Relations between the IAEA and North Korea continued to deteriorate during the early months of the Clinton administration. In February 1993, the IAEA requested permission to conduct "special inspections" at the two facilities at Yongbyon that inspectors believed were possible nuclear waste storage sites. North Korea again refused this request based on its assertion that these buildings were military warehouses and not associated with its nuclear energy program. An impasse developed between the IAEA and North Korea with DPRK officials repeating more frequently that the IAEA was nothing more than a tool of the United States as evidenced by the increased pressure that the IAEA was bringing to bear on North Korea.[8]

In mid-March, the UN Security Council voted 13–0 to adopt a resolution calling on the DPRK to allow IAEA inspectors access to the two suspected nuclear waste sites with only China and Pakistan abstaining in the Security Council vote. North Korea responded that such inspections would be "an interference in its internal affairs and a grave infringement of its sovereignty."[9] When the IAEA, now backed by the Security Council, continued to press for these special inspections, North Korea announced on March 14, 1993, that it intended to withdraw from the nuclear NPT at the conclusion of the 90-day notification period as required by the treaty. This was the first time a signatory country officially announced its intention to withdraw from the NPT.[10]

The administration took the North Korean threat to withdraw from the NPT very seriously because of the direct implications for American national security and also because of the likely effects on international nonproliferation initiatives. Compounding the difficulties confronting the administration was the lack of consensus on whether the North Koreans already had enough plutonium to build nuclear weapons. For example, former Secretary of State Lawrence Eagleburger testified before a congressional committee that he believed North Korea already had at least one weapon. However, James Woolsey, the director of the Central Intelligence Agency, expressed the view that the DPRK had enough plutonium to build a bomb, but had not yet done so.[11] International diplomacy continued in May 1993 when the Security Council passed another resolution calling on the DPRK to allow the IAEA inspections and to rescind its decision to withdraw from the NPT. The vote was 13–0 with China and Pakistan again abstaining.[12]

In late May, the United States and North Korea agreed to hold high-level talks in the effort to resolve some of the outstanding issues between them. The 90-day NPT notification deadline was due to expire in mid-June, and this deadline provided a sense of urgency to the negotiations. North Korea was represented by Kang Sok Ju, first deputy minister of foreign affairs, and the United States by Robert L. Gallucci, assistant secretary of state for political–military affairs. As is obvious from this description of the negotiators involved, the discussions that began in May 1993 were bilateral with only the United States and the DPRK directly involved. That is not to suggest that the United States was opposed to multilateral involvement, and in fact the IAEA and the UN were major players as the negotiations progressed. The most significant point is that North Korea insisted on negotiating directly with the United States, and there were not many other options open. However, it is important to keep this point in mind because whether the majority of negotiations were bilateral or multilateral would come to be one of the major differences between the strategies of the Clinton and Bush administrations.

The negotiations beginning in May 1993 took place in New York and Geneva and lasted for the next 2 months. In an agreement announced in June, North Korea stated its decision "to suspend as long as it considers necessary the effectuation of its withdrawal from the Treaty on the Non-Proliferation of Nuclear Weapons."[13] Keeping the North Koreans in the NPT was a major goal of the Clinton administration. After the discussions concluded in July, the negotiators released another statement. They addressed some of the agreements reached in June, and the United States specifically pledged not to threaten the use of force, including nuclear weapons, against North Korea. In another significant development, both sides recognized the importance of the DPRK's intention to replace its aging graphite nuclear reactors with LWRs. This was an important understanding because although it is possible to reprocess plutonium from the spent fuel of LWRs, it is much more difficult than from the spent fuel of graphite reactors. The United States indicated it was willing to assist North Korea in obtaining LWRs, and the DPRK agreed to begin consultations with the IAEA on safeguard inspections. There also was a statement by North Korea that it would meet with representatives from South Korea on bilateral issues to include nuclear weapons.[14]

Even though progress was made in that North Korea agreed "to suspend" its withdrawal from the NPT, IAEA inspections did not immediately resume. There was growing concern that if the inspectors were not allowed access to DPRK nuclear power facilities, then the film, batteries, and other equipment the IAEA had installed to monitor North Korean sites would no longer be operational, and the agency would not be able to guarantee "the continuity of its safeguard inspections" that was so critical.[15] In December 1993, the DPRK offered to allow the inspectors access to five of the seven declared nuclear facilities to change the film and batteries in the cameras. However, the Korean authorities would not permit the inspectors to visit the nuclear reactor at Yongbyon or the suspected nuclear reprocessing plant there. This offer was unacceptable to the IAEA because it was against its policy that a signatory country could not stipulate which of its declared nuclear sites were eligible for inspections.[16]

The impasse over inspections continued in early 1994. During May, the DPRK shocked the international community when it announced it had begun to remove the estimated 8,000 spent fuel rods from its 5 MW reactor at Yongbyon. Prior to that time, the IAEA had demanded its inspectors be present before the North Koreans removed any fuel rods. DPRK officials justified their decision to remove the fuel rods without an IAEA presence because of its "unique status" following its temporary suspension of its withdrawal from the NPT. According to this interpretation, there was no requirement for an IAEA presence other than the cameras that were operating. From the IAEA perspective, this removal of the fuel rods was totally unacceptable because it would impede the agency's ability to verify the plutonium-laden fuel was not being diverted for use in building nuclear weapons.[17]

In early June, the Clinton administration announced its intentions to pursue global economic trade sanctions against North Korea if the North did not permit IAEA inspectors to be present for the examination of the spent fuel rods at Yongbyon. The DPRK foreign minister responded that the implementation of economic sanctions would be treated as an act of war by his country.[18] As the crisis deepened, Kim Il Sung told a visiting American delegation that he would be willing to forgo the extraction of plutonium from the spent fuel rods if the United States would provide a firm commitment to assist the North Koreans to develop other types of nuclear power plants.[19]

However, shortly after Kim's offer, the DPRK announced that it was withdrawing from the IAEA. In response, the United States moved ahead with its plans to introduce a sanctions resolution in the Security Council. The proposed draft called for a 1-month grace period before the sanctions went into effect. During this month, the DPRK would have to reestablish its relationship with the IAEA. If the North failed to do so, the United States would move to ban the export of all weapons to North Korea plus halt economic, technical, and cultural assistance programs.[20] Just as the crisis appeared to be spiraling out of control, Jimmy Carter intervened by traveling to North Korea and attempting to provide the impetus for continued negotiations.

The Clinton administration did not initiate the Carter visit to Pyongyang although President Clinton did approve it just before the former president began his journey. This visit remains controversial, but the meeting between Kim Il Sung and Jimmy Carter on June 16, 1994 was an important factor in the resumption of negotiations between the two countries. In a news conference after his meeting with Kim, Carter stated his view that the administration's plans to introduce economic sanctions against North Korea were a mistake. He also granted an interview to CNN in which he repeated his concern that economic sanctions would be a serious error.[21] After Carter left North Korea, the administration announced its willingness to grant a 30-day grace period before introducing any sanctions resolution against North Korea. Shortly thereafter, representatives of the two countries related that high-level talks would resume. In return for scheduling negotiations, the DPRK agreed not to extract any plutonium from the spent fuel rods, not to refuel the 5 MW reactor, and to allow IAEA inspectors to remain at Yongbyon. These concessions were contingent on productive negotiations with the United States.[22] The negotiations began on July 9 in Geneva with Robert Gallucci once again representing the United States and Kang Sok Ju representing North Korea. These talks were almost immediately suspended due to the unexpected death of Kim Il Sung on the same day the talks began. President Clinton expressed his sympathy to the North Korean people, and Gallucci signed a condolence book at the DPRK's mission in Geneva.[23] These gestures were very important in contributing to the resumption of negotiations in August. They continued until October when the two sides finalized what became known as the Agreed Framework.

The complete title of this document was the "Agreed Framework Between the United States of America and the Democratic People's Republic of Korea" and was signed on October 21, 1994 (see appendix B, Document 2). The specifics of the Agreed Framework called for North Korea to freeze its graphite reactors and replace them with LWRs having a generating power of 2,000 MW. The completion date for the LWRs was tentatively set for 2003. The United States assumed responsibility for the formation of an international consortium to finance and supply the LWRs. In order to make up for the energy lost from the closing of the one operating graphite reactor, the United States pledged to provide 500,000 tons of HFO per annum. The DPRK agreed to allow the IAEA to monitor the freezing of its graphite reactors and their eventual dismantlement once the LWRs came on line. The spent fuel rods from the 5 MW reactor also were to be stored in North Korea under the supervision of the IAEA during the construction of the LWRs and then were to be disposed of in a safe manner. On the political and economic fronts, both sides pledged to reduce trade and investment barriers and to open liaison offices in each other's capital as the first step toward establishing diplomatic relations.

The United States agreed to provide formal assurances that it would not use nuclear weapons against the DPRK. North Korea promised to take steps to implement the North–South Joint Declaration on the Denuclearization of the Korean Peninsula and to engage in dialogue with the ROK. Finally, the DPRK agreed to remain in the NPT and to allow the implementation of the stipulated safeguards called for in the NPT. Pending completion of a supply agreement regarding the LWRs, North Korea promised to allow ad hoc and routine inspections of facilities not subject to the freeze of the graphite reactors. This was an important point because of suspicions that the North Korea might have other nuclear facilities or had stored plutonium from earlier times. Finally, the DPRK and the United States agreed that when a "significant portion" of the LWR project was finished but "before delivery of key nuclear components," North Korea would come into full compliance with IAEA safeguards including steps deemed necessary by the agency to verify "the accuracy and completeness of the DPRK's initial report on all nuclear material in the DPRK."

President Clinton provided a "letter of assurance" to be given to the DPRK at the time of the signing of the Agreed Framework pledging to use the "full powers of his office" to meet the requirements the United States agreed to in this document.[24] This letter was significant because in the U.S. general elections held in November 1994, the Republicans gained control of the House of Representatives to go along with their majority in the Senate. This electoral victory set the stage for the development of a contentious relationship between the executive and legislative branches of government to influence policy toward the Korean peninsula. In 1995, the United States took the lead as it pledged to do in the Agreed Framework to establish KEDO that also included Japan, South Korea, and later the European Union. KEDO's primary purpose was to oversee the completion of the LWR project.[25]

There is no question that the Agreed Framework was an incomplete document and a controversial one. Part of the problem involved ambiguous language and nonspecific timelines in the document itself. Examples of some of these problems were the lack of details concerning the final disposition of the spent fuel rods and exactly when "a significant portion" of the LWR project would be completed. In addition, issues developed in the United States after the mid-term elections of 1994, and funding for the American requirement to provide 500,000 tons of HFO each year sometimes became embroiled in partisan appropriation battles within the Congress and conflicts over political turf between the executive and legislative branches. An interesting side note is that the Agreed Framework was so named instead of the Framework Agreement in part because the latter would possibly indicate some requirement for congressional ratification while the former did not.[26] Difficulties also developed with the establishment of diplomatic and more normal economic relations between the two countries with each side bearing some of the responsibilities. Finally, labor problems occurred in the DPRK associated with the LWR project in part because of the North Korean paranoia over having foreign workers in the country, especially those from South Korea.[27] At the end of the Clinton administration, the completion date for the LWRs had been moved back from 2003 to perhaps as late as 2008.

In 1999, Richard Armitage, who had served in the first Bush administration, and some of his associates wrote a critique of the Clinton administration's policies toward North Korea with specific reference to the Agreed Framework. The critique became known commonly as the "Armitage Report" and was published by the National Defense University as part of its Strategic Forum series.[28] In his report, Armitage challenged some of what he described as the basic assumptions of the Agreed Framework. He was particularly critical of the assumption that the Agreed Framework and its implementation would have terminated North Korea's nuclear weapons program and induced the DPRK to open up to the outside world. He observed that the Agreed Framework should be viewed as the beginning of a policy toward North Korea and not as the end of the nuclear weapons problem. He proposed a more "comprehensive and integrated" approach that would also address issues such as the DPRK's missile program, conventional military buildup, and human rights violations.

Armitage paid particular attention to North Korea's developing missile technologies and the threats he believed these technologies brought to the region and the international community. In addition, he charged that little progress had been made since the Agreed Framework was signed on identifying and inspecting other suspected nuclear sites beyond the Yongbyon complex or removing the spent fuel rods from North Korea. He proposed a series of "red lines" be drawn that would outline what DPRK behavior was unacceptable to the United States and its allies, although he did not specify exactly what such behavior would include. Finally, he proposed a six-party meeting be held involving the United States, both Koreas, China, Japan, and Russia to address particular security concerns that the DPRK had expressed. This report became very important not only because it was a lucid critique of the Clinton administration's policies toward North Korea, but more significantly because Richard Armitage would become deputy secretary of state in the administration of George W. Bush and a major player in the development of the new administration's policies toward North Korea as will become evident later in this chapter.

Robert Gallucci, the principal American negotiator of the Agreed Framework, has defended this document effectively over the years against criticisms such as those of Armitage and others. In a 2003 interview with the author and in *Going Critical: The First North Korean Nuclear Crisis,* the book he co-authored with Joel Wit and Daniel Poneman, he indicated that President Clinton considered three options to deal with the nuclear crisis in 1993 and 1994. One option was a military attack on North Korea that would concentrate on the Yongbyon facility using air power to take out the operating nuclear reactor, reprocessing plant, and the cooling ponds holding the 8,000 spent fuel rods. The likely result of such an attack was thought to be a second Korean war and massive destruction in South Korea although the administration was confident that the United States and ROK would eventually prevail. The second option was a variant of the containment policy in which the United States would maintain its "nuclear umbrella" over South Korea and keep North Korea in check much as the two super powers had done to each other during the Cold War period. The problem with this option was that it would have no effect on the nuclear capabilities that North Korea already had or might develop. The third option was to negotiate with North Korea employing a combination of carrots and sticks in the effort to convince Kim Il Sung and then Kim Jong Il that giving up their nuclear weapons would result in important political and economic rewards. Since the North Koreans demanded bilateral negotiations and there were few other possibilities for multilateral talks because countries such as China expressed little interest and the ROK was unacceptable to the DPRK, the negotiations option was limited to the bilateral approach. President Clinton also was convinced that if he began negotiations with North Korea, and this course failed to resolve the problem, he could escalate his approach as necessary.[29]

In his book, Robert Gallucci suggested that one way to evaluate the Agreed Framework was to ask this basic question: did the agreement support and enhance American national security objectives at an acceptable price?[30] A strong argument can be made that the answer to this question should be in the affirmative. The plutonium producing facilities at Yongbyon and Taechon were shut down and remained under the control of the IAEA throughout the Clinton years in office. The DPRK stayed in the NPT and IAEA with all of the associated responsibilities.

In August 1998, U.S. intelligence sources suggested that North Korea may be building a secret underground nuclear facility at Kumchangri north of Yongbyon near the China border that could include a nuclear reactor and reprocessing plant.[31] In May 1999, after some difficult negotiations with North Korea, a U.S. inspection team was allowed access to the Kumchangri site and found only a large underground shelter with no evidence of a nuclear weapons program.[32] Without the good will that had been established from the Agreed Framework, it is unlikely that North Korea would have allowed this inspection. In addition, some progress was made between the two countries to establish more normal diplomatic and economic relations although definite limits remained in place. The LWR project made progress under the supervision of KEDO despite delays that occurred in the construction of these reactors. The bottom line is that the Agreed Framework prevented the DPRK from reprocessing any additional plutonium or building any more nuclear weapons at the Yongbyon site while it remained in effect. This outcome is what President Clinton charged Gallucci to accomplish, and that is what he did.

While arguably successful in addressing the DPRK plutonium program, the United States was less successful during the Clinton presidency in controlling the North Korean missile initiatives. This lack of success became patently obvious in late August 1998 when the DPRK test fired a Taepodong 1 missile over Japan. This launch resulted in much controversy both in Northeast Asia and in the U.S. Congress.[33] The Congress passed legislation requiring President

Clinton to appoint a North Korea policy coordinator to conduct a thorough review of American policy toward the DPRK.[34] Based on this requirement, Clinton selected William J. Perry, who had served as the president's second secretary of defense, to this position.

In October 1999, after a visit to North Korea the previous May, Perry and his team submitted their report to the president and secretary of state.[35] Perry recommended that America's focus should remain to end the North Korean nuclear weapons program as well as its long-range missile development. In September, North Korea had announced a self-imposed moratorium on ballistic missile tests as long as the negotiations with the United States continued.[36] Perry outlined three "constraining facts" that should influence U.S. policy. First, despite severe economic problems in North Korea, there was little evidence that the Kim Jong Il regime would collapse any time soon. Second, the 37,000 American service members stationed in South Korea as well as the South Korean population would be at grave risk if another war on the Korean peninsula broke out. Third, the Agreed Framework had been successful in verifiably freezing the DPRK's plutonium production at Yongbyon. Based on this analysis of the Agreed Framework, Perry recommended that U.S. policy should supplement this document rather than undermine of supplant it.

Perry and his team concluded their report by proposing a "two path" negotiating strategy. The first path was designed to achieve "complete and verifiable assurances" that North Korea did not have a nuclear weapons program. Presumably, Perry's intent with this stipulation was to go beyond the known plutonium production facilities at Yongbyon and Taechon. This first path also required North Korea to cease its "testing, production, and deployment of missiles exceeding the parameters of the Missile Technology Control Regime" as well as the export of missiles and equipment exceeding those limits. The Missile Technology Control Regime limits for missiles are a payload of 500 kg over a distance of 300 km. Restrictions such as these went considerably beyond the self-imposed moratorium on testing that North Korea had in place at the time of the Perry Report. In response to these actions, the United States would normalize diplomatic relations with the DPRK, relax economic sanctions, and take other steps that would benefit North Korea, although Perry did not give specific examples. In reality, the carrots Perry offered were very similar to those pledged in the Agreed Framework.

The second path would be taken if North Korea did not continue to cooperate on both the nuclear weapons and missile programs. If this lack of cooperation occurred, then it would not be possible for the United States to pursue a new relationship with the DPRK, and the United States and its allies "would have to take other steps to assure their security and contain the threat." Perry was vague as to what these "other steps" would be, but one can infer that economic sanctions, diplomatic isolation, and possibly military actions were among the choices considered. Perry concluded his report by pointing out that these recommendations supported American allies in the region, played to American diplomatic strengths, and built upon the basic premises of the Agreed Framework. It was clear from his report that Perry viewed the Agreed Framework as the central component of U.S. policy toward North Korea.

In large part because of the improved bilateral relationship between the two countries, the Clinton administration invited Vice Marshall Cho Myong Rok, director general of the General Political Bureau and the KPA and a close adviser to Kim Jong Il, to visit Washington. This visit took place in October 2000, and at its conclusion, both sides stated there was "no hostile intent" from one to the other and agreed that resolution of the missile issue would contribute to even better relations. Vice Minister Cho presented a letter from Kim Jong Il to President Clinton inviting him to come to Pyongyang.[37] Secretary of State Madeleine Albright did visit North Korea later in October. In her discussions with Kim, Albright continued to press for an official agreement on North Korea's long-range ballistic missiles. However, the specific details remained elusive, and an agreement on verification in particular could not be reached before the Clinton presidency came to an end even though the president continued to express interest in accepting Kim's invitation for a visit right until he left office.

For the Clinton administration, there was a central belief that bilateral negotiations with North Korea held the promise of better relations and provided at least the chance to resolve the nuclear weapons and missile programs in a manner favorable to the United States and its allies in the region. The Agreed Framework remained at the core of this policy approach offering rewards for good North Korean behavior and threatening punishment for bad behavior. Although Kim Jong Il remained a bad actor, there was little expectation in the Clinton White House that regime change would occur any time soon regardless of what the administration did or did not do. But as George W. Bush prepared to assume the presidency in January 2001, it soon became apparent that another approach to North Korea was in the offing.

THE BUSH ADMINISTRATION AND THE NORTH KOREAN NUCLEAR WEAPONS PROGRAM

Once in office, the new president took what became known as an "ABC" policy orientation on a number of foreign policy issues–meaning "anything but Clinton." There certainly is evidence to support this new orientation in East Asia. Instead of describing China as a strategic partner as his predecessor had done, Bush referred to China as a strategic competitor. Consequently, the bilateral relationship deteriorated appreciably as the new administration agreed to additional arms sales to Taiwan, and then the EP-3 incident occurred in April 2001. It was not until the terrorist attacks in New York and Washington that the United States and China began to rebuild their relationship based on congruent counter terrorism goals. Similarly, regarding North Korea, the Bush administration was critical of the effectiveness of the Agreed Framework and the Clinton efforts to restrict the DPRK missile program. President Bush announced it would be necessary to conduct a thorough review of the policies toward North Korea before determining what course to follow.[38]

In March 2001, President Kim Dae Jung, the political leader of South Korea, visited President Bush. By almost all accounts, this meeting did not go well. Part of the explanation was the wide gap in experience levels between the two presidents. Kim was a long-time dissident leader against the authoritarian governments in the ROK and the driving force behind his government's "sunshine policy" toward North Korea. One of Kim's goals with this policy was to separate economic and political policies between the two Koreas and to encourage the United States, Japan, and others to assist with the economic development of the DPRK. President Bush told Kim that his policy review was still underway, but he expressed serious reservations about negotiating with Kim Jong Il.[39] This meeting was symptomatic of the increasing differences that continue to the present between the United States and South Korea concerning how the nuclear weapons program in North Korea should be most effectively addressed.

President Bush announced the results of his administration's policy review in June. He directed his national security team to conduct "serious discussions" with the DPRK, but he expanded the agenda for negotiations in addition to nuclear weapons to also include constraints on the North's missile program and a ban on missile exports. Further, he added the DPRK's large conventional forces and its human rights record as topics for future negotiations. Bush referred to a comprehensive approach to North Korea that was similar to what Richard Armitage had recommended in 1999 and is a good indication of Armitage's influence in the policy review as deputy secretary of state. In his concluding comments, President Bush stated that if the DPRK responded affirmatively to the actions addressed in the policy review, the United States would expand its efforts to assist the North Korean people by easing sanctions and taking other nonspecific political steps.[40] The results of the policy review were not particularly well received on either side of the 38th parallel because of the perceptions that the American administration had raised the bar for successful negotiations too high for North Korean compliance.

In 2002, the administration published two documents that were of particular importance to the evolving relationship with North Korea. The first was the Nuclear Posture Review released to the public in January and the second was the National Security Strategy of the United States of America published in September. The Nuclear Posture Review outlined a "new triad" for the United States that would include both nuclear and nonnuclear offensive strike systems, active and passive defensive weapons, and a revitalized defense infrastructure to meet emerging threats. This report also contained references to developing conventional and nuclear weapons that would be able to attack deep underground bunkers, and specifically mentioned North Korea as one of seven countries that could be targeted.[41]

The National Security Strategy was more specific concerning the DPRK. It identified the very real danger that the United States and other countries confronted from terrorist organizations that have global reach and support from nation states possessing WMD. This document also described current dangers to be more "complex and dangerous" than those during the Cold War at least in part because of rogue states and their possible support for terrorist organizations. In this context, the National Security Strategy specifically mentioned North Korea as being one of these rogue states and described the DPRK as "the world's principal purveyor of ballistic missiles" and also as a country "developing its own WMD arsenal." To counter the threats associated with such rogue states and terrorist organizations, this report indicated that more traditional forms of deterrence were no longer effective, and the United States would incorporate preemptive attacks as a more appropriate way to deal with these threats.[42] The Nuclear Posture Review and the National Security Strategy were both important documents, and the implications for North Korea were unmistakable.

President Bush made his position even more clear in his State of the Union address in late January 2002 when he identified North Korea as a member of his "axis of evil" along with Iran and Iraq.[43] In an August 2002 interview with Bob Woodward, Bush went even farther when he expressed his visceral dislike or even hatred for Kim Jong Il because of Kim's mistreatment of his own people through starvation, prison camps, and torture.[44] Based on the above policy review, the views expressed in the two policy documents, and the president's own statements, it is not surprising that little or no contact with North Korea occurred during the first almost 2 years of the Bush presidency.

Part of the reason for the delay in contacts with the DPRK was the understandable desire of the new administration to conduct the policy review, a common occurrence for incoming presidents. However, this review process was complicated because of deep divisions within the Bush camp concerning the proper approach that should be taken toward North Korea. On one side representing the more hard line position were among others Vice President Dick Cheney, Secretary of Defense Donald Rumsfeld, and Undersecretary of State for Arms Control and International Security Affairs John Bolton. For these individuals, any negotiations with North Korea would be counterproductive because the North could not be trusted to comply with any agreement its officials might enter into. Cheney and his allies also believed that time was on the American side because continued pressure on North Korea could lead to the collapse of the Kim regime. Those supporting this position were adamantly opposed to any concessions to the DPRK because such concessions would be perceived as rewards for bad behavior since these officials believed that North Korea clearly had violated its previous commitments stipulated in the Agreed Framework and other negotiations. They also were convinced that concessions would contribute to the regime staying in power longer than would otherwise be possible.

Those on the other side of the debate took a more pragmatic approach and opined that it was possible to reach some type of an agreement with the DPRK on its nuclear weapons program through multilateral negotiations and engagement. They were of the opinion that time probably was not on the American side because the longer it took to resolve this problem, the more time North Korea would have to expand its cache of nuclear weapons. Secretary of State Colin Powell and his deputy Richard Armitage were reportedly in this camp along with Assistant Secretary of State for East Asia and Pacific Affairs James Kelly.[45] Basically, these differences came down to those who supported regime change in North Korea (Cheney et al.) and those who supported behavior change (Powell et al.) in Kim Jong Il's policies.

The administration did decide to break the ice when it dispatched Assistant Secretary Kelly to Pyongyang in October 2002 although the intent was not necessarily to begin the negotiations process. Secretary Powell had met briefly with Paek Nam Sung, his North Korean counterpart, at the annual meeting of the Association of South East Asian Nations Regional Forum (ARF) in Brunei during late July, and this meeting may have set the stage for the Kelly visit. Kelly's trip to North Korea was very important because he presented evidence to his hosts indicating that the DPRK was constructing a clandestine uranium enrichment facility. To the surprise of many, the North Koreans admitted they were developing such a facility after an initial denial. Subsequently, North Korean officials would again reverse themselves and argue that they had the right to build a HEU facility because of the Bush administration's "hostile policies," but they had not yet done so. Perhaps more important, the North Koreans indicated to Kelly that from their perspective, the Agreed Framework was no longer in effect.[46]

Although it is impossible to know for certain why the DPRK would initially admit to having this HEU program, it may well be that the evidence Kelly presented was so compelling that North Korean officials could not deny the existence of the program. Another possible explanation is that North Korea saw its admission as a means to force the United States to enter into bilateral negotiations using the HEU program as a potential bargaining chip for American political and economic concessions. However, Kelly made it clear that there now was a "precondition" for any further discussions, and that requirement was North Korea's termination of its HEU efforts. To the DPRK's excuse that its program was a response to hostile Bush policies, Kelly retorted that his intelligence information indicated that North Korea had begun its HEU program considerably before President Bush took office. In fact, a Department of Energy report stated that the DPRK began the process of developing nuclear weapons through uranium enrichment as early as 1999 if not earlier.[47] Whatever the reasons, the North Korean admission set in motion a series of events that in many ways were very similar to those in 1993–1994 and once again raised the very real possibility of conflict on the Korean peninsula.

For those in the administration and Congress who opposed negotiations with the DPRK, the North's announcement regarding the HEU program in violation of the Agreed Framework and the Joint Declaration with South Korea only reinforced their position. Their anger increased when the DPRK demanded certain conditions be met before it would negotiate with the United States. These conditions included the need for the United States to "recognize" North Korean sovereignty, to "assure" the North that the United States had no aggressive intentions, and not to hinder the North's economic development. The recognition of Korean sovereignty probably referred to some sort of assurance that the United States would not try to overthrow the Kim regime. The DPRK wanted to enter into a form of nonaggression agreement with the United States that would preclude an invasion, and the economic reference most likely meant the United States would provide economic assistance and not block North Korean membership in international lending institutions such as the World Bank, IMF, and Asian Development Bank. In return for these concessions, the DPRK indicated it would be willing to negotiate the possible termination of its HEU program.[48]

In November 2002, the KEDO Executive Board, including representatives from the United States, South Korea, Japan, and the European Union, met and condemned the DPRK's nuclear weapons program. More significantly, the board announced its decision to suspend future HFO shipments to North Korea beginning in December, and the LWR program came to a stop for all intents and purposes. Reinstatement of these HFO shipments would be contingent on the termination of the HEU program.[49] A South Korean authority on the DPRK has referred to this KEDO decision as a "tactical blunder" because it forced North Korean to respond.[50] The DPRK took a number of steps that caused even more concern in the United States and international community. In December, its representatives once again declared the Agreed Framework to be null and void, announced the restarting of the 5 MW reactor at Yongbyon and the continuation of the construction of the 50 and 200 MW reactors, and the expulsion of the IAEA inspectors from North Korean nuclear weapons sites. They also stated that North Korea intended to retrieve the 8,000 spent fuel rods that had been in cooling ponds at Yongbyon and begin reprocessing plutonium from them. Finally, in January 2003, North Korea declared its decision to withdraw from the NPT and IAEA safeguards agreement. This withdrawal became effective in April, and North Korea is the only country to have withdrawn from the NPT to this point.[51]

Dr. Mohamed ElBaradei, the director general of the IAEA, reported to his Board of Governors in February that the actions the DPRK had taken were clearly in violation of the NPT and IAEA safeguards, and he called on North Korea to comply with its safeguards and nonproliferation commitments. The Board of Governors responded to ElBaradei's report by adopting a resolution deploring the actions of the DPRK and demanding compliance with all of its obligations. Perhaps more important, the board directed ElBaradei to notify the UN Security Council and the General Assembly of North Korea's violations.[52] The DPRK responded to these IAEA actions in a letter to the member countries of the NPT stating that it "has no intention of making nuclear weapons" and that its efforts "will be confined only to power production and other peaceful purposes."[53]

The Bush administration took a relatively low-key approach to the North Korean actions in late 2002 and early 2003. The most likely explanation for this approach was that the White House placed a higher priority on the Iraqi threat and did not want to confront another crisis that would detract from the efforts underway to remove Saddam Hussein from power. In an attempt to distinguish between the Iraqi and North Korean challenges, President Bush indicated that North Korea had not used WMD against its own people or neighbors and was not in violation of Security Council resolutions. He continued that the DPRK also did not have established links to terrorist groups and remained somewhat susceptible to pressure from other countries in Northeast Asia, particularly China. All of these factors suggested to the president that North Korea was a more manageable problem than that represented by Iraq.[54]

Although North Korea insisted that any future negotiations involve only the United States and the DPRK, bilateral negotiations were not acceptable to the administration. President Bush made it clear that he believed multilateral negotiations offered the better chance for success because there were other Northeast Asian countries that had a direct stake in the negotiations and should be involved. Further, Bush surmised that based on his understanding of the problems associated with implementing the Agreed Framework, the more countries involved in the process, the less chance for confusion over what was agreed to and by whom. In a recent book on the Bush administration's diplomacy with North Korea, Charles L. (Jack) Pritchard argued there were other factors that influenced the president to support multilateral negotiations. Pritchard, who had served as senior director for Asian affairs on the National Security Council under President Clinton and then continued to serve under President Bush as special envoy for negotiations with North Korea and U.S. representative to KEDO until 2003, wrote that President Bush favored multilateral negotiations because negotiations involving several countries would prevent or at least limit American bilateral contacts with the regime in Pyongyang. Pritchard also related that when the DPRK offered to assist the United States with counter terrorism information after the September 11 attacks on Washington and New York, the administration refused because this cooperation could also lead to bilateral contacts.[55]

Because of China's long-time relationship with North Korea, President Bush and others in his administration pressured China to use its influence to convince Kim Jong Il to engage in multilateral negotiations. This initiative apparently worked because in April 2003, officials from the United States, China, and North Korea met in Beijing. Assistant Secretary of State Kelly was the lead American official and, according to Jack Pritchard, was instructed to have no bilateral contacts with his North Korean counterpart.[56] The DPRK took a rather belligerent position during the negotiations, and one of its representatives stated that the DPRK already had two nuclear weapons, was reprocessing additional plutonium, threatened to export nuclear weapons in the future, and indicated North Korea might consider some sort of "physical demonstration" of its capabilities.[57] This latter threat was taken to mean the DPRK might conduct some sort of nuclear weapons test although the DPRK did not specifically make such a claim. Secretary Kelly restated the American position that no concessions would be made until the North completely and verifiably terminated both of the nuclear weapons programs. Although the North Korean official stated that the DPRK had two nuclear weapons, this statement was not taken as an official declaration on North Korea's nuclear weapon status.

China hosted a subsequent series of negotiations in August 2003 and February 2004 that were expanded to include South Korea, Japan, and Russia in addition to the three countries participating in the April talks. This expansion of the negotiations was seen as both a victory for the United States and further evidence of China's influence over the DPRK. Very little was accomplished in Beijing during these talks, and North Korea once again alleged that it had nuclear weapons and threatened to test one of them. Secretary Kelly responded that any test would be taken very seriously in Washington and could well result in economic sanctions that might include the interdiction of Korean ships at sea. During the February negotiations, the participants did agree to establish WGs in the effort to schedule future talks and establish agendas in advance of these meetings.[58]

Part of the difficulty evident in the negotiations that occurred in 2003 and 2004 was the fact that the United States and North Korea remained so far apart on crucial issues. Those differences became very clear in the working level discussions that took place after the February negotiations. For the United States, to achieve its political goals required the CVID (complete, verifiable, irreversible dismantlement) of the North Korean nuclear weapons programs. These policy goals quickly became known by the acronym CVID. The Bush administration had been explicit as to what was entailed with each of these components. "Complete" meant that both the DPRK's plutonium and uranium enrichment programs must be included. Since North Korean officials denied the existence of an HEU program after their initial admission, there was a definite problem of agreement on this point. "Verifiable" for the Americans stipulated that any inspections of North Korean sites must go beyond the normal IAEA safeguards requirements or even the IAEA Additional Protocol. However, since the DPRK is such a closed society and paranoid over external threats, particularly from the United States, it was not likely that a comprehensive verification regime could be achieved that would be acceptable to both countries. "Irreversible" for the Bush administration referred to both the North Korean nuclear weapons programs and its nuclear energy capabilities. The DPRK resisted every effort to force it to give up its nuclear power program seeing this issue as one largely involving national sovereignty. Finally, "dismantlement" for the United States meant the immediate accomplishment of this goal not some subsequent eventuality for future negotiations. North Korea wanted a more incremental approach to this end.[59]

Despite these serious and fundamental differences between the United States and North Korea, China was able to arrange another round of six-party talks in Beijing between June 23 and 26, 2004. President Bush found he was under some pressure from both external and internal sources to be more accommodating toward the DPRK. The external pressure came from South Korea and Japan, both of which encouraged the administration to be more specific as to what North Korea would gain if it agreed to terminate its nuclear weapons programs. The two American allies also suggested that the CVID term not be used because it was so unacceptable to the North Koreans. The internal pressure came during the 2004 presidential campaign when Senator John Kerry criticized President Bush for not making more progress in reducing the DPRK threat.[60]

At the June 2004 negotiations, Assistant Secretary of State Kelly proposed a two-stage process that was designed to enunciate clearly the benefits North Korea would achieve if it cooperated to terminate its nuclear weapons programs. First, the DPRK would make a unilateral declaration of its intent to dismantle all of its nuclear programs to include plutonium and HEU facilities. All nuclear weapons, weapons components, centrifuge equipment, fissile material, and fuel rods would be among the materials removed from North Korea, and a long-term monitoring regime would be employed. Second, after the DPRK declaration of intent, the other negotiating parties would draft a detailed implementation agreement that would include provisional multilateral security assurances, a study to determine what North Korea's energy requirements were and how the parties could best address at least some of these needs, a promise to begin discussions for the lifting of the remaining economic sanctions against North Korea, and consideration of the steps that would be necessary to remove the DPRK from the Department of State's list of state sponsors of terrorism.[61]

In response, North Korean negotiators offered what became known as the "rewards for freeze" proposal. The "freeze" referred specifically to the operations of the 5 MW reactor and reprocessing plant at Yongbyon, both of which would be placed under some sort of international inspections. The "rewards" would include specific details concerning the resumption of the HFO shipments and other energy assistance programs for the DPRK. Mutual suspicions and distrust between the United States and North Korea plus substantive differences on the proposed solutions prevented further progress at the June negotiations.[62] The presidential elections in the fall of 2004, the reassignment of important administration foreign policy advisers after the Bush victory and the beginning of his second term on the American side and continued delays by the North Koreans resulted in more that a year passing before the next six-party talks occurred. It was not until July 2005 that the Chinese were able to bring all the parties back to Beijing. Initially, very little progress was made in the first few weeks of talks, and a recess was called until mid-September. However, when negotiations resumed, one of the more successful sessions of the six-party process took place.

As President Bush began his second term in office, there were a few new influences that began to affect his policies involving North Korea. Although the administration would not admit this, it is probable that some advisers close to the president realized that the policies followed during the first term had largely failed and a new course was necessary. Another factor was the selection of Condoleezza Rice as secretary of state. This is not a criticism of Secretary Powell but rather recognition that Rice was closer to Bush than was Powell and could exercise more influence. Similarly, the selection of Christopher Hill as the new assistant secretary of state for East Asia and Pacific affairs and lead negotiator with North Korea was significant. Hill was a seasoned diplomat with much negotiating experience in difficult areas such as the Balkans. In addition, he had been the American ambassador in Seoul prior to his selection and was very familiar with the issues associated with North Korea's nuclear weapons. Lastly, China continued to put pressure on Kim Jong Il to return to the negotiations, and this pressure eventually brought results.[63]

When the negotiations reconvened in mid-September 2005, more progress was achieved than in the July session. On September 19, the negotiating parties agreed to a Joint Statement that concluded round four of the six-party talks[64] (see Appendix B, Document 3). This statement contained several important provisions although a number of specifics remained to be negotiated. On the North Korean side, the DPRK agreed to abandon all of its nuclear weapons programs and return to the NPT to include allowing IAEA safeguard inspections. However, regarding both the termination of its nuclear weapons and returning to the NPT, North Korea would only commit to doing each "at an early date," with nothing more specific concerning a timeline in the statement. Further, the DPRK maintained that it had the right to develop the peaceful uses of nuclear energy and to have LWRs as part of this capability. In return, the United States affirmed that it had no intensions of using nuclear weapons against North Korea or of conducting an invasion. The Americans and North Koreans pledged to respect each other's sovereignty and to begin the process of normalizing diplomatic relations. All of the parties agreed to provide the DPRK with energy assistance with South Korea being more specific with its pledge of 2 million kW of electric power. However, the other parties did not concur with the North Korean argument that it deserved to have LWRs. They promised only to discuss this issue "at an appropriate time."[65]

Despite some initial optimism, relations between the United States and DPRK began to deteriorate almost before the ink was dry on the Joint Statement. The inclusion of any reference to LWRs caused serious concerns for the Americans. There also was the basic problem sometimes referred to as "sequencing" regarding which side goes first with concessions and what specifically are the rewards. When there is as much mistrust among the negotiating partners as there is with the six-party talks, sequencing can be a major issue. More important, the U.S. Department of the Treasury acting under Article 311 of the U.S. Patriot Act designated BDA (Banco Delta Asia), a bank in Macao in which North Korea had approximately $25 million on deposit, to be "a primary money laundering concern." This designation effectively froze the North Korean funds in this bank and reinforced what the DPRK believed was a deliberate attempt by the Bush administration to cause additional financial harm to the DPRK. A former member of the administration has written that at the time of the 2005 negotiations, President Bush was pursuing two different tracks in interactions with North Korea. One was the diplomatic effort as evidenced by the completion of the Joint Statement. The other was a more punitive approach aimed at cracking down on the DPRK for its illegal activities such as counterfeiting and money laundering.[66] The real issue was whether these different approaches to North Korea were coordinated or just two different departments working independently and possibly at cross purposes. The effect on the negotiations was that when the parties reconvened in November, their meeting lasted only a very short time before being adjourned over the BDA problem. It would be more than a year before these negotiations resumed.

During this hiatus in negotiations is when North Korea resumed its ballistic missile launches in July 2006 and the nuclear weapons detonation the following October as discussed in chapter 4. After the missile tests, the United States, Japan, and other countries introduced a resolution in the United Nations Security Council that passed unanimously later in July.[67] The unanimous passage was significant because China and Russia, two of North Korea's strongest supporters, voted in favor of the resolution further isolating the DPRK. UNSC Resolution 1695 condemned the missile launches and called on North Korea to reimpose the missile moratorium, rejoin the NPT and IAEA safeguards regime, and continue with the six-party negotiations. This resolution also applied a series of sanctions against North Korea related to its missile programs and the exports of missiles and technologies.

After the October nuclear detonation, the United Nations Security Council responded by passing a stronger resolution condemning the nuclear test than it passed in July. Security Council Resolution 1718, dated October 14, 2006, was again passed unanimously and under Chapter VII, Article 41 of the UN Charter and described the test "as a threat to international peace and security." Article 41 allows for the use of nonmilitary measures to enforce the resolution's provisions including interruption of economic interchanges and the severance of diplomatic relations.[68] This resolution demanded that North Korea return to the NPT and IAEA safeguards agreement, not conduct any more ballistic missile launches, and to abandon its WMD programs (chemical, biological, and nuclear). It banned the sale or provision of major conventional arms to the DPRK as well as luxury goods. The latter was significant because Kim Jong Il has long used luxury items as gifts to keep the military and other elites in North Korea loyal to him. Two experts on North Korea have referred to this resolution as "the toughest international sanctions against North Korea since the end of the Korean War."[69]

Under major pressure from China since the nuclear weapon test, North Korea began to move back to the negotiating track. Shortly after the nuclear detonation, Tang Jiaxuan, China's state counselor, met with Kim Jong Il in Pyongyang. Kim reportedly told Tang that the DPRK was ready to return to the negotiations but requested some sort of bilateral meeting with an American representative before doing so.[70] In late November 2006, Assistant Secretary of State Christopher Hill traveled to Beijing and met with Kim Gye Gwan, North Korea's vice foreign minister. Hill and Kim were the lead representatives at the fourth round of six-party talks and have continued in those positions. According to press reports, during this meeting in Beijing, Hill offered food assistance and promised help in resolving the BDA bank deposit problem if North Korea would agree to give up its nuclear weapons.[71]

An even more important bilateral meeting took place between Hill and Kim this time in Berlin in mid-January 2007. Again according to media accounts, the two negotiators began to develop an agenda that could be used in the next round of six-party negotiations. In exchange for American economic and energy assistance as well as relief from the BDA imbroglio, North Korea would agree to suspend certain nuclear programs to include the 5 MW reactor. These bilateral discussions were given more prominence when Secretary of State Rice passed through Berlin just after the conclusion of the Hill–Kim meetings and indicated her support for resuming negotiations as soon as possible.[72] There were also some changes within the Bush administration that facilitated returning to negotiations just as had been true in 2005. After the Democratic Party's victory in the November 2006 congressional elections, Bush accepted the resignation of Secretary of Defense Donald Rumsfeld. John Bolton, the U.S. ambassador to the United Nations also resigned as did Robert Joseph, under secretary of state for arms control. These three men were among the harshest critics of negotiating with Kim Jong Il, and now they were out of the administration.[73]

The fifth round of the six-party negotiations took place in Beijing between February 8 and 13, 2007. At the conclusion of the discussions, the representatives signed the North Korea-Denuclearization Plan[74] (see Appendix B, Document 4). This plan was largely designed to implement the September 2005 Joint Statement in a phased manner to resolve the sequencing problem that had bedeviled earlier negotiations. The principle of "action for action" was to be spelled out so that all the parties would know who was to do what when. In the initial phase that would last from 60 days of the signing, North Korea was to shut down and seal the reprocessing plant and nuclear reactors at Yongbyon and invite back the IAEA inspectors to monitor and verify these actions. The DPRK agreed to discuss with the other parties a list of all nuclear programs to include the plutonium extracted from the spent fuel rods. The United States pledged to hold bilateral talks with North Korea to consider removing the DPRK from the Department of State's state sponsor of terrorism list and to terminate the application of the Trading with the Enemy Act to North Korea. These actions could enable the two countries to establish more normal economic relations and could lead to the DPRK gaining membership to international lending organizations such as the World Bank and IMF. To assist the DPRK with its energy requirements, the other countries agreed to supply 50,000 tons of HFO within the 60-day period.

In the second phase (a specific time period was not established in the Plan of Action), the DPRK pledged to disable the nuclear facilities at Yongbyon and provide a complete declaration of all its nuclear programs. The other countries would supply a total of 950,000 tons of HFO in addition to the 50,000 tons in the initial phase. The February agreement established five WGs to oversee the implementation of these provisions. The first three were multilateral including the Denuclearization of the Korean Peninsula group headed by China; the Economy and Energy group headed by South Korea; and the Northeast Asia Peace and Security Mechanism group headed by Russia. The other two WGs were bilateral in structure; one was the normalization of DPRK–U.S. relations group and the other was the normalization of the DPRK–Japan group. The Bush administration accepted the February agreement with apparently little debate. Some observers have suggested that since this agreement was basically the implementation phase of the 2005 Joint Statement, Secretary of State Rice and Assistant Secretary of State Hill avoided the normal interagency process and thereby deprived Vice President Cheney and his supporters the opportunity to scuttle the deal.[75] Whatever the truth to this report, it still remained for the United States and North Korea to resolve the BDA problem with the sequestered $25 million in the DPRK accounts.

In separate negotiations that took place concurrently with the February six-party talks, U.S. Treasury officials told the North Koreans that the United States no longer objected if Macao decided to return the $25 million to the DPRK. Although this American concession seemed to clear the way for the release of the North Korea accounts, technical problems developed within the international banking system. As a result, the 60-day period of the initial phase of the February agreement came and went with the DPRK refusing to shut down and seal its nuclear facilities at Yongbyon until its funds were released. North Korea also demanded that its funds be transferred through a third party financial institution so that its access to the international financial system would be restored. This demand caused problems because most banks were not willing to handle funds that the United States had designated as being tainted because of the money laundering allegation. Finally, in June 2007, a deal was consummated whereby BDA would release the funds to the Federal Reserve Bank of New York that would in turn transfer these funds to Russia's central bank. The Russian central bank then would make the final transfer to the Russian Far Eastern Commercial Bank where North Korea maintains accounts.[76]

As the funds changed hands, North Korea reportedly sent a letter to the IAEA inviting inspectors to come to Pyongyang to discuss plans for shutting down the its 5 MW reactor. On hearing this news, South Korea made public its plans to begin procuring the 50,000 tons of HFO it had agreed to provide to the DPRK. Christopher Hill announced in June that he thought China would convene the next round of six-party negotiations in early July for the purpose of discussing in more detail the second phase requirements of the February Action Plan. This announcement occurred after Hill visited Pyongyang to discuss the proposed agenda with his North Korean counterparts. This visit to the North Korean capital was the first by an American of his status since the Kelly mission in October 2002.[77] Ten IAEA inspectors traveled to Yongbyon in mid-July to observe the North Korean shutdown of its reactor and to install monitoring equipment. The arrangement agreed to by the DPRK and IAEA was for two inspectors to remain at Yongbyon after the certification that the reactor has been idled. South Korea shipped 6,200 tons of HFO to North Korea at this same time as the first installment of the 50,000 tons pledged. China then announced that the next round of six-party talks would convene in Beijing between July 18 and 20 to discuss the implementation of the remainder of the February 2007 agreement.[78]

At the conclusion of the July 2007 six-party negotiations, the parties agreed that the five WGs established in February 2007 would meet over the next several weeks to work out the details for the timing and sequencing of the following steps. Christopher Hill indicated that substantial progress had been made on the permanent disabling of the nuclear reactor complex at Yongbyon, the required comprehensive declaration of its nuclear programs that North Korea must provide to the other parties, and the beginning of the deliveries of a million tons of HFO to the DPRK. The next round of six-party talks would convene sometime in September 2007.[79] What remains unclear is whether North Korea will list the number of nuclear weapons it has in its comprehensive declaration as well as definitive information on its HEU program. Both Alexander Vershbow, the

American ambassador in Seoul, and Christopher Hill cautioned the ROK not to move too far ahead on its efforts to improve bilateral relations with North Korea unless the DPRK was willing to continue to make progress in the denuclearization negotiations.[80] There was some speculation that Roh Moo Hyun desired to hold another leadership summit involving Kim Jong Il before Roh left office.

CONCLUSION

In evaluating the Clinton and Bush administrations' efforts to curb the North Korean nuclear weapons and missile programs, the evidence suggests that President Clinton was the more successful. At the end of his term of office, the DPRK had at most enough plutonium to make one or two nuclear devices. More important, the North Koreans remained in the NPT and IAEA inspectors were on the ground at all the known plutonium-related sites. The Agreed Framework was far from a perfect document, and bilateral negotiations presented some difficult challenges, particularly keeping the South Koreans apprised of what was taking place since they have so much at stake. If North Korea decided to cheat on the Agreed Framework and other agreements with the ROK, there was little the United States could do other than stay vigilant with the effective use of intelligence assets. That is exactly what happened in detecting the clandestine HEU program. By the end of the Clinton administration, North Korea had imposed a ballistic missile moratorium on testing, and the relationship had progressed to the point that the secretary of state visited Kim Jong Il in Pyongyang.

President Bush and others in his administration have stated on numerous occasions that nuclear weapons in North Korea are intolerable and unacceptable. When then Japanese Prime Minister Junichiro Koizumi visited the president at his Crawford, Texas ranch in May 2003, Bush stated "we (Bush and Koizumi) will not tolerate nuclear weapons in North Korea...we will settle for nothing less than the complete, verifiable, irreversible elimination of North Korea's nuclear weapons program." President Bush made similar comments after a meeting with South Korean President Roh Moo Hyun in October 2003.[81] Despite this rhetoric, North Korea has proceeded to reprocess plutonium, build a nuclear arsenal, and test one nuclear devise. It no longer is a member of the NPT and the IAEA inspectors were expelled in December 2002. No one can be sure what the status of the HEU program is at this point. The ballistic missile moratorium was rescinded and the DPRK tested missiles in July 2006.

Part of the problem President Bush confronted was the serious divisions among some of the most powerful members of his administration regarding whether or not to negotiate with North Korea. These divisions made the development of a consistent negotiating strategy very difficult. There is no question that multilateral negotiations have some advantages in that more pressure can be brought to bear on North Korea and the costs associated with any agreement can be shared.

However, multilateral negotiations also have some limitations too. In the instance of the six-party negotiations, South Korea, China, and Russia have taken more conciliatory positions regarding North Korea because of their own national security interests. The United States and Japan have been less willing to compromise with the DPRK again based on their national security interests. The differences in approach among the other five negotiating partners have presented Kim Jong Il and his team with opportunities to divide the others to the benefit of North Korea. This DPRK negotiating strategy will become more evident in the next chapter as we examine the relationships between the two Koreas, North Korea and the United States, and the United States and South Korea.

NOTES

1. For an earlier version of this chapter that ended with the September 2005 Statement of Principles among the six parties participating in negotiations concerning the North Korean nuclear program, see William E. Berry, Jr., "The North Korean Nuclear Weapons Program: A Comparison of the Negotiating Strategies of the Clinton and Bush Administrations," in *Perspectives on U.S. Policy Toward North Korea: Stalemate or Checkmate?* ed. Sharon Richardson (New York: Lexington Books, 2006), 1–27. For Soviet pressure on North Korea, see Michael Mazarr, *North Korea and the Bomb: A Case Study in Nonproliferation* (New York: St. Martin's Griffin, 1997), 29.

2. Kongdam Oh and Ralph Hassig, "North Korea's Nuclear Program," in *Korea and the World Beyond the Cold War,* ed. Young Whan Kihl (Boulder: Westview Press, 1994), 234–35 and Mazarr, *North Korea and the Bomb: A Case Study in Nonproliferation,* 35–54.

3. David Sanger, "North Korea Reported Near Nuclear Ability," *New York Times* (September 14, 1991): 2.

4. The Joint Declaration on the Denuclearization of the Korean Peninsula, January 20, 1992 can be found on the South Korean Ministry of Unification web site http://www.unikorea.go.kr/interkorean.

5. Oh and Hassig, "North Korea's Nuclear Program," 237–38.

6. Ibid., 238.

7. Larry A. Niksch, "North Korea's Nuclear Weapons Program," CRS Issue Brief, Congressional Research Service (May 2, 1994): 1–2.

8. Selig S. Harrison, *Korean Endgame: A Strategy for Reunification and U.S. Disengagement* (Princeton: Princeton University Press, 2002), 208–09. Mazarr, *North Korea and the Bomb: A Case Study in Nonproliferation,* 104.

9. Reuters, "Pyongyang Stung by Vote, Warns UN Not to Seek Sanctions," *International Herald Tribune* (March 12, 1993): 6.

10. Nicholas D. Kristof, "Abandoning Treaty, North Korea Warns Against Nuclear Ban," *International Herald Tribune* (March 13–14, 1993): 1. Article X.1 of the NPT requires the 90-day notification before a signatory country can withdraw from the treaty.

11. Paul F. Horwitz, "U.S. Sees 'Danger' in North Korean Shift," *International Herald Tribune* (March 15, 1993): 1.

12. Joel S. Wit, Daniel B. Poneman, and Robert L. Gallucci, *Going Critical: The First North Korean Nuclear Crisis* (Washington: Brookings Institution Press, 2004), 45–46.

13. "U.S.–North Korean Joint Statement," June 11, 1993 is available in its entirety in Wit, Poneman, and Gallucci, *Going Critical: The First North Korean Nuclear Crisis,* 419–20.

14. For a copy of the "U.S.–North Korea Agreed Statement, July 19, 1993" see *The U.S.–Korea Review,* 2, no. 5 (September–November 1993): 6.

15. Tim Weiner, "U.S. and North Korea Hold Quiet Talks on Nuclear Inspections," *New York Times* (October 27, 1993): 4.

16. Michael R. Gordon, "UN Atom Agency Rejects Offer By North Korea," *New York Times* (December 7, 1993): 4.

17. Wit, Poneman, and Gallucci, *Going Critical,* 103–04.

18. Michael R. Gordon, "White House Asks Global Sanctions on North Koreans," *New York Times* (June 3, 1994): 1.

19. Paul F. Horwitz, "The North Koreans Send a Conciliatory Message," *International Herald Tribune* (June 13, 1994): 1. One of the visiting Americans to see Kim Il Sung was Selig Harrison.

20. Wit, Poneman, and Gallucci, *Going Critical,* 210–12.

21. Ibid., 221–28.

22. Jeffrey Smith, "Before Sanctions, a Grace Period," *International Herald Tribune* (June 16, 1994): 1 and Michael R. Gordon, "Back From Korea, Carter Declares the Crisis in Over," *New York Times* (June 20, 1994): 1.

23. Wit, Poneman, and Gallucci, *Going Critical,* 255–59.

24. Jonathan D. Pollack, "The United States, North Korea, and the End of the Agreed Framework," *Naval War College Review,* 56, no. 3 (May 5, 2003): 19.

25. "Agreement on the Establishment of the Korean Peninsula Energy Development Organization" signed by representatives of United States, Japan, and South Korea on March 9, 1995. For a copy of this document, see http://www.kedo.org.

26. I am indebted to Ralph Cossa for this insight. See his "North Korea: Digging Deeper Holes," PacNet 37, September 2, 2003. The PacNet series is published by the Pacific Forum in Honolulu and available through its web site at http://www.csis.org/pacforum.

27. Several of these issues are outlined in Pollack, "The United States, North Korea, and the End of the Agreed Framework," 19–20.

28. Richard L. Armitage, "A Comprehensive Approach to North Korea," Institute for National Security Studies, National Defense University, Strategic Forum No. 159, March 1999. The details that follow are taken directly from this report.

29. Author's interview with Robert L. Gallucci, Dean of the School of Foreign Service, Georgetown University, Washington, DC, July 17, 2003 and Wit, Poneman, and Gallucci, *Going Critical: The First North Korean Nuclear Crisis,* 383–87.

30. Wit, Poneman, and Gallucci, *Going Critical,* 387–96.

31. David E. Sanger, "North Korea Site An A-Bomb Plant, U.S. Agencies Say," *New York Times* (August 17, 1998): 1.

32. Philip Shenon, "Suspected North Korean Atom Site is Empty U.S. Finds," *New York Times* (May 28, 1999): 3.

33. For coverage of this missile launch and the immediate reactions, see Sheryl Wu Dunn, "North Korea Fires Missile Over Japanese Territory," *New York Times* (September 1, 1998): 6 and Barbara Crossette, "North Korea Draws Anger with Test of Missile," *New York Times* (September 2, 1998): 4.

34. This account of the appointment of the North Korea Policy Coordinator can be found in "North Korea: A Phased Negotiation Strategy," *International Crisis Group Asia Report No. 61,* dated August 1, 2003, 9.

35. "Review of United States Policy Toward North Korea: Findings and Recommendations," an unclassified version of this report is available at http://www.state.gov/regions/eap/

991012_northkorea_rpt.html. For more on the Perry mission as reported in the press, see Philip Shenon, "Panel Urges Stepped-Up Attention to Ties with North Korea," *New York Times* (September 15, 1999): 14 and David Sanger, "Trade Sanctions on North Korea Are Eased by U.S.," *New York Times* (September 18, 1999): 1

36. Pollack, "The United States, North Korea, and the End of the Agreed Framework," 22.

37. Ibid., 22–23 and "North Korea: A Phased Negotiation Strategy," *International Crisis Group Asia Report No. 61,* dated August 1, 2003, 9. For media coverage at the time of the Cho visit, see David Sanger, "North Korean at White House, Continuing a Warming Trend," *New York Times* (October 11, 2000): 3.

38. Ibid., 24.

39. For a good review of the Bush–Kim meeting in March 2001, see Morton I. Abramowitz and James T. Laney, "Meeting the North Korean Nuclear Challenge," Report of the Independent Task Force sponsored by the Council on Foreign Relations, June 2003, 12.

40. Statement of the President, June 11, 2001. This statement is available at http://www.whitehouse.gov/news/releases/2001/06/20010611-4.html.

41. The Nuclear Posture Review can be found at http://www.globalsecurity.org/wmd/library/policy/dod/npr.htm. The reference to the new triad is on p. 1 and attacking underground bunkers on page 4. See also Abramowitz and Laney, "North Korean Nuclear Challenge," 12.

42. The National Security Strategy of the United States of America, September 2002, 6–15. In the 2006 National Security Strategy, the administration referred to North Korea as a tyrannical government and one that continues to destabilize the region. It also listed the DPRK as "a serious nuclear proliferation challenge." While this report still supported preemptive actions as a last resort, there was more emphasis n multilateral diplomacy than in the 2002 edition. See The National Security Strategy of the United States of America, March 2006, 3, 19, and 21.

43. For a good review of Bush's State of the Union address and how it was received in both Pyongyang and Seoul, see John Larkin, "Axis of Uncertainty," *Far Eastern Economic Review* (February 14, 2002): 12–15.

44. Bob Woodward, *Bush at War* (New York: Simon and Shuster, 2002), 340.

45. Larry A. Niksch, "Korea: U.S.–Korean Relations-Issues for Congress," Issue Brief for the Congress, Congressional Research Service, May 1, 2003, 2. Niksch made similar arguments in an interview with the author in Washington, DC, July 15, 2003. For another good description of the divisions within the administration and effects on policies toward North Korea, see Sebastian Harnisch, "U.S.–North Korean Relations Under the Bush Administration: From 'Slow Go' to "No Go,'" *Asian Survey,* 42, no. 6 (November/December 2002): 856–82.

46. For a series of articles on the Kelly visit, see David Sanger, "North Korea Says It Has a Program on Nuclear Arms," *New York Times* (October 17, 2002): 1; David Sanger and James Dao, "U.S. Says Pakistan Gave Technology to North Korea," *New York Times* (October 18, 2002): 1; and Howard French, "North Korea's Confession: Why?" *New York Times* (October 21, 2002): 6. See also Murray Hiebert, "Still Stuck in Stalemate," *Far Eastern Economic Review* (October 17, 2002): 22–23 and Murray Hiebert, "Consequences of a Confession," *Far Eastern Economic Review* (October 31, 2002): 14–19.

47. Pollack, "The United States, North Korea, and the End of the Agreed Framework," 35–36 has some excellent insights into the Kelly visit as Larry A. Niksch, "North Korea's

Nuclear Weapons Program," Issue Brief for Congress, Congressional Research Service, November 27, 2002, 8.

48. Ibid., 37–38. See also a series of *New York Times* articles including Elisabeth Buimiller, "Bush Sees Korean Nuclear Effort as Different from Iraq's," October 22, 2002, 6; Julie Preston, "North Korea Demands U.S. Agree to Nonaggression Pact," October 26, 2002, 8; and Philip Shenon, "North Korea Says Nuclear Program Can Be Negotiated," November 3, 2002, 1.

49. KEDO Executive Board Meeting Notes, November 14, 2002 can be found on the KEDO web site at http://www.kedo.org.

50. B.C. Koh, "A Breakthrough or An Illusion?: An Assessment of the New Six-Party Agreement," The Institute for Far Eastern Studies, February 16, 2007, 4 available at http://ifes.kyungnam.ac.kr/eng/activity/print_ifesforum.asp?ifesformumNO=197&page=1.

51. "North Korea: A Phased Negotiation Strategy," International Crisis Group Asia Report No. 61, August 1, 2003, 13 and a series of *New York Times* articles including David Sanger, " U.S. Criticizes North Korea for Rejecting Inspections" (December 5, 2002): 23; Howard French and David Sanger, "North Korea to Reactivate An Idled Nuclear Reactor" (December 13, 2002): 16; David Sanger and James Dao, "North Korea Says It Regains Access to Its Plutonium" (December 23, 2002): 1; Richard Stevenson, "North Korea Begins to Reopen Plant for Processing Plutonium" (December 24, 2002): 1; and James Brooke, "North Korea Says It Plans to Expel Nuclear Monitors" (December 28, 2002): 1.

52. ElBaradei's Introductory Statement to the Board of Governors, dated February 12, 2003 can be found at http://www.iaea.org/worldatom/Press/Statement/2003/ebsp2003n004.shtml, and the IAEA Board of Governor Adopts a Resolution of Safeguards in North Korea dated February 14, 2003 can be found at the IAEA web site http://www.iaea.org/worldatom/Press/ P_release/2003/med-advise_048.shtml.

53. Jean du Preez and William Potter, "North Korea's Withdrawal from the NPT: A Reality Check," Monterey Institute of International Studies, April 9, 2003 available at http:// cns.miis.edu/pubs/week/030409.htm.

54. Pollack, "The United States, North Korea, and the End of the Agreed Framework," 38–39.

55. Charles L. Pritchard, *Failed Diplomacy: The Tragic Story of How North Korea Got the Bomb* (Washington: The Brookings Institution Press, 2007), 55–58.

56. Ibid., 64.

57. For a series of *New York Times* articles covering the 3-party talks, see David Sanger, "North Koreans and U.S. Plan Talks in Beijing" (April 16, 2003): 1; David Sanger, "Bush Takes a No-Budge Stand in Talks With North Korea" (April 17, 2003): 11; Joseph Kahn, "North Korea May Be Angering Its Only Ally" (April 26, 2003): 5. For a positive op ed article on the talks, see Brent Scowcroft and Arnold Kanter, "A Surprising Success on North Korea" (May 1, 2003): 31.

58. See again *New York Times,* Joseph Kahn and David Sanger, "North Korea Says It May Test an A-Bomb" (August 29, 2003): 6 and Joseph Kahn, "Korea Arms Talks Close With Plans for a New Round" (August 30, 2003): 1. See also, Murray Hiebert, "An Alliance Under Stress," *Far Eastern Economic Review* (February 26, 2004): 18–19.

59. Ralph A. Cossa, "CVID: Does Everyone Agree?" PacNet 20, Pacific Forum, May 6, 2004, 1–2.

60. "North Korea: What Next for the Nuclear Talks," International Crisis Group Asia Report No. 87, November 15, 2004, 7–9.

61. "Ending the North Korean Nuclear Crisis," The Center for International Policy and the Center for East Asian Studies, University of Chicago, November 2004, 9–10.

62. Joseph Kahn, "North Korea Is Studying Softer Stance From the U.S.," *New York Times* (June 24, 2004): 13.

63. Pritchard, *Failed Diplomacy,* 107–09. For more information on Rice's bureaucratic skills regarding the six-party talks, see Marcus Mabry, "Condoleezza Rice," *Foreign Policy* (May/June 2007): 22–28. In 2000 before joining the Bush administration, Rice wrote a critical article in *Foreign Affairs* regarding the Agreed Framework and Clinton policies toward North Korea in general. See Condolleeza Rice, "Promoting the National Interest," *Foreign Affairs* 79, no. 1 (January/February 2000): 45–62.

64. Joint Statement of the Fourth Round of the Six-Party Talks, Beijing, September 19, 2005. This statement is available at http://www.state.gov/r/prs/ps/2005/53490.htm.

65. For a somewhat guardedly optimistic assessment of the Joint Statement, see Ralph A. Cossa, "Six-Party Statement of Principles: One Small Step for Man," PacNet 41, September 19, 2005, Pacific Forum. For a more pessimistic appraisal, see John Tkacik, "North Korea's Bogus Breakthrough," *Far Eastern Economic Review,* 168, no. 8 (September 2005): 21–23.

66. Julia Choi and Karin Lee, "North Korea: Economic Sanctions and U.S. Department of Treasury Actions 1955—September 2006," The National Committee on North Korea, 14–16 available at http://www.ncnk.org. For a critical analysis of the BDA sanctions, see Glyn Ford, "Dead Talks Walking: North Korea and Removing the Bomb," Policy Forum Online 06-104A, December 14, 2006, Nautilus Institute available at http://www.nautilus.org/fora/security/06104Ford.html. Jack Pritchard is the former administration official. See his book *Failed Diplomacy: The Tragic Story of How North Korea Got the Bomb,* 130–31.

67. United Nations Security Council Resolution 1695, "United Nations Security Council Condemns Democratic People's Republic of Korea's Missile Launches," dated July 15, 2006 available at http://www.state.gov/p/eap/rls/prs/69022.htm.

68. UN Security Council Resolution 1718, "UN Security Council Resolution on North Korea," dated October 14, 2006 available at http://www.state.gov/p/eap/rls/ot/74010.htm.

69. Ilsoo David Cho and Meredith Jung-En Woo, "North Korea in 2006: The Year of Living Dangerously," *Asian Survey,* XLVII, no. 1 (January/February 2007): 68–73.

70. Pritchard, *Failed Diplomacy,* 156.

71. Helene Cooper and David Sanger, "U.S. Offers North Korea Aid for Dropping Nuclear Plans,"*New York Times* (December 6, 2006): 11.

72. Mark Landler and Thom Shanker, "North Korea and U.S. Envoys Meet in Berlin," *New York Times* (January 18, 2007): 3. See also Jonathan D. Pollack, "North Korea's Nuclear Weapons Program to 2015: Three Scenarios," *Asia Policy,* no. 3 (January 2007), National Bureau of Asian Research, 109.

73. David Sanger, "Sensing Shift in Bush Policy, Another Hawk Joins the Exodus," *New York Times* (March 21, 2007): 1.

74. North Korea-Denuclearization Action Plan, February 13, 2007 is available at http://www.state.gov/r/pa/prs/ps/2007/february/80479.htm.

75. David Sanger and Thom Shanker, "Rice Said to Have Speeded North Korean Deal," *New York Times* (February 16, 2007): 3.

76. Steven R. Weisman, "U.S. Close to Deal to Release Frozen North Korean Funds," *New York Times* (June 12, 2007): 4.

77. "North Korea Says It Has Invited Team to Discuss Closing Reactor," *New York Times* (June 17, 2007): 10 and Norimitsu Onishi, "Money Dispute's End Paves Way For North Korean Nuclear Talks," *New York Times* (June 21, 2007): 8. For Hill's June 2007 visit to North

Korea, see Donald G. Gross, "U.S–Korea Relations: Finally Progress on the February 13 Joint Agreement," *Comparative Connections,* 9, no. 2 (July 2007): 47–52.

78. Choe Sang Hun, "Oil Is Shipped to North Korea Under Nuclear Shutdown Pact," *New York Times* (July 13, 2007): 9.

79. Howard W. French, "North Korean Nuclear Talks Fail to Set Disarmament Timetable, but Yield Agreement on Goals," *New York Times* (July 20, 2007): 13.

80. Donald G. Gross, "U.S.–North Korea Relations: Finally Progress on the February 13 Joint Agreement," *Comparative Connections,* 9, no. 2 (July 2007): 47–52.

81. See http://www.whitehouse.gov/news/releases/2003/05/20030523-4.html and http://www.whitehouse.gov/news/releases/2003/10/print/20031020-2.html.

CHAPTER 6

Evolving Security Environment on the Korean Peninsula

In evaluating North Korean foreign policy, one of the most important conclusions to be gained is how well the DPRK has linked the goals of enhancing its national security, fostering economic development opportunities, and preserving its political legitimacy, particularly in its competition with South Korea. Also evident is what Samuel Kim has referred to as implementing "the power of the weak" and playing the "collapse card" whereby North Korea uses geographical considerations to gain maximum advantage.[1] Both of these negotiating tactics will be evident in the section on inter-Korean relations that follows.

As related in chapter 1, geography has been and remains an important factor for both Koreas because they are relatively small nation states situated in a dangerous neighborhood including China, Japan, and Russia. However, the DPRK has learned how to play its geographic location to its maximum advantage because the other major powers in the region have to take North Korea seriously. Any conflict on the Korean peninsula or collapse of the Kim dynasty could result in economic disruptions that would adversely affect these countries. In this chapter, our focus will be on the relationship between the two Koreas, the troubled history of North Korean–American contacts, and the long-standing ties between South Korea and the United States. The final section will explore some possible reunification scenarios.

INTER-KOREAN RELATIONS

During the first two decades following the Korean War, the two Koreas were locked in a deadly competition for political legitimacy and to be perceived domestically as well as internationally to represent true Korean nationalism. These circumstances began to change in the early 1970s in part because of or in reaction to the policies of the Nixon administration in Washington. The removal of one of the two U.S. Army infantry divisions from South Korea certainly got the attention of President Park Chung Hee in Seoul. Perhaps more important, the 1972 visit of President Nixon to meet with Mao Zedong in China marked the beginning of a period of rapprochement with the communist regime in Beijing. This new relationship with China caused growing feelings on insecurity on both sides of the 38th parallel. In response, the two Korean governments began to consider means by which they might be able to improve their relations with each other.

The first substantive discussions occurred in August 1971 when representatives of the two Korean Red Cross societies met in Panmunjom along the DMZ. These discussions were held in the highest secrecy and did not accomplish much in and of themselves. However, they did provide an opportunity for high-level contacts between officials of the KCIA and the DPRK's KWP. On May 4, 1972, Lee Hu Rak, the director of the KCIA, met with Kim Il Sung in Pyongyang, a meeting that would not be officially confirmed until late in the 1980s. In this meeting, both sides expressed their displeasure with the policies of "big powers" that had contributed to the division of the Korean peninsula. Kim also apologized for the 1968 KPA commando raid on the Blue House in Seoul and the attempt to assassinate Park Chung Hee. In a return visit in late May, Park Sung Chul, the North Korean deputy prime minister, traveled to Seoul and met with President Park.[2]

As a result of these events, the two sides released a Joint Statement on July 4, 1972.[3] Included in this Joint Statement were three principles:

1. Reunification should be achieved independently, without reliance upon outside force or its interference.
2. Reunification should be achieved by peaceful means without recourse to the use of arms against the other side.
3. Great national unity should be promoted first of all as one nation, transcending the differences of ideology, ideal, and system.

Both Koreas also pledged to refrain from slandering the other and from committing armed provocations. They agreed to install direct telephone communications between the two capitals to prevent military incidents from escalating. Finally, the negotiators expressed the intent to form a North–South Coordination Committee to promote the implementation of the points expressed in the Joint Statement. Although somewhat nebulous, this statement outlined the Korean perception that the division of the country was the responsibility of outside powers and expressed a desire to resolve the problems through negotiations between the two Koreas.

Despite initial optimism, little long-term progress resulted. Part of the reason for this lack of success was that Kim Il Sung saw the agreement with the ROK as a means to reduce the American presence in South Korea, particularly the U.S. military forces there. In a confidential presentation to the East German government shortly after the Joint Statement was published, the DPRK ambassador stated that this reduction in the American commitment to South Korea was a major North Korean goal. He went on to state that he was confident that the Park Chung Hee government would be weaker as a result of this negotiating ploy, and the perceived improvement in relations could lead to an opportunity for a North Korean victory.[4] This incident provides a good example of North Korean efforts to use negotiations to enhance its national security.

Relations between North and South Korea deteriorated later in the 1970s and early 1980s. The discovery of the underground DPRK tunnels south of the 38th parallel, the 1976 ax murders in the DMZ, and the attempt in 1983 to assassinate Chun Doo Hwan in Rangoon, Burma among other incidents all contributed to this deterioration. However, in September 1984, an act of nature intervened that provided an opportunity for additional contacts. Severe floods hit South Korea resulting in significant losses of life and property. North Korea responded with an offer of assistance including rice, cement, clothing, and medical supplies. To the surprise of many, the Chun Doo Hwan administration accepted this offer, and several hundred North Korean trucks crossed the DMZ to deliver the promised supplies. Red Cross officials on both sides took advantage of this improvement in relations to press their governments to move forward on family reunions. As a result of these efforts, thirty-five South Korean family members traveled to Pyongyang to meet with relatives in September 1985. Thirty North Koreans journeyed to Seoul to meet their relatives at the same time.[5]

Again, the optimism associated with the North Korean assistance to the ROK and the subsequent family reunions was short lived. Conflicts developed over the holding of the Team Spirit military exercise in 1986 with North Korea voicing its opposition to this exercise that it described as war preparation for an invasion of the DPRK. Actually, Team Spirit, a joint and combined exercise involving United States and South Korean military forces began in 1976 as a means to show that the United States was still capable of fulfilling its military commitments to allies such as the ROK after the collapse of South Vietnam and Vietnamese reunification under communist control in 1975. Team Spirit also had a demonstration effect on North Korea because it was a practical example of the American logistical capabilities to move thousands of troops and their equipment to South Korea to reinforce those forces already there. Nonetheless, the holding of the Team Spirit exercise in 1986 and the North Korean shoot down of the KAL jetliner in 1987 leading up to the 1988 Olympics in Seoul brought to an end the improved relations that had occurred earlier in the 1980s.

Although President Roh Tae Woo's Nordpolitik policy was perhaps best known for the initiatives to establish normal diplomatic relations with the Soviet Union, China, and several communist countries in Eastern Europe, another intent was to increase contacts with North Korea. Specific policies called for more exchanges involving North and South Koreans from a variety of occupations, improved humanitarian interactions to include reuniting separated families, and enhanced trade between the two countries to improve both economies. Finally, Roh encouraged improved relations between North Korea and the United States and Japan. From the North Korean perspective, the ROK's success in establishing diplomatic relations with the Soviet Union and China had a tremendous effect on the DPRK's national security. These developments plus the eventual collapse of the USSR and the communist governments in Eastern Europe served to convince Kim Il Sung and Kim Jong Il that improved relations with South Korea might be a wise course.

In late 1991 and early 1992 toward the end of the Roh presidency, the two Koreas entered into two very important agreements. The first was the Agreement on Reconciliation, Nonaggression, and Exchanges and Cooperation Between South and North Korea that was signed on December 13, 1991, and went into effect on February 19, 1992.[6] The parties agreed not to use force against each other and to resolve any differences through dialogue and negotiation. Similar to the 1972 Joint Statement, they pledged to establish a South–North Joint Military Commission to discuss mutual problems and promote confidence building measures to include phased reductions in armaments leading to the elimination of WMD. The two Koreas also stipulated their desire to replace the 1953 Armistice Agreement negotiated at the end of the Korean War with a "firm state of peace" and agreed to reconnect rail and road connections across the DMZ. This agreement would prove difficult to implement, but it was much more comprehensive than the 1972 statement.

In early January 1992, North and South Korea signed the Joint Declaration of the Denuclearization of the Korean Peninsula that entered into effect in February of that year (see Appendix B, Document 1).[7] In this document, the two Koreas pledged not to "test, manufacture, produce, receive, possess, store, or use nuclear weapons." They also promised to use nuclear energy only for peaceful purposes and not to possess nuclear reprocessing or uranium enrichment facilities. To verify compliance, both countries agreed to permit inspections and to establish a South–North Joint Nuclear Control Commission. In 2002 when the United States accused the DPRK of developing a HEU program, this Joint Declaration along with the 1994 Agreed Framework were the two documents very important in substantiating North Korean misbehavior.

When Kim Young Sam became South Korea's president in early 1993, the nuclear weapons issue was just becoming the dominant problem between the two Koreas and between the United States and DPRK. One of the outcomes of

Jimmy Carter's discussions with Kim Il Sung in June 1994 was to provide the impetus for a possible summit meeting between the two Korean presidents. In subsequent negotiations, the two sides established July 25, 1994 as the date for this summit in Pyongyang. Unfortunately, Kim Il Sung died in early July, and the plans for the summit collapsed. Kim Young Sam's other major negotiating initiative involving North Korea centered on proposals for four-party talks that would include the two Koreas, the United States, and China. One of Kim's major concerns with the bilateral negotiations then underway between the DPRK and United States over nuclear weapons was that South Korean interests would not be fully represented even though American officials did all possible to ensure that South Korea was fully aware of the negotiating specifics. In any event, the four-party talks provided an opportunity for direct ROK involvement. These discussions began in Geneva during December 1997 and would continue on and off for some time although there was little substantive progress.[8]

South Korea responded favorably to North Korean requests for assistance as the economic crisis intensified in the mid-1990s by providing food aid. However, in September 1996, the DPRK launched a major military provocation against the ROK. A South Korean taxi driver detected a North Korean submarine that had run aground near Kangnung on the east coast of the ROK. A subsequent manhunt captured one of the infiltrators and killed the other twenty-five who were loose in the South Korean countryside and refused to surrender. This major effort to infiltrate KPA special purpose forces into the ROK shocked Kim Young Sam and his government based on its audacity and because the South Korean military had not been able to prevent this incursion or even detect the presence of the submarine and its crew in ROK territory.[9]

It was difficult to determine what the Kim Jong Il regime was trying to accomplish by this brazen violation on South Korean sovereignty, particularly at a time when the DPRK's economy was in tatters, and Kim Young Sam had offered assistance. Some experts suggested that this represented normal North Korean behavior and reflected a lack of coordination between the KPA and other government agencies. Others opined that those in the government who were critical of improved relations with Seoul may have used this infiltration as a means to scuttle those relations. Still others expressed the view that this incursion just represented another KPA attempt to measure the readiness of South Korean defenses.[10]

Whatever the motivations, Kim Young Sam responded forcefully by announcing that his government was reviewing all of its policies and programs toward North Korea. These programs included economic cooperation and ROK support for KEDO's continuing construction of LWRs in the DPRK under the provisions of the 1994 Agreed Framework. Kim demanded an apology from North Korea before he would continue these programs. In late December 1996, the North Korean government did express its "deep regret" over the submarine incursion and promised that "such an incident would not recur."[11] This apology cleared the way for extended negotiations in 1997 leading to the beginning of the four-party discussions in December of that year.

Kim Dae Jung had a long history of attempting to reduce tensions and support engagement with North Korea during his years as an opposition leader. When he assumed the presidency of South Korea in February 1998, his orientation toward engagement was reinforced by the dire financial situation the ROK found itself in as the Asian economic crisis intensified for South Korea and several other Asian countries. Kim was even more convinced that the German model of reunification was not applicable for the Korean peninsula, at least at that time, because of the tremendous costs that would be involved. As related in chapter 2, Kim announced his Sunshine Policy toward North Korea during his inaugural address. There were three main components to this policy. First, South Korea would not tolerate armed provocations from the DPRK such as the submarine incursion in 1996. Second, the ROK had no intention to undermine or absorb North Korea. Third, the ROK would promote reconciliation and cooperation between the two Koreas focusing on those areas where agreement was most likely. A key part of Kim's policy was to attempt to separate political issues from economics so that South Korean business leaders could take the lead in establishing contacts with North Korea and improving economic cooperation.[12]

The Sunshine Policy achieved its greatest success during Kim Dae Jung's presidency in June 2000 when President Kim traveled to Pyongyang for a summit meeting with Kim Jong Il. At the conclusion of this 3-day summit, the two leaders issued the South–North Joint Declaration on June 15.[13] The Joint Declaration included the following points:

1. The South and North have agreed to resolve the question of reunification independently and through the joint efforts of the Korean people, who are the masters of the country.

2. For the achievement of reunification, we have agreed that there is a common element in the South's concept of a confederation and the North's formula for a loose federation. The South and the North agreed to promote reunification in that direction. (Note to Readers: the differences between the two Korean proposals on reunification will be discussed at the end of this section.)

3. The South and North have agreed to promptly resolve humanitarian issues such as exchange visits by separated family members and relatives on the occasion of the August 15 National Liberation Day and the question of unswerving communists serving prison sentences in the South.

4. The South and North have agreed to consolidate mutual trust by promoting balanced development of the national economy through economic cooperation and by stimulating cooperation and exchanges in civic, cultural, sports, health, environmental, and all other fields.

5. The South and North have agreed to hold a dialogue between relevant authorities in the near future to implement the above agreements expeditiously.

At the conclusion of the Joint Declaration, President Kim invited Kim Jong Il to visit Seoul, and Kim accepted the invitation although he would only commit to making the visit "at an appropriate time." This declaration was signed by Kim Dae Jung as president of the ROK and Kim Jong Il as chairman of the National Defense Commission.

One of the most significant elements of this declaration was that the two Koreas expressed their confidence that they would be able to work out the details of reunification on their own—a good example of the significance of Korean nationalism to both sides and perhaps a slap at outside powers. The Joint Declaration also appeared to put to rest the long-standing competition for political legitimacy between the two Koreas, but it did not raise the very important issue of how to achieve security on the Korean peninsula. The reference to economic cooperation and sports exchanges has paved the way for some of the economic initiatives pursued by both the Kim Dae Jung and Roh Moo Hyun administrations and laid the groundwork for the possibility of a joint Korean Olympic Team at the 2008 Games in Beijing.

During conversations between the two leaders, Kim Dae Jung tried to convince Kim Jong Il to continue the missile moratorium in place and to respect the provisions of the Agreed Framework. He also emphasized the importance he saw in North Korea improving relations with the United States in the context of enhanced inter-Korean ties. Finally, Kim Dae Jung reported that Kim Jong Il agreed that the retention of an American military presence in the ROK was a worthwhile goal and that he would not oppose the continuation of this presence. However, the North Korean leader emphasized that the mission of these forces should be changed to reflect a regional peacekeeping function rather than be directed at the DPRK.[14]

After the summit, the Clinton administration announced the implementation of the easing of economic sanctions against North Korea. When Vice Marshall Cho Myong Rok visited Washington in October 2000, the two sides issued a United States–DPRK Joint Communiqué that specifically mentioned the summit as a major event that would influence Washington–Pyongyang relations in the future. Both countries stated they had no hostile intent towards the other and pledged to develop a new relationship "free from past enmity." North Korea also promised to maintain its ballistic missile moratorium as long as negotiations with the United States continued, and the two governments affirmed their intentions to achieve a nuclear free Korean peninsula under the terms of the Agreed Framework.[15] Shortly thereafter, Secretary of State Madeleine Albright made her trip to meet Kim Jong Il in North Korea.

The 2000 summit and its aftermath remain controversial both because of the allegations that the Kim Dae Jung government bought the rights to hold the summit through secret payments to Kim Jong Il and also because there have been major criticisms in South Korea that the North has not reciprocated for the benefits the Kim regime has received. For example, Kim Jong Il has never made the promised return visit to Seoul. However, the summit had and continues to have a major effect on South Koreans as far as relations with their northern cousins are concerned. The way in which many South Koreans looked upon North Koreans and Kim Jong Il in particular was dramatically changed, and the DPRK was no longer viewed as the enemy but rather as disadvantaged relatives.[16] This changed perception of North Korea would not only affect inter-Korean relations, but also the bilateral ties between Seoul and Washington as will be evident later in this chapter.

Roh Moo Hyun initially attempted to differentiate his administration from that of Kim Dae Jung when he came into office in early 2003 by changing the name of his policy toward North Korea to the Peace and Prosperity Policy. The emphasis here on prosperity was meant to signal to the South Korean populace that more attention would be paid to reciprocity on the part of North Korea and thereby more benefits to the ROK. Roh also indicated his intent to concentrate more efforts on broadening support for his policy among South Koreans in general and the National Assembly in particular. This has proved to be a difficult task in part because of the impeachment proceedings brought against Roh in 2004 and shifting party allegiances that have cost him his majority in the legislature. In addition to the demands for increased reciprocity, President Roh expressed his interest in replacing the 1953 Armistice Agreement with a more permanent security regime, but little progress has been made although the six-party negotiations have now addressed this issue if only to indicate a new security regime should be the subject of separate discussions.[17]

What becomes evident in our discussion of the evolving South Korean policy toward North Korea is the gradual development of engagement strategies from the time of Roh Tae Woo to the current administration, but most noticeably under Kim Dae Jung and Roh Moo Hyun. In December 2007, South Korea will conduct its next presidential election, and early polling data suggested the GNP, the major opposition party, is favored to win the presidency. The GNP tends to be more conservative than the Roh administration on many issues to include relations with the DPRK. On many occasions, the GNP has been critical of the Peace and Prosperity Policy based on the party's perception that North Korea has not lived up the specifics of many of the promises the North has made in bilateral and multilateral negotiations. At present, the GNP is attempting to develop its own policy on North Korea that it has named the Vision for Peace on the Korean Peninsula. However, this process of developing a coherent policy has proven to be difficult because of substantive differences within the party. Particularly difficult has been resolving issues such as denuclearization and peace mechanisms on the Korean peninsula, economic initiatives and desired outcomes, humanitarian cooperation, and human rights in North Korea.[18] Obviously, the outcome of the 2007 presidential election could have a definite effect on inter-Korean relations, but the argument here is that there has been a fundamental positive shift in how a majority of South Koreans view their northern neighbors, and this shift will limit the range of policy initiatives any party in the ROK can initiate.

One quantitative method to measure the effectiveness of South Korean engagement policies with North Korea over the past several years is to evaluate the economic interactions that have occurred between the two Koreas. For our purposes, we will concentrate on bilateral Korean trade relations and South Korea direct investments in North Korea with a specific focus in the KIC. Beginning in 2001, as the ROK was emerging from the worst of the Asian financial crisis, total trade between the two Koreas was $403 million with South Korea enjoying a $50.617 million surplus. Over the next 5 years, through 2006, bilateral trade more than tripled to a total of $1.350 billion with the ROK again having a $310.635 million surplus. South Korea has become the DPRK's second largest trading partner following only China. Significantly, in 2006, approximately $420 million of the ROK's $830 million in exports to the DPRK were food, fertilizers, and other humanitarian assistance products. One estimate is that in 2005, South Korea supplied $385 million in humanitarian assistance including 500,000 tons of rice on a deferred payment arrangement.

Since the 2000 summit, the ROK has averaged 300,000 tons of fertilizer and 400,000 tons of food per year supplied to the DPRK. In addition to these goods, other South Korean exports included chemicals, textiles, machinery, steel, and metal. North Korea's major exports to Seoul were fish and forestry products, textiles, and electronics.[19] As an important component of Kim Dae Jung's and Roh Moo Hyun's Sunshine and Peace and Prosperity policies, increased trade with North Korea would hopefully result in more integration of the DPRK into the international economy. The desired end result would be that an improved North Korean economy would not only lead to an enhanced standard of living for the people, but would eventually reduce the costs of reunification, the preferred "soft landing."

The KIC is a joint ROK and DPRK economic initiative managed by South Korea's Hyundai Asan and Korea Land Corporation entities. One of the major goals of the KIC is to attract medium and small South Korean companies that do not have the resources to invest in China or other countries with cheaper labor costs to become involved in the KIC instead. North Korean labor and land costs are more than competitive with those in China and enhance overall ROK competitiveness with some other countries in the region by reducing labor and land expenditures. By early 2007, fifteen ROK companies are operating in the KIC employing 8,746 North Korean workers directly with another more than 2,000 working on construction projects. The end goal is to attract more that 2,000 South Korean businesses that will employ around 300,000 North Koreans. In December 2006, the ROK's Korean Electric Power Corporation provided a 100,000 kW power transmission line that has become the source of electricity for the businesses operating in the KIC. Of the $374 million in investments to this point, the South Korean government has put up $223 million. During 2006, the companies operating in the KIC produced on average $7.5 million in merchandise each month.[20]

From the South Korean perspective, investing in the KIC brings both political and economic benefits. Politically, the KIC opens up new channels of communication with North Korea and exposes thousands of North Koreans not only to capitalist economic practices but also to South Korean culture. Many in the ROK have become concerned by the fact that a significant percentage of North Korean defectors to South Korea have had major problems with integration into the ROK society. Even though there are no major language problems involved, the life experiences of North and South Koreans are so different that integration has proved difficult.[21] One of the desired outcomes of exchanges such as the KIC is that the differences in these life experiences will diminish over time.

Economically, the access to the DPRK's labor force and land allows ROK companies to be more competitive as discussed previously. For North Korea, the KIC and the opening to the ROK address some of the major economic problems the country confronts, particularly shortage of food, energy, and foreign exchange. Managerial and technical experiences gained through the KIC also are extremely important. Although these initiatives fly in the face of the DPRK's long held Juche principles of self-reliance, it is a testament to the dire straits the North Korean economy finds itself that Kim Jong Il has decided to follow this path. Perhaps the most significant problem Kim confronts regarding the KIC is trying to determine how to take advantage of the potential economic reforms while still exercising the domestic political and social controls that have been a hallmark of the Kim dynasty.[22] This is a difficult challenge that will go a long way toward determining the fate of the regime in North Korea.

The changes that have occurred and continue to develop in South Korea influencing relations with North Korea are largely associated with the democratization process that began in earnest during the 1980s. Among the most important are political developments particularly since the late 1990s, generational changes among the population, media diversification, and the growth of a viable and vibrant civil society.[23] A fundamental outcome of all these changes and others is that for many South Koreans, they no longer view North Korea as the threat that it once represented, and they are convinced that the DPRK will neither attack the ROK with conventional forces nor its WMD. This change in how North Korea is viewed by many South Koreans cannot be overstated in its importance. For these ROK citizens, they have become convinced that South Korea should play a more definitive role in negotiating with the DPRK and working toward the eventual reunification of the Korean peninsula.

The political changes of most importance were the elections of Kim Dae Jung in late 1997 and Roh Moo Hyun in late 2002 along with significant differences in those South Koreans elected to the National Assembly during this same time period. For both Kim and particularly Roh, they came to office without some of the more traditional backing of earlier administrations. Consequently, both men were able to bring in many new individuals to fill important positions in their governments who were mostly younger and more progressive in their opinions about North Korean relations. These younger political operatives are frequently referred to as the 386/486 generation in that they are mostly in their thirties and forties, came of age politically in the 1980s during the struggles to achieve democracy, and were born in the 1960s. In addition to their expanding roles in the executive branch, this new generation of political leaders has had a significant influence in the National Assembly too. For example, the percentage of the 386/486 generation elected to the legislature has increased from 24.3 percent of the members in 1996 to 32.9 percent in 2000 to 45.9 percent in 2004.[24] This generation obviously has no personal experience with the Korean War era, and many of them view North Korea far differently than those older Koreans who experienced the DPRK invasion and resulting turmoil in the 1950s.

Changes in the ROK media refer to the significant expansion of the use of the Internet as a source of the news. The major print media including the three major newspapers, *Chosun Ilbo, Dong-a Ilbo, and Joongang Ilbo,* remain largely conservative in their orientation toward North Korean policy. For those in the younger generations, more and more of them rely on Internet sources for information rather than read the major dailies or watch television news. Many NGOs (nongovernmental organizations) have decided to use the Internet to circulate their views and positions on critical issues such as policies involving North Korea. One of the most popular of the Internet-based journalism sources is OhmyNews (http://english.ohmynews.com). The bottom line is that with so many sources of information present, it is no longer possible for those opposed to improved relations with the DPRK to dominate the coverage and analysis available. One of the outcomes is far more diversity in bilateral policy options expressed by the media.

The generational changes in play in South Korea already has been alluded to with the rise of the 386/486 group in both the executive and legislative branches, but this change also plays out in the general population. The even younger age cohorts, sometimes referred to as "X" and "Y" generations, appear to be less politicized than their elders and more interested in pursuing their chosen careers. Therefore, regional stability is considered very important as a stimulus for the ROK economy, and many of these younger Koreans place a high value on developing strong economic ties with the DPRK to enhance South Korean international competitiveness. The growth of civil society groups in the ROK is another outcome of the democratization movement. During the Kim Dae Jung administration, President Kim was very effective in mobilizing many of these civil action groups that supported his Sunshine Policy to form the Council on

Reconciliation and Cooperation. This council brought together unification activists and religious groups among others to support programs such as exchange visits with North Korean counterparts that have made the integrative effort more effective. Roh Moo Hyun has continued this practice particularly among more progressive civil action groups.

All of these political, generational, media, and civil society changes in South Korea over the past several years have direct influence on ROK policies toward North Korea. Therefore, whatever the outcomes of the 2007 presidential election and the following election for the National Assembly in early 2008, the policies developed by the Kim and Roh administrations supporting increased engagement with North Korea will be difficult to change even if the new government chooses to reverse course.

One aspect of the Sunshine Policy sometimes overlooked by outside observers is the increased bureaucratic or intergovernmental contacts that have originated. For example, during the spring and summer of 2007, the 15th round of family reunions took place at Mt. Kumgang. In order to facilitate these reunions, the pertinent bureaucracies on both sides have to negotiate many issues before the reunions can take place. The ECPC (Economic Cooperation Promotion Committee) held its 13th meeting in Pyongyang in April 2007 to try to enhance economic ties between the two Koreas. Perhaps more significant, the ECPC organized an inter-Korean team with seven members from each country that visited a number of South Korean businesses established in China and Vietnam to learn more about their operations and business models. One of the goals with these visits is to determine if it might be possible to start some joint Korean investments abroad. The most recent cabinet-level ministerial meetings took place in Seoul during late May. This meeting was the 21st meeting in a long series of senior contacts between the two countries. Resumption of the six-party talks and the continuation of rice and fertilizer shipments to North Korea were major discussion items. Last but not least, the two Koreas in May finally were able to reestablish railroad connections across the DMZ for the first time since these connections were cut during the Korean War. Although regular service still is not occurring, the promise of improved rail transportation across the DMZ has both economic and political implications.[25] The point here in not necessarily the substance of these meetings and discussions as much as it is about the relationships established between bureaucratic entities and the interpersonal contacts developed among government officials. The hope is that these relationships will pave the way for the settlement of difficult issues between North and South Korea in the future.

The final topic to be addressed in this section on inter-Korean relations is a brief analysis of the two different approaches the DPRK and ROK have posited regarding the possible reunification of the Korean peninsula. In truth, neither of these proposals is particularly well thought out, and both have been used more for propaganda purposes than as a serious vehicle to bring about reunification.

Kim Il Sung first introduced his concept that he called the DCRK (Democratic Confederal Republic of Koryo) in 1960 and then again in 1980. This proposal called for the creation of basically a "one country, two systems" solution in that both Koreas would continue their present political and economic systems and would be responsible for maintaining their foreign relations. In time, the two countries would form a Supreme National Committee that would have authority over certain common issues. One of the catches to this concept and a good indicator of its propaganda value was the provision that no foreign military forces or nuclear weapons would be permitted in the DCRK. Since the United States maintained both in South Korea during this period, it obviously was a nonstarter from the American and South Korean perspectives but played well to Kim Il Sung's claims to represent true Korean national identity.[26]

The most extensive South Korea reunification proposal came during the presidency of Roh Tae Woo in the late 1980s and early 1990s that he called the Korean National Commonwealth. Under this proposal, both the ROK and DPRK would continue as sovereign nation states, but there would be created a Council of Ministers that would be co-chaired by the prime ministers of both countries. This council would include about ten cabinet-level officials from each side. A number of standing committees created by the council would address diplomatic, political, and military issues. A Council of Representatives composed of equal numbers from the legislatures of the two Koreas would be responsible for drafting a constitution for the unified country and for developing the procedures necessary to bring about reunification. This process would eventually lead to the holding of general elections under democratic circumstances. The rub here was the call for a democratic process that more than likely would not be acceptable to the Kim dynasty.[27]

To return to the point made at the beginning of this chapter concerning North Korea's ability to use its geographic characteristics effectively, inter-Korean relations tend to bear out this tactic. South Korean trade, aid, and investment policies are designed in part to ensure to the extent possible that North Korea does not collapse largely out of concern for South Korea's own national interests. The collapse of the DPRK would simply be more costly than the ROK is willing to countenance.

NORTH KOREAN–AMERICAN RELATIONS

The details of American–North Korean relations involving the DPRK's nuclear and missile programs were presented in chapter 5. In this section, we will concentrate on the North Korean views of American policy and the American efforts to restrict North Korea's alleged illicit activities. In June 2007 at the annual Asia–Pacific Roundtable in Kuala Lumpur, Malaysia, An Song Nam, the executive director of North Korea's Institute of Disarmament and Peace in

Pyongyang made a presentation that is informative because it expressed the DPRK's views of what the North Koreans have described as American "hostile policies" toward North Korea. While this presentation may well be viewed as a propaganda exercise, it remains important if for no other reason than it provided specific examples of how many in North Korea perceive American policy.[28] In his presentation, An indicated that specific examples of American hostile policies included the threat to use nuclear weapons going all the way back to the Korean War, employing economic sanctions, conducting military exercises in South Korea, and opposing the replacement of the 1953 Armistice Agreement with a more permanent peace mechanism.

Regarding nuclear weapons, An alleged that beginning in the early 1950s, American administrations have repeatedly threatened to use nuclear weapons against the DPRK. An made no mention of the fact that the first Bush administration removed all tactical nuclear weapons from the ROK before leaving office. He went on to state that the United States aggravated the tense situation at the beginning of the Clinton administration by charging that North Korea was developing a nuclear weapons program—a charge that An denied. His example of the second American hostile policy was the imposition of economic sanctions against the DPRK after the 2005 Joint Statement was issued. The resulting freeze of North Korean accounts in Macao's BDA caused the suspension of the six-party talks for several months and delayed the successful resolution of the nuclear weapons issue. Therefore, from the North Korean perspective, all delays in the negotiating process were the results of American actions. Since An was speaking before this issue was resolved, he indicated that North Korea would gage American intentions by the outcome of the BDA controversy.

The third hostile policy An identified was the conducting of military exercises in South Korea. He did not mention the Team Spirit exercise that lasted from 1976 to 1994, but instead referenced the Foal Eagle joint and combined exercise. An described this as a war exercise and maintained that such exercises and negotiations were mutually exclusive from his perspective. His final argument was the 1953 Armistice Agreement was a relic of the Cold War and should be replaced with a more contemporary lasting peace arrangement. The U.S. resistance to such a peace arrangement was unacceptable to North Korea. He closed his presentation by asserting that Kim Il Sung's last instruction before his death was to reiterate his ultimate goal of establishing a nuclear free Korean peninsula. An's point was that North Korea stood ready to proceed with dialogue and negotiations to resolve this issue peacefully as soon as the United States dropped its hostile policies.

Although few American officials would refer to U.S. policies toward North Korea as being hostile, most would agree that these policies are tough primarily because of the alleged DPRK illicit activities that include production and sale of illegal drugs, distribution of counterfeit cigarettes, money laundering, and the counterfeiting of U.S. currency. Despite the fact that North Korea consistently denies involvement in these activities, there are numerous reports that Bureau 39 or Office 39 operates in the center of Pyongyang as the government headquarters overseeing the DPRK's global criminal enterprises. Reportedly, Bureau 39 is under the direction of the Central Committee of the KWP. The most informed estimates are that North Korea earns more than $1 billion per year from these illegal activities. A significant percentage of these funds are used by Kim Jong Il to provide rewards to civilian and military elites in order to maintain their loyalty. One reporter has referred to this source of funding as "the palace economy of Kim Jong Il."[29]

North Korea grows most of its opium in North Hamgyong Province. After harvesting, the opium is transported by government vehicles to a plant outside of Pyongyang where some of it is converted into heroin. North Korean diplomats are a major courier source for delivering the heroin and other drugs such as crystal methamphetamines outside the country. Part of the reason for using diplomats in addition to their diplomatic immunity is that since 1975 when North Korea began to default on many of its foreign loans, DPRK embassies have become "self financing" meaning each embassy had to raise its own operating expenses. Serving as couriers for drugs and other illegal items became part of this "self financing" process.[30]

The bulk opium is transported by ocean-going vessels to ports such as Vladivostok, Russia, and Hong Kong where criminal networks take it from there. China and Russia are two of the largest markets for North Korean narcotics, but there is evidence that even Europe receives some shipments. One of the major concerns of American and other officials is that the DPRK may be able to use some of the same routes and criminal gangs it has developed for bulk narcotics to ship WMD. These concerns are compounded by the suspicion that the North Korean government may actually be losing some of its control over these illicit activities as the government relies more on criminal elements for transportation.

Contraband cigarettes have become another major source of illegal funding for the Kim dynasty. The DPRK has built ten to twelve factories to produce an estimated 41 billion fake cigarettes each year. These cigarettes are transported out of the country on large vessels, and then the cigarettes are off loaded on smaller fishing boats for final delivery to a variety of ports in the region. There are credible reports that Subic Bay in the Philippines has become a major distribution port for North Korean cigarettes both for within the Philippines and to other countries in the region. Estimates range between $80 million to $160 million per year that the Kim regime receives through the sale of contraband cigarettes.[31]

The illicit North Korean activity most galling to the United States is the counterfeiting of U.S. currency, particularly $100 Federal Reserve notes, the infamous supernotes. Although the exact amount of these counterfeit notes is not known, the best estimates are that between $45 to $48 million are in circulation.

These notes are of extremely high quality and very difficult to identify particularly overseas. Again, North Korean diplomats and employees of government owned trading companies are primary couriers for the fake currency. The amount of this money in circulation is disturbing to the Bush administration, but the more difficult fact to accept is that counterfeit American currency is being used to support the Kim dynasty and helps to keep this regime in power. Although North Korea denies its involvement in counterfeiting, it was largely because of money laundering allegations that the Bush administration applied Section 311 of the USA Patriot Act to force the freezing of the North Korean accounts in Macao's BDA. The U.S. government has estimated that approximately half of the $25 million in the Macao bank accounts was directly attributable to illicit activities.[32]

In March and July 2003, the United States and ten other countries came together to form the PSI (Proliferation Security Initiative). The Chairman's Statement issued in Brisbane, Australia in July 2003 made it clear that the primary goal of the PSI was "to stop the flow of WMD, missiles, and related items to and from proliferators." The PSI members pledged to interdict suspected WMD and missile shipments "at sea, in the air and on land." In addition to actual interdiction operations, the member states agreed to share intelligence and to conduct interdiction training exercises.[33] Even though the PSI has expanded with more than sixty countries participating in some form by 2006, South Korea expressed concerns about the PSI. Along with Russia and China, the ROK has not become a member because by so doing it might result in a confrontation between naval vessels of the two Koreas. The Roh Moo Hyun government does not want to take the chance that such a confrontation would occur and adversely affect the efforts to bring about improved inter-Korean relations. Although the primary goal of the PSI was directed at WMD and missiles, the application of interdiction operations could also be used against the other North Korean illegal shipments outlined above in support of the Bush administration's 2003 Illicit Activities Initiative.[34]

This section concludes by examining some of the options the United States has as it attempts to develop its relationship with North Korea over the next several months. The fundamental assumption that must come to fruition before these options have any value is that North Korea does in fact comply with the pledges it made in the September 2005 Joint Statement and the February 2007 Denuclearization Action Plan (Appendix B, Document 3). In addition to denuclearization, it would be very useful if the DPRK rejoined the NPT and the IAEA with all the requirements involved. If North Korea does comply, then the other partners to the six-party negotiations have a responsibility to respond "action for action." The Bush administration and the new American administration that will assume power in January 2009 might want to give consideration to the following options.

First, begin the process of establishing normal diplomatic relations with the DPRK. Both of the documents referred to above call on the two countries to take this basic step. In the period after the 1994 Agreed Framework came into effect, the Clinton administration and North Korea began this process and pledged to establish liaison offices in each capital, but this did not happen because of administrative issues associated with travel across the DMZ and other details. It may well be that following this model of establishing liaison offices is the better choice at present because it is possible that many Americans might object to normalizing relations with the Kim Jong Il regime. They may perceive recognition as acceptance of the human rights and other egregious policies this regime practices. But the United States has diplomatic relations with a number of countries that follow policies and practices that are objectionable. Diplomatic relations would establish a whole series of contacts that could provide additional sources of information to the North Korean government and people that may work to pry open this closed society and integrate it more effectively into the international community.

Second, remove the DPRK from the State Department's list of nation states that sponsor terrorism and from the Trading With the Enemy Act. The United States agreed to take both of these steps in the 2007 Denuclearization Action Plan. While there is no question that North Korea deserved to be on the State Department's list, the last known terrorist act occurred in 1987 with the shoot down of the KAL passenger jet just prior to the 1988 Olympics in Seoul. Nonetheless, current American legislation requires the United States to oppose international loans to countries that are on the State Department's list. One of the major advantages of removing the DPRK from this list is that it would open the way for North Korean application for membership to international financial institutions such as the World Bank, IMF, and Asian Development Bank. In order to obtain loans and other forms of assistance from these institutions, North Korea will have to open its economy and provide information that will reveal the answers to many questions. The visits to conduct surveys and assessments of projects will open the DPRK's society more than is currently the case if North Korea wants to take advantage of membership in these organizations.

Third, negotiate a trade agreement with the DPRK that eventually will provide for normal trade relations for both countries. Since normal trade relations do not exist currently, the few products that North Korea exports to the United States are subject to tariffs that may be as high as 90 percent. This trade agreement should also cover American investments in the DPRK so that U.S. businesses could consider investing in ventures such as the KIC. Finally, and in conjunction with the other members of the six-party process, the United States should support the replacing of the 1953 Armistice Agreement with a permanent peace mechanism for the Korean peninsula. The 2007 Denuclearization Plan established a WG to address this issue and calls for all parties "to negotiate a permanent peace regime" at an appropriate, but separate proceeding from the six-party talks. Some experts have suggested that if the six-party process is eventually successful in resolving the nuclear weapons issue, then it might be converted into a broader security forum that could address issues like a permanent peace mechanism for Korea.[35] This is a possibility worth pursuing.

None of these recommendations will necessarily be easy to accomplish. But the United States and the other negotiating partners must keep in mind that a final objective of negotiations is to convince Kim Jong Il that the best way to maintain regime survivability is to give up his nuclear weapons programs and cooperate with the rest of the international community. To continue with developing nuclear weapons only will jeopardize political and economic progress and contribute to the eventual collapse of the North Korean political system. If Kim accepts this logic, then it may be possible to resolve these problems and eventually achieve the goal of peaceful reunification of the two Koreas. In the end, Kim Jong Il and his government remain concerned about the goals and aspirations of the other countries in Northeast Asia and the possible effects on the DPRK's national security. Improved relations with the United States then may make more sense if the result is that North Korea views this relationship as being valuable enough to sacrifice its nuclear weapons to achieve this improvement in official ties.[36]

SOUTH KOREAN–AMERICAN RELATIONS

The security bonds between the United States and South Korea remain remarkably strong more than 50 years after the conclusion of the Korean War. The 1954 MDT continues in effect and the deployment of thousands of American troops in the ROK provides a very tangible example of the American commitment to the defense of South Korea. It is only normal that this security relationship is undergoing some fundamental revisions on both sides. The South Korea at present is far different from the country devastated by war in 1953 and almost completely dependent on the United States for its defense and economic viability. Now, the ROK is a full-fledged democracy with one of the most vibrant economies globally. It has developed a military capability that is far superior to that of North Korea with the exception of the North's WMD. In this section, we will examine some of the factors influencing the security relationship to include South Korean democratization, the generational changes occurring in the ROK, the roles of American military forces on the peninsula and in the region, and differing threat perceptions between the two allies regarding North Korea.

In many ways, it was easier to manage the bilateral ties during the more autocratic period in South Korean political history. For Park Chung Hee and Chun Doo Hwan, they did not have to pay much attention to popular criticisms of their policies because the Korean public was limited in how it could voice its opposition without suffering unpleasant consequences. The situation now is much different with civil action groups and NGOs acting as major players in the policy process. The growth in the number of NGOs is remarkable going from 10,000 in 1996 to 20,000 in 1999, to more that 25,000 in 2002. That number is no doubt even higher at present. Since political parties are generally considered to be weak in the ROK, many of these NGOs have taken on the roles of being political advocates for a considerable percentage of the South Korean population in bringing pressure to bear on the executive and legislative branches of government.[37]

An example of the growing power and influence of NGOs and civil action groups occurred in the second half of 2002. In June of that year, two American soldiers were driving a large military vehicle north of Seoul that struck and killed two Korean school girls. The American military command and United States embassy immediately apologized for the accident and offered to pay compensation to the families of the girls. Since the soldiers were performing official military duties at the time of the accident, the United States claimed jurisdiction over them according to the provisions of the SOFA despite the fact that South Korean authorities wanted to try the Americans in the Korean judicial system. Both the death of the girls and the jurisdictional question resulted in large anti-American demonstrations in Seoul and elsewhere organized by NGOs and civil action groups. The American command charged the soldiers with negligent homicide and proceeded with courts-martial arrangements.[38]

In late November, the courts-martial proceedings concluded with both soldiers acquitted of the charges against them. More demonstrations occurred and the South Korean media also demanded that the SOFA be renegotiated to provide ROK courts with more jurisdiction over American troops. Since the 2002 presidential election campaign was underway at the time of the acquittals, this issue became part of that campaign with the result that the acquittals became even more politicized. Roh Moo Hyun was elected at least in part because he had opposed the American military presence earlier in his political career and was seen as more of a political outsider than his main opponent. This background allowed him to take advantage of some of the anti-American sentiment evident at that time.[39] The point here is that NGOs, civil action groups, and the Internet media were effective in mobilizing support against what many Koreans perceived as an injustice.

One leading authority has identified the generational change in South Korea as the most important factor contributing to the polarization of the Korean population toward the United States.[40] Those older South Koreans who remember the Japanese occupation or the dire conditions associated with the Korean War and its aftermath tend to view the United States with great respect and appreciate the continuation of the security relationship as being critical to the defense of the country. For many younger Koreans who did not directly experience these events, their view of the United States is less charitable in part because of American support for authoritarian ROK political regimes in the 1960s to the early 1980s. Many in the younger group are convinced that the ROK has established clear political, economic, and military superiority over North Korea. The North Koreans are then seen as poor cousins needing assistance rather than as a viable threat to attack South Korea.[41]

Korean nationalism is also a factor in that there is a fundamental desire to reunite the two Koreas so that the Korean nation can achieve its full potential. These same sentiments are factors for many younger South Koreans who object to American dominance in the relationship and want to be treated more as equals with the United States. As discussed earlier in this chapter, many of the 386/486 generation have now come of age politically and have taken important positions in the Roh administration and the National Assembly so that their orientations on ROK–United States relations have definite policy implications. The Sunshine Policy of Kim Dae Jung and Peace and Prosperity Policy of Roh Moo Hyun have tended to present a favorable view of North Korea that affects the general population. The 2000 summit in Pyongyang has only reinforced these perceptions most importantly among the younger cohort of the population.

American policies toward North Korea have been factors in influencing the bilateral ties with South Korea. As the following examples make clear, sometimes ROK government officials have been critical of American policies because they perceive these policies as being too lenient on the DPRK. At other times, these officials may see American policies as being too harsh. During the Clinton administration, as the negotiations were nearing a conclusion on the Agreed Framework, President Kim Young Sam gave an interview to the *New York Times*.[42] In this interview, Kim accused the administration of being "naïve and overly flexible" in its approach to North Korea. He encouraged the negotiators to stiffen their resolve and press the North Koreans to abandon their nuclear weapons program and improve the DPRK's human rights performance. From his perspective, a harder line approach could drive the DPRK into a corner and perhaps cause the collapse of the Kim Jong Il regime.

The reporter conducting this interview was of the opinion that President Kim was very frustrated because his government had only a limited role to play in the negotiations, but yet would be stuck with paying for some of the concessions made to the DPRK such as the construction of LWRs. The Clinton administration was not happy with Kim's interview, and the coordination between the two countries as the final details of the Agreed Framework was strained as a result.[43]

As we have seen in chapter 5, the governments of Kim Dae Jung and Roh Moo Hyun have been critical of the Bush administration for being too harsh with North Korea and not willing to offer effective incentives for improved behavior. The Bush–Kim meeting in March 2001 provides a good example of the differences in both style and substance. President Bush's designation of the DPRK as a member of his "axis of evil" conflicts with the efforts of Kim and Roh to present North Korea in a more favorable light so as to encourage improved relations.

Another more recent example involves the KORUSFTA (Korea–U.S. Free Trade Agreement) that was completed in June 2007, but not yet ratified. There is significant opposition to this agreement in the U.S. Congress especially among Democrats who object to some of the provisions on automobiles and agricultural products. Whether or not the KORUSFTA is ratified remains problematic.

In the negotiations leading up to this agreement, the ROK argued strongly that goods produced in the KIC should be considered as made in the ROK and thereby eligible for preferential treatment under the KORUSFTA.[44] Since the KIC is one of the major achievements of the Kim and Roh policies to engage North Korea, the current South Korean government believes this inclusion of KIC products to be important. The Bush administration opposes including these goods in the KORUSFTA primarily because of concerns over North Korean workers' conditions in the KIC and because North Korea receives valuable foreign exchange from its involvement at Kaesong. In the end, the provision was not included in the KORUSFTA and deferred for future negotiations.[45]

Even though the ROK is now directly involved with the six-party negotiations, policy issues continue to arise that influence not only those negotiations but the bilateral relations between the two allies too. For many South Koreans, they find themselves in a zero sum game in which any improvement in relations with North Korea frequently results in the creation of strains in their ties with the United States.[46]

The final issue to be discussed that influences ROK–United States ties are the roles that American military forces perform while serving in South Korea. The U.S. ground force presence in South Korea has been a mainstay of the security commitment since the end of the Korean War. Many of those forces traditionally have been deployed along the major invasion routes and have served a "trip wire" effect. When Donald Rumsfeld became secretary of defense at the beginning of the Bush administration, he announced that he intended to transform the U.S. military. One of his goals was to make the Army in particular lighter, more mobile, with increased lethality. Rumsfeld also desired to change the dependency of American military units on large overseas bases in Europe, Japan, and South Korea. The GPR published early in the Bush presidency provided more details.

Specifically referring to the ROK, the new strategy was coined "strategic flexibility" meaning that American forces in Korea would have other missions in the region in addition to contributing to the defense of South Korea. There were three specific ramifications of this changed strategy. First, the United States stated its intention to remove most of the forces north of Seoul that had performed the "trip wire" mission for more that 50 years. The ROK and United States would construct additional facilities at Osan and Pyongtaek considerably south of Seoul for these redeployed forces. Second, the total American troop presence would be reduced by approximately 12,500 soldiers as one of the brigades of the 2nd Infantry Division was deployed to Iraq. This redeployment resulted in the reduction of American troop strength in the ROK to approximately 25,000. Third, the Bush administration committed to spending $11 billion for additional equipment and facilities in the ROK over a 3-year period. This additional equipment would include advanced Patriot missiles, Apache helicopters, Stryker armored vehicles, and improved "buster busting" bombs for possible use against North Korea's underground facilities. The two allies also agreed to establish the Future of the Alliance Initiative as a long-term means to address specific issues associated with the redeployments and changing roles of both countries within the alliance context.[47]

These changes to the alliance have contributed to a couple of major divisions within the South Korean population. The first is between those referred to as "pro alliance" against those referred to as "pro independence." For the former, it is essential for South Korea to remain close to the United States because of the perceived security threats. For the latter, the American military presence restricts efforts for the ROK to become a truly independent country. The second division refers to two different perspectives on the redeployment of American forces in the ROK. One group of Koreans is concerned about this redeployment because they view it as the first step in the eventual removal of the U.S. military presence from the country. This is the abandonment school. The second group sees the establishment of "strategic flexibility" and the redeployment of American troops as having the potential to involve the ROK in U.S. conflicts that may not be in the national interest. For example, possible American attacks on North Korea or involvement in a conflict between China and Taiwan would be among these conflicts from the ROK perspective. This is the entanglement school.[48]

One other ongoing issue is the transfer of wartime operational control of Korean military forces to a South Korean command arrangement. During the Clinton administration in 1994, peacetime operational control was transferred to South Korea, but an American would still exercise control over ROK forces under the CFC in the case war broke out on the Korean peninsula. Roh Moo Hyun has wanted to change this command relationship since he became president, but he has encountered some resistance from his defense community, particularly retired generals. Many of these retired officers remain concerned that the transfer of wartime operational control might send the wrong message to North Korea, and they also question whether the ROK armed forces are adequately prepared to exercise the associated responsibilities. South Korea has begun a major military equipment buildup, but it will take time for this new equipment to come on line.[49] However, in October 2006 at the annual SCM, the two sides agreed that South Korea will assume wartime operational control sometime between October 2009 and March of 2012. The CFC will cease to exist once this transfer is made and will be replaced by a Military Cooperation Center that will be responsible for overseeing combined military operations.[50]

Despite the many changes that have occurred over the life of the security relationship between the United States and South Korea, this relationship remains strong. The most difficult challenges for the present and immediate future will be the evolving North Korean threat perceptions involving the two allies and basic questions as to what the security relationship should be or if the relationship should continue once Korean reunification occurs.

POSSIBLE REUNIFICATION SCENARIOS

Any discussion of Korean reunification must take into consideration significant unknowns regarding North Korea and the Kim dynasty. While there is no question of the seriousness of the economic crisis beginning in the mid-1990s, the regime has survived without a serious institutional challenge. Several experts on North Korea were convinced as this crisis deepened that Kim would not be able to consolidate his power after the death of his father. They were proved wrong. As pointed out in chapter 3, Kim Jong Il is wary of the KPA and has developed the military first policy as a means to keep the armed forces loyal. What follows is at best an educated guess as to how reunification may occur on the Korean peninsula and under what timeline.

The first possibility is what we could call the "status quo" or "soft landing" outcome. Much of the groundwork for this outcome has been put in place by the administrations of Kim Dae Jung and Roh Moo Hyun in South Korea. Their policies have been designed to assist with the gradual improvement of the North Korean economy and the integration of the North's economy into the international system. The KIC serves as an example of efforts to accomplish both of these goals as well as the establishment of enhanced linkages between the bureaucracies of the two Koreas.

The Chinese economic model of introducing market reforms might also eventually have more influence on the DPRK. For several years, China has been attempting to convince Kim Jong Il to follow its example although without much success. If the DPRK would introduce more effective economic reforms, then there could be political ramifications over time. As the economy improves, a more vocal middle class may develop and put increasing pressure on the regime for additional political participation. If these reforms are successful over several years, then the two Koreas may be able to negotiate a final settlement leading to reunification. There are obviously several hurdles to achieving this peaceful outcome with the Juche ideology of self-reliance and Kim Jong Il's paranoia over the reduction of political control being strong points of resistance, but for South Korea, this is the preferred endgame.

A second model for reunification involves the implosion and collapse of North Korea and the subsequent absorption of the DPRK by the South along the lines of German reunification in the late 1980s and early 1990s. Although the Kim regime appears to have survived the worst of the economic deprivations, some experts on the DPRK believe that this is only a brief respite. Andrei Lankov argues that there are major changes affecting North Korea that could well result in the collapse of the government. Among these are increased access to outside sources of information for the North Korean people through VCRs and DVDs from South Korea and the increasing availability of cell phones; the introduction of some economic reforms such as the KIC that expose North Korean workers to new ideas; and reduced political and social controls through rampant government corruption and an expansion of the gap between the rich and poor in the DPRK.[51]

Robert Kaplan points out what he calls the "seven phases of collapse in North Korea."[52] This collapse begins with severe resource depletion, energy supplies in particular, that contributes directly to the deterioration of critical infrastructure around the country. As this situation grows worse, "independent fiefs" develop that work around the declining central government and begin to present a fundamental threat to Kim Jong Il. The final phases result in splits within the government and its inevitable collapse leading to the formation of a new national leadership.

Again, the closed nature of North Korea makes it difficult to determine the probability of either of these collapse scenarios actually occurring. Basic questions concerning how the succession from Kim Jong Il to the leader who follows him may present increased opportunities for elite conflict in Pyongyang. Reports in the South Korean press in July 2007 suggested that based on photos published after the North Korean leader met with Yang Jiechi, the new Chinese foreign minister, Kim appeared gaunt, disheveled, and in poor health.[53] If Kim Jong Il were to die suddenly with no designated successor named, then the possibility of conflict among those competing to gain political control could lead to chaos and the collapse of governmental effectiveness.

From the South Korean perspective, the implosion and absorption model based on the German reunification example is a nightmare in the making. Most observers believe that the costs to the ROK if North Korea collapses would far surpass the costs to West Germany as East Germany imploded based on the differences in comparative gross national product terms. For example, the North Korean population as a percentage of the South Korean population is larger than a similar comparison of the two Germanys' population. Also the discrepancies between the North Korean and South Korean economies are greater than was true for East and West Germany. Finally, although the ROK's economy is the tenth largest in the world, West Germany's economy was stronger at the time of reunification, but even so, the costs continue to be a major drain on the German gross national product many years after reunification took place. For all of these reasons, the South Korean government does not want to see the North Korean regime collapse any time soon.

The third reunification scenario would entail an all out North Korean attack on the ROK using its conventional forces, special operations units, and WMD. This attack would be one final roll of the dice by Kim Jong Il in an attempt to reunify the country by force as his father attempted in 1950. The United States and ROK have developed Operations Plan 5027 over many years and have conducted innumerable exercises on how to implement this plan if the DPRK ever would attack. Although North Korea has the capabilities to cause tremendous destruction in South Korea, it could not prevail in the longer term. The two allies responding under OPLAN 5027 would destroy Pyongyang and other major DPRK cities and infrastructure through the use of airpower. A massive invasion of North Korea would follow designed to remove the government and reunify the country under South Korean control. If Kim Jong Il places as much emphasis on regime survival as we have suggested, then this type of all out attack would result in regime suicide rather than regime survival.

Based on these three reunification scenarios, it is not hard to understand why most South Koreans prefer the first option even though it may well take many years to achieve. No matter how reunification occurs, the final topic of this book will examine what the relationship of the United States to a unified Korea may be. The basic assumption in this discussion is that a unified Korea will be under South Korean dominance. There appear to be two primary options for this relationship: some sort of continued alignment or nonalignment.[54] If reunification occurs through the first scenario of a long peace process as described above, then nonalignment may be more attractive particularly if the countries of Northeast Asia establish some sort of a security organization that is effective in resolving regional issues. Korean nationalism would make it difficult for the United States to maintain military forces in a unified Korea unless the external threats are strong.

If reunification takes place under scenarios two or three where much more chaos is involved, then alignment with the United States may be more attractive to Korea, at least until the situation stabilizes. If alignment results in the continuation of an American military presence in Korea, this would most likely cause problems with both China and Russia. Both of these countries would not appreciate having at least the potential for U.S. forces to be stationed near their borders. There are ways to mitigate these concerns such as having no American forces north of the 38th parallel, but just as is evident with discussions to resolve NATO expansion in Europe, these negotiations would be protracted and difficult.

In conclusion, it is safe to say that the long established security relationship between the United States and South Korea will almost certainly be fundamentally changed after reunification. It is only natural for this to occur. But this reality should not detract from the fact that the MDT and all that has followed after the Korean War not only assisted with the defense of South Korea, but also contributed to eventual democratization (although perhaps not as quickly as some Americans and South Koreans would have liked) and the economic dynamism of the ROK.

NOTES

1. Samuel S. Kim, *North Korean Foreign Relations in the Post–Cold War World* (Carlisle Barracks: Strategic Studies Institute, April 2007), 81–84. For an excellent analysis of North Korean negotiating strategies, see Scott Snyder, *Negotiating on the Edge: North Korean Negotiating Behavior* (Washington: United States Institute of Peace Press, 1999), particularly 65–96.

2. Don Oberdorfer, *The Two Koreas: A Contemporary History* (New York: Basic Books, 2001), 11–24.

3. Joint Statement of North and South, July 4, 1972 available at http://www1.korea-np.co.jp/pk/011th_issue/97100103.htm.

4. Oberdorfer, *The Two Koreas,* 25.

5. Ibid., 147–48. For journal accounts at the time, see John Burgess, "North Korea Delivers Aid to South," *International Herald Tribune* (October 1, 1984): 1 and Shim Jae Hoon, "A Thaw in the North?" *Far Eastern Economic Review* (October 4, 1984): 30–32. On the family reunions, see Young H. Lee, "A Generation Later, Reuniting in Korea," *International Herald Tribune* (September 23, 1985): 1 and Paul Ensor, "Hello and Farewell," *Far Eastern Economic Review* (October 10, 1985): 22.

6. Agreement on Reconciliation, Nonaggression, and Exchanges and Cooperation Between South and North Korea, December 13, 1991 and available at http://www.isop.ucla.edu/eas/documents/korea-agreement.htm.

7. The Joint Declaration of the Denuclearization of the Korean Peninsula, January 20, 1992 available at http://www.state.gov/t/ac/rls/or/2004/31011.htm.

8. Oberdorfer, *The Two Koreas,* 338–39 and 393. See also the International Crisis Group Asia Report No. 89, "Korea Backgrounder: How the South Views Its Brother From Another Planet," December 14, 2004, 1–2.

9. Nicholas D. Kristof, "Koreans Search for Infiltrators From Wrecked Sub," *New York Times* (September 19, 1996): 1 and Nicholas D. Kristof, "North Korean Infiltrators Still Elude Search," *New York Times* (September 21, 1996): 5.

10. Nicholas D. Kristof, "North Korea's Mission Failed, But At What?" *New York Times* sect. 4 (September 22, 1996): 4.

11. Nicholas D. Kristof, "Deep Regret Sent by North Koreans," *New York Times* (December 30, 1996): 1. This article contains a verbatim transcript of the North Korean apology. See also Oberdorfer, *The Two Koreas: A Contemporary History,* 387–93 for good coverage of the submarine incursion.

12. Oberdorfer, *The Two Koreas,* 407–8.

13. South–North Joint Declaration, Pyongyang, June 15, 2000 available at http://www.usip.org/library/pa/n_skorea/n_skorea06152000.html. For newspaper coverage, see Howard W. French, "2 Korean Leaders Speak of Making A Day in History," *New York Times* (June 14, 2000): 1 and Howard W. French, "Koreans Reach Accord Seeking Reconciliation After 50 Years," *New York Times* (June 15, 2000): 1.

14. Oberdorfer, *The Two Koreas,* 432–33.

15. U.S.–DPRK Joint Communiqué, Washington, DC, October 12, 2000 available at http://www.armscontrol.org/Events/communique.asp.

16. Calvin Sims, "New Friendly Craze in South Korea: The North," *New York Times* (June 20, 2000): 8.

17. International Crisis Group Asia Report No. 89, "North Korea Backgrounder: How the South Views Its Brother From Another Planet," 3–4.

18. Lee Byong Chul, "GNP's New North Korean Policy Is a Tall Order," *OhmyNews,* July 10, 2007 available at http://english.ohmynews.com/articleview/article_print.asp?menu=c10400&no=371291&re. For more information on OhmyNews as a news source, see Jennifer Veale, "Seoul Searching," *Foreign Policy,* 158 (January/February 2007): 94–96.

19. Dick K. Nanto and Emma Chanlett-Avery, "The North Korean Economy: Overview and Policy Analysis," Congressional Research Service (RL32493) updated April 18, 2007, 27–30. See also Jae Kyu Park, "North Korea Since 2000 and Prospects for Inter-Korean Relations," Woodrow Wilson Center for International Scholars, January 17, 2006, 4. Professor Jae presented a lecture to the Woodrow Wilson Center on this date.

20. Ibid., 11–13.

21. For a good article on this problem of integration into South Korean society, see Normitsu Onishi, "From a Lead Role in a Cage to Freedom and Anomie," *New York Times* (June 23, 2007): 4.

22. Bradley O. Babson, "Economic Perspectives on Future Directions for Engagement With the DPRK in a Post-Test World," The Stanley Foundation Policy Analysis Brief, December 2006, 2–6.

23. This discussion unless otherwise cited is based largely on the analysis found in the International Crisis Group Asia Report No. 89, "Korea Backgrounder: How the South Views Its Brother From Another Planet," 6–17.

24. Sunhyuk Kim and Wonhyuk Lim, "How to Deal With North Korea," The *Washington Quarterly* 30, no. 2 (Spring 2007): 74–75.

25. Aidan Foster-Carter, "North Korea–South Korea Relations: On Track?" *Comparative Connections* 9, no. 2 (July 2007): 103–14.

26. B.C. Koh, "A Comparison of Unification Policies," in *Korea and the World: Beyond the Cold War,* ed. Young Whan Kihl (Boulder: Westview Press, 1994), 153–65 and Bruce Cumings, *Korea's Place in the Sun: A Modern History* (New York: W.W. Norton & Company, 1997), 489.

27. Lee Hong Koo, "Unification Through a Korean Commonwealth: Blueprint for a National Community," in *Korean Under Roh Tae Woo: Democratization, Northern Policy, and Inter-Korean Relations,* ed. James Cotton (Canberra: Allen & Unwin Publishers, 1993), 308–10.

28. An Song Nam, "Process of Denuclearization on the Korean Peninsula and the Challenges," Policy Forum Online 07-049A, June 29, 2007, Nautilus Institute, pages 1–6 available at http://www.nautilus.org/fora/security/07049Nam.html. All of the discussion regarding American hostile policies comes from this presentation unless otherwise cited.

29. For three excellent articles on the North Korean illicit activities, see Raphael F. Perl and Dick K. Nanto, "North Korean Counterfeiting of U.S. Currency," Congressional Research Service Report for Congress (RL33324), March 22, 2006, 1–18; Stephen Mihm, "No Ordinary Counterfeit," *New York Times Magazine* (July 23, 2006): 36–41; and Bill Powell and Adam Zagorin, "The Sopranos State," *Time* (July 23, 2007): 45–48. The $1 billion estimate is from Powell and Zagorin, "The Sopranos State," 45 and the quote regarding the "palace economy" is from Mihm, "No Ordinary Counterfeit," 40.

30. Sheena Chestnut, "Illicit Activity and Proliferation," *International Security* 32, no. 1 (Summer 2007): 85–86.

31. Powell and Zagorin, "The Sopranos State," 48. For more information on possible North Korean government control over the shipment of illicit items, see Chestnut, "Illicit Activity and Proliferation," 95–97.

32. Perl and Nando, "North Korean Counterfeiting," 1–9 and Powell and Zagorin, "The Sopranos State," 46.

33. Chairman's Statement, Proliferation Security Initiative, Brisbane, Australia, July 9–10, 2003 available at http://www.dfat.gov.au/globalissues/psi/index.html.

34. Myung Jin Kim, "South Korea–North Korea Relations: Influence of the PSI on North Korea," *Strategic Insights,* vol. V, no. 7 (August 2006). This is a bimonthly electronic journal published by the Center for Contemporary Conflict at the Naval Postgraduate School. For more information on the 2003 Illicit Activities Initiative, see Chestnut, "Illicit Activity and Proliferation," 107–08.

35. Keun Sik Kim, "The Prospects for Institutionalizing the Six-Party Talks," Policy Forum Online 07-051A, July 12, 2007, Nautilus Institute available at http://www.nautilus.org/fora/security/07051Kim.html.

36. Peter Hayes makes a similar argument in his article "The Stalker State: North Korean Proliferation and the End of the American Nuclear Hegemony," Policy Forum Online 06-82A, October 4, 2006, Nautilus Institute, 1–13 available at http://www.nautilus.org/fora/security/0682Hayes.html.

37. Sook Jong Lee, *The Transformation of South Korean Politics: Implications for U.S.–Korea Relations,* (Washington, DC: The Brookings Institution, September 2004), 22.

38. Donald G. Gross, "U.S.–Korean Relations," *Comparative Connections,* 4, no. 3, 3rd Quarter (October 2002): 38. *Comparative Connections* is an online quarterly published by the Pacific Forum. The web site is http://www.csis.org/pacfor/ccejournal.html.

39. Ralph A. Cossa, "U.S.–Korea Relations: Trials, Tribulations, Threats, and Tirades," *Comparative Connections,* 4, no. 4, 4th Quarter (January 2003): 42.

40. Lee, "The Transformation of South Korean Politics: Implications for U.S.–Korea Relations," 16.

41. L. Gordon Flake, "Same Bed, Different Nightmares: Diverging U.S. and South Korean Views of North Korea," Policy Forum Online 05-47A, June 7, 2005, Nautilus Institute, available at http://www.nautilus.org/fora/security/0547AFlake.html.

42. James Sterngold, "South Korea President Lashes Out at the U.S." *New York Times* (October 8, 1994): 3.

43. Joel S. Wit, Daniel B. Poneman, and Robert L. Gallucci, *Going Critical: The First North Korean Nuclear Crisis* (Washington, DC: The Brookings Institution Press, 2004), 314–15.

44. Mark E. Manyin and William H. Cooper, "The Proposed South Korea–U.S. Free Trade Agreement (KORUSFTA)," Congressional Research Service Report to Congress (RL33435), May 24, 2006, 18–20.

45. Choe Sang Hun, "U.S. and South Korea Agree to Sweeping Trade Deal," *New York Times* (April 3, 2007), sec. C: 1.

46. Scott Snyder, "South Korea's Squeeze Play," *The Washington Quarterly* 28, no. 4 (Autumn 2005): 99–100.

47. Chae Jin Lee, *A Troubled Peace: U.S. Policy and the Two Koreas* (Baltimore: Johns Hopkins University Press, 2006), 256–61.

48. Taik Young Hamm, "The Self-Reliant National Defense of South Korea and the Future of the U.S.–ROK Alliance," Policy Forum Online 06-49A, June 20, 2006, Nautilus Institute, 2 available at http://www.nautilus.org/fora/security/0649Hamm.html.

49. For a good discussion of South Korean military modernization, see Kim Jung Soo, "The Proactive Grand Strategy for Consensual and Peaceful Korean Reunification," Masters Thesis, Naval Postgraduate School, March 2007, 64–65.

50. Donald A. Gross, "U.S.–Korea Relations: North Korea Tests a Nuke and Returns to the Six-Party Talks," *Comparative Connections,* 8, no. 4, 4th Quarter (January 15, 2007): 7–8.

51. Andrei Lankov, "The Natural Death of North Korean Stalinism," *Asia Policy,* no. 1 (January 2006): 95–121.

52. Robert D. Kaplan, "When North Korea Falls," *The Atlantic Monthly* 298, no. 3 (October 2006): 64–73.

53. Foster-Carter, "North Korea–South Korea Relations: On Track?" 112–13.

54. Lee, *A Troubled Peace: U.S. Policy and the Two Koreas,* 289–95.

Epilogue

During the summer and early fall of 2007, two events occurred related to the North Korean nuclear weapons program and relations between the two Koreas that deserve attention. As outlined in chapter 5, after the resolution of the BDA (Banco Delta Asia) financial problem, North Korea shut down its nuclear facilities at Yongbyon to include the 5 MW reactor, nuclear reprocessing unit, and the nuclear fuel fabrication plant. The IAEA (International Atomic Energy Agency) sent inspectors to Yongbyon to verify that these facilities had in fact been shut down, and the inspectors provided such assurances in July. Later that month, the respective country representatives reconvened in Beijing for the first session of the Sixth Round of the six-party talks and stipulated that the working groups established in February would meet over the next few months to address issues and then report their results to another six-party meeting in September.

During early September, Ambassador Christopher Hill and North Korea's Vice Foreign Minister Kim Kye Gwan met in Geneva representing both sides in the United States–North Korean Normalization Working Group. According to Ambassador Hill, he and Minister Kim agreed that the DPRK would make a full declaration of all its nuclear programs and disable its nuclear facilities at Yongbyon by the end of 2007. In return according to North Korean sources, the United States would agree to withdraw the DPRK from the State Department's state sponsor of terrorism list and remove restrictions under the Trading with the Enemy Act as applied to North Korea.[1]

The second session of the sixth round of the six-party talks convened in Beijing between September 27 and 30. At the conclusion of this session, the representatives traveled to their home countries to gain approval for the agreements reached. On October 3, the Chinese Foreign Ministry released the "Second-Phase Actions for the Implementation of the September 2005 Joint Statement."[2] This statement contained the following points:

1. On the Denuclearization of the Korean Peninsula

   - The DPRK agreed to disable all existing nuclear facilities subject to abandonment under the September 2005 Joint Statement and the February 13 agreement. The disablement of the 5 MW experimental reactor at Yongbyon, the Reprocessing Plant (Radiochemical Laboratory) at Yongbyon and the Nuclear Fuel Rod Fabrication Facility at Yongbyon will be completed by December 31, 2007. Specific measures recommended by the expert group will be adopted by heads of delegation in line with the principles of being acceptable to all Parties, scientific, safe, verifiable, and consistent with the international standards. At the request of the other Parties, the United States will lead the disablement activities and provide the initial funding for those activities. As a first step, the U.S. side will lead the expert group to the DPRK within the next 2 weeks to prepare for disablement.

   - The DPRK agreed to provide a complete and correct declaration of all its nuclear programs in accordance with the February 13 agreement by December 31, 2007.

   - The DPRK reaffirmed its commitment not to transfer nuclear materials, technology, or know-how.

2. On Normalization of Relations between the Relevant Countries

   - The DPRK and the United States remain committed to improving their bilateral relations and moving toward a full diplomatic relationship. The two sides will increase bilateral exchanges and enhance mutual trust. Recalling the commitments to begin the process of removing the designation of the DPRK as a state sponsor of terrorism and advance the process of terminating the application of the Trading with the Enemy Act with respect to the DPRK in parallel with the DPRK's actions based on consensus reached at the meetings of the Working Group on Normalization of DPRK–U.S. relations.

   - The DPRK and Japan will make sincere efforts to normalize their relations expeditiously in accordance with the Pyongyang Declaration, on the basis of the settlement of the unfortunate past and the outstanding issues of concern. The DPRK and Japan committed themselves to taking specific actions toward this end through intensive consultations between them.

3. On Economic and Energy Assistance to the DPRK

   - In accordance with the February 13 agreement, economic, energy, and humanitarian assistance up to the equivalent of 1 million tons of HFO (heavy fuel oil) (inclusive of the 100,000 tons of HFO already delivered) will be provided to the DPRK. Specific modalities will be finalized through discussion of the Working Group on Economy and Energy Cooperation.

4. On the Six-Party Ministerial Meeting

   - The Parties reiterated that the Six-Party Ministerial Meeting will be held in Beijing at the appropriate time.

   - The Parties agreed to hold a heads of delegation meeting prior to the Ministerial Meeting to discuss the agenda of the meeting.

This is an important document that moves the process of denuclearization of the Korean peninsula considerably forward in conjunction with North Korea closing its facilities at Yongbyon earlier this year. Although not specifically defined, disablement is believed to mean that the facilities would be incapacitated or rendered inoperable for at least 3 years if not forever.[3] This stipulation represents an improvement over the 1994 Agreed Framework that only entailed shutting down the facilities at Yongbyon. When the problems developed in 2002 and 2003 between the United States and North Korea over the alleged HEU (highly enriched uranium) program, the DPRK was able to restart its nuclear facilities in a relatively short period of time. Another issue remaining with the most recent agreement involves the declaration of North Korea's nuclear programs. Since the DPRK denies the existence of a HEU capability, it remains to be seen how thorough this declaration will be at least from the American perspective. One other issue of extreme importance that has not been resolved is what will North Korea be willing to do with the plutonium and nuclear weapons it already possesses? Whether Kim Jong Il will ever be agreeable to give up these weapons and materials is the most important issue in the overall goal to achieve a nuclear free Korean peninsula and remains a fundamental unanswered question. On the American side, removal of North Korea from the terrorist list will require congressional approval. The Export Administration Act stipulates that the executive branch must notify Congress of its intention to remove a country from this list. Congress can then enact legislation to prevent this removal from occurring. To the present, the executive branch has not attempted to remove any country, so Congress has not exercised this authority.[4]

North Korea's pledge not to transfer nuclear materials has taken on new significance based on an incident involving Israel and Syria in September 2007. In the middle of that month, articles began to appear in the American press reporting an Israeli air attack on suspected nuclear sites in Syria.[5] Subsequent reports suggested that North Korea was involved in providing either equipment or technical assistance to the Syrian program in part because the DPRK has a long history of assisting Syria's missile programs.[6] By October, intelligence analysts in both Israel and the United States had concluded that Syria was attempting to build a nuclear reactor based on the North Korean 5 MW model at Yongbyon. Although these analysts would not go so far to suggest that the DPRK had supplied parts or other equipment, the suspicions were that such transfers had occurred.[7] Vice Minister Kim Kye Gwan emphatically denied any North Korean involvement stating that "lunatics have created these rumors about a nuclear deal between us and Syria."[8] Nonetheless, this incident has rekindled the old debate within the Bush administration concerning whether or not to negotiate with North Korea reportedly pitting Vice President Cheney against Secretary of State Rice and Secretary of Defense Gates.[9] Since both Israel and the United States are treating this incident and the intelligence surrounding it with the highest security, it is difficult to know what the facts are. What is clear is that this incident has added another bit of uncertainty to the ongoing negotiations regarding North Korea's nuclear weapon programs and whether or not the DPRK can be trusted to comply with any agreement it makes.

On August 8, the two Koreas announced that the second leaders' summit would take place between August 26 and 28 with President Roh Moo Hyun traveling to Pyongyang to meet with Chairman of the Military Commission Kim Jong Il. This proposed meeting proved controversial since Kim had promised to visit the ROK at the time of the first summit in June 2000 but had not done so. Further, there were questions raised about the timing of the summit because Roh was approaching the end of his term in office, and opposition leaders questioned whether any agreements Roh entered into would be considered valid by his successor. Another issue was the venue in Pyongyang. Some South Korean critics suggested that if Kim was not going to reciprocate by coming to Seoul, then at least the meeting ought to take place at a neutral site. Later in August, severe floods occurred in North Korea, and the two sides agreed to postpone the summit until early October.[10]

At the conclusion of the 3-day summit on October 4, 2007, the two leaders signed "The Declaration on the Advancement of South–North Korean Relations, Peace and Prosperity."[11] In the initial paragraphs of this declaration, Roh and Kim stated their firm desire "for the establishment of peace on the Korean peninsula and denuclearization of the peninsula." They also pledged "to speed up the construction of a common economic bloc for the South and North to seek coprosperity through economic cooperation in various fields." These statements outline the two most important aspects of this declaration focusing on security issues and economic cooperation that the eight points of the document then address in more detail.

On the security front, Roh and Kim agreed to work in concert "to end their hostile military relations, reducing tension, and securing peace on the Korean peninsula." To put more substance to this pledge, the two leaders agreed that each country's defense minister will meet in Pyongyang in November to discuss specific confidence building measures. In addition, the two Koreas will create "a special peace and cooperation zone in the West Sea" with the goal of reducing military tensions. The West Sea, also known as the Yellow Sea, has been a frequent area of conflict involving competing North and South claims for rich fishing zones including armed clashes that occurred in 1999 and 2002. Finally, Roh and Kim promised "to end the current armistice regime and build a permanent peace regime." The two Koreas "agreed to work together with the other countries directly involved in this matter to declare an end to the Korean War...." This declaration did not go into any further specifics as to how this peace regime would be established but implies that future multilateral negotiations will be necessary.

On the economic front, the West Sea "peace and cooperation zone" most likely will focus on the DPRK's southwestern port of Haeju and development projects there.[12] The Koreas also will expedite the completion of the first phase construction efforts at the KIC (Kaesong Industrial Complex) and move on to the building of the second phase as well as opening rail service to the complex and improving highway connections between the KIC and Pyongyang. Additional infrastructure development will include the construction of joint shipbuilding facilities at the North Korean ports of Nampo and Anbyon. To oversee economic cooperation and the forging of "an economic community" on the Korean peninsula, the Inter-Korean Economic Cooperation Promotion Committee will be upgraded to a Joint Committee for Inter-Korean Economic Cooperation with deputy prime ministers from each country responsible for implementation.

Serious issues remain to be resolved with both the Six-Party process and the evolving relations between North and South Korea. However, there does appear to be the prospects for favorable outcomes in both areas if domestic politics permits, particularly in the ROK, and if regional partners along with the United States continue to play supportive roles.

NOTES

1. Donald G. Gross and Hannah Oh, "Agreement With the North, Progress with the South," *Comparative Connections* (October 2007): 4 available at http://www.csis.org/pacfor/ccejournal.html.

2. Second-Phase for the Implementation of the September 2005 Joint Statement can be found at http://www.nautilus.org/fora/security/07075JointStatement.html.

3. Ralph A. Cossa, "Korean Peninsula Denuclearization: So Far, So Good," *PacNet 40*, October 5, 2007 available at http://www.csis.org/media/pubs/pac0740.pdf.

4. Larry Niksch and Raphael Perl, "North Korea: Terrorist List Removal," Congressional Research Service Report for Congress (RL30613), updated April 6, 2007, 11.

5. Mark Mazzetti and Helene Cooper, "U.S. Official Says Syria May Have Nuclear Ties," *New York Times* (September 15, 2007): 7.

6. Mark Mazzetti and Helene Cooper, "Israeli Nuclear Suspicions Linked to Raid," *New York Times* (September 18, 2007): 12.

7. David E. Sanger and Mark Mazzetti, "Analysts Find Israel Struck A Syrian Nuclear Project," *New York Times* (October 14, 2007): 1.

8. Gross and Oh, "Agreement with the North, Progress with the South," 6.

9. Mark Mazzetti and Helene Cooper, "An Israeli Strike On Syria Kindles Debate in U.S.," *New York Times* (October 10, 2007): 1.

10. For a good review of the decision to hold the summit and the advantages that each leader perceived in going forward with this meeting, see Eric J. Ballbach, "Summit Spirit on the Korean Peninsula," Nautilus Institute Policy Forum Online 07-071A, September 20, 2007 available at http:www.nautilus.org/fora/security/07071Ballbach.html.

11. The Declaration on the Advancement of South–North Korean Relations, Peace and Prosperity is available at http://english.president.go.kr/cwd/en/archive/popup_archive_print.php?meta_id=en_peace.

12. For a good review of the security and economic projects outlined in this declaration, see Aidan Foster-Carter, "North Korea–South Korea Relations: Summit Success?" *Comparative Connections* (October 2007): 6–8 available at http://www.csis.org/pacfor/ccejournal.html.

Biographies

SYNGMAN RHEE

Syngman Rhee was born Lee Seungman in the southern part of Korea on March 26, 1875. As the Japanese gained influence in Korea, Lee opposed this hegemony and was subsequently arrested and imprisoned in 1897. He was released in 1904 and went into exile in the United States gaining an undergraduate degree from George Washington University and a PhD from Princeton. While in the United States, Lee Seungman anglicized his name to Syngman Rhee. In 1910, Rhee returned to Korea just after the Japanese annexation of the country. He remained there until 1912 when he traveled to China. In 1919, Rhee became the president of the Korean Provisional Government in Shanghai and held this position until 1925. Then, he returned to the United States where he would remain for the remainder of the Japanese colonial occupation of Korea.

In 1945 after the Japanese surrender at the end of World War II, Rhee returned to Korea where he became a favorite of many in the American occupation because of his fluency in English and strong anticommunist sentiments. Some regional experts in the State Department questioned his leadership abilities to serve as a unifying force in an increasingly divided Korea because of his doctrinaire positions. Nonetheless, he was elected the first South Korean president in May 1948 and took over political control when the ROK was formed on August 15, 1948. During his first term in office and before the beginning of the Korean War in June 1950, Rhee initiated what many believed were dictatorial powers, and he took strong measures against those Koreans he accused of being communists or North Korean agents. In 1952, he was reelected president and subsequently amended the

South Korean Constitution so that he was exempt from the 8-year term limit. This amendment allowed him to run again successfully in 1956 aided by the unexpected death of the major opposition candidate during the campaign. Perhaps more important, in 1953, as the Armistice Agreement ending the Korean War was being finalized, Rhee refused to sign it because he viewed the Armistice as serving to prolong the division of the Korean peninsula.

In April 1960, Rhee ran again for reelection even though he was well into his 80s and achieved an overwhelming margin of victory. The much closer election was for vice president. When Rhee's candidate was declared the winner, there were major claims of voter fraud and intimidation. Student-led demonstrations occurred throughout the ROK and the increasingly isolated Rhee resigned on April 26, 1960. He once again went into exile this time in Honolulu, Hawaii where he died of a stroke on July 19, 1965.

KIM IL SUNG

Kim Il Sung was born Kim Song Ju near Pyongyang on April 15, 1912. In 1920, he and his family moved to Jilin Province in northern China (Manchuria) primarily because of increasing famine in Korea under the Japanese occupation. As Kim grew older, he became involved with anti-Japanese guerrilla groups in China including the anti-Japanese United Army from 1935 to 1941 that was under the supervision of the Chinese Communist Party. It was during this period that Kim Song Ju took the nom de guerre of Kim Il Sung after a famous Korean nationalist figure. As the Japanese pressure became overwhelming in China, Kim and other guerrilla fighters fled across the border into the Soviet Union. The Soviets sent Kim to a military camp near Khabarovsk where he underwent training. He became a captain in the Soviet Red Army and served until the end of World War II. Through his anti-Japanese guerrilla exploits and his years in the Soviet army, Kim Il Sung became known and respected among many Koreans for his military experiences.

Kim Il Sung returned to Korea in September 1945 with Soviet military forces. The Soviets appointed him head of the Provisional People's Committee in their zone of occupation, and Kim also was instrumental in forming the NKPA (North Korean People's Army), later the KPA, that was made up largely of former guerrilla fighters and soldiers. The Soviet Union provided the new North Korean military with modern equipment and training that helped to make the NKPA a relatively formidable fighting force. In September 1948, Kim was appointed prime minister of the newly formed DPRK. He also held the position of general secretary of the KWP and was the head of the NKPA.

In the spring of 1950, Kim was able to convince Joseph Stalin and Mao Zedong that North Korea was strong enough to reunite the Korean peninsula under the DPRK's control. Kim further persuaded Stalin and Mao that the

United States would not intervene to rescue South Korea once the invasion began. This judgment turned out to be a serious mistake, and the Korean War ensued with tremendous loss of life and property on both sides. After the war ended with the Armistice Agreement in 1953, Kim conducted a series of very harsh purges to rid North Korea of people who would be a source of opposition to the Kim regime. He also established a cult of personality and a sense of leadership infallibility that pervaded North Korean society and developed a prison/gulag system to punish anyone and their families who might threaten the regime. In 1955, Kim introduced the Juche principle of self-reliance that would make the DPRK one of the most isolated countries in the world. Despite this isolation, North Korea under Kim's tutelage played off China and the Soviet Union, the DPRK's major allies, for maximum advantage. The end of the Cold War and the collapse of the USSR came as major blows to Kim Il Sung near the end of his life. Through a series of policy errors, acts of nature, and the reduction of major external support, North Korea saw its fragile economy collapse soon after Kim's death.

At the Sixth Party Congress in 1980, Kim announced that his oldest son, Kim Jong Il, was his designated successor. Kim had consolidated his own political power in 1972 when he gave up the prime minister position to assume the presidency of the DPRK. From the time of the Sixth Party Congress until Kim Il Sung's death from a heart attack in July 1994, the younger Kim began to take on more of the responsibilities for running the country. In 1998, 4 years after his death, the Supreme People's Assembly designated Kim Il Sung "eternal president" of North Korea. Kim Il Sung's legacy outside of North Korea is that of one of the world's most inhumane tyrants who also developed WMD that threatened all of Northeast Asia. Inside North Korea, Kim is still treated as an infallible leader by many if not most North Koreans even though his rule was marred by terrible inefficiencies and terror. He is still referred to as the "Great Leader." Statues of Kim are prevalent throughout the country, and his dominance over North Korea for over 45 years remains a major source of political legitimacy for his son more than 10 years after the death of Kim Il Sung.

PARK CHUNG HEE

South Korea's longest serving president so far in its history was Park Chung Hee who was born near Taegu on November 14, 1917. The youngest of seven children, Park attended Taegu Teachers College from 1932 until his graduation in 1937. After graduating, he taught school for a few years. In 1940, he was accepted to attend a Japanese military training school in Manchukuo, the Japanese name for Manchuria during the Japanese occupation of that part of China. Park graduated in 1942, and the Japanese then selected him to attend the Imperial Military Academy in Tokyo. After graduating in 1944, he became a lieutenant in the Imperial Japanese Army until the end of World War II. After returning to Korea, Park joined the army in the southern part of Korea being formed by the United States. Despite some allegations of leftist sentiments and involvement in the 1948 Yosu rebellion, Park survived with the assistance of some American military officers and the intervention of Syngman Rhee. He served in the Korean War and rose to the rank of brigadier general. By 1961, he had been promoted to major general in the ROK Army.

After Syngman Rhee was forced to resign in April 1960, an interim government under Prime Minister Chang Myon proved to be ineffective in addressing and resolving some of the major political and economic problems it confronted. On May 16, 1961, Major General Park Chung Hee led a bloodless coup against the government and seized power under the rubric of the Supreme Council for National Reconstruction. As chairman of this council, Park exercised real political power and also established the KCIA in June 1961 to help him control the country. In a presidential election held in 1963, Park was elected and then reelected in 1967.

Two of President Park's lasting legacies during his presidency were the development of the South Korean economy by implementing the Japanese model of export-led industrialization and the gradual slide of the ROK's political system into increasing authoritarianism. On the economic front, Park was convinced that South Korea must be able to provide more of the industrial might to meet its own national security needs because he had become suspicious that the United States might not always be there as the guarantor of the ROK. He designed the Heavy and Chemical Industries Promotion Plan to promote the growth of six major industries he believed necessary for South Korea to become more self-sufficient. The ROK economy also was assisted in the 1960s by the normalization of diplomatic relations with Japan and Park's decision to send military forces to support the American war effort in Vietnam. Establishing relations with Japan resulted in an infusion of Japanese aid and an expanded market for Korean exports. President Johnson responded to Park's offer of troops with increased economic and military assistance programs.

Park ran for another term as president in 1971 against Kim Dae Jung and won although there were significant charges of voter fraud and intimidation. After this election, Park declared a state of emergency and wrote a new constitution that came to be known as the Yushin Constitution. This document provided the executive with even more sweeping powers than Park already exercised. The presidential term was increased to 6 years with no limits on the number of terms a president could serve. Under these new rules, Park won again in the 1972 and 1978 elections with little or no opposition. Park became increasingly authoritarian and isolated by the end of the 1970s as the domestic and international demands for reforms increased. On October 26, 1979, Kim Jae Kyu, the director of the KCIA, assassinated Park during a dinner in the Blue House compound ending more than 18 years in office. Kim claimed that he killed Park because he had become an obstacle to democratic development in the ROK, but Kim's real motives remain obscure. He was tried, convicted, and executed soon after the assassination. One of Park Chung Hee's lasting legacies is that his oldest daughter, Park Geun Hye, became a leading candidate of the GNP for the December 2007 presidential election.

KIM DAE JUNG

One of the great political survivors of the twentieth century, Kim Dae Jung was born in the Cholla region of southern Korea on January 6, 1925. Kim became a leading opposition figure during the presidency of Park Chung Hee and ran a strong campaign against Park in the 1971 presidential election. Many South Koreans still believe that if that election had been free and fair, Kim would have won. After Park initiated the Yushin Constitution in 1972, Kim became an even more vocal critic of Park's authoritarian government. In response, the KCIA kidnapped Kim in August 1973 while he was in Japan and probably would have killed him on the return trip to Seoul if the American ambassador had not intervened.

The Park regime imprisoned Kim in 1976 for antigovernment activities until he was placed under house arrest in 1978. After Park's assassination, Kim Dae Jung's political rights were reinstated, and he was allowed to participate in the political process again. However, when Chun Doo Hwan came to power after the Kwangju incident in 1980, Kim was again arrested and this time charged with sedition and conspiracy. The court sentenced him to a death sentence, but this sentence raised such international condemnation, that the Chun government commuted the sentence to 20 years and then allowed Kim to go into exile in the United States for "health reasons." Kim Dae Jung returned to the ROK in the mid-1980s as the democratization movement was underway.

In the 1987 direct presidential election, Kim Dae Jung and Kim Young Sam were unable to decide which of them should run against Roh Tae Woo. Consequently, the two Kims split the opposition vote, and Roh won. In the 1992 presidential election, Kim Dae Jung ran against Kim Young Sam and lost. Many Koreans believed this defeat, his third effort at the presidency, probably ended his political career. However, Kim decided to run again in December 1997, and this time he won by a narrow margin over Lee Hoi Chang. Kim served as president from February 1998 until February 2003. Two dominant issues defined the Kim presidency. The first was the ROK's efforts to recover from the Asian financial crisis of the late 1990s including implementing the reforms mandated by the IMF in return for a $57 billion loan. The second was Kim's initiatives to engage North Korean through his Sunshine Policy. This effort to engage the DPRK culminated in the June 2000 summit between Kim and Kim Jong Il in Pyongyang.

Although Kim and his Sunshine Policy have been criticized by many for the lack of DPRK reciprocity, he has never wavered in his belief that engaging North Korea is the best policy to move toward eventual reunification. Because of his long history of resisting authoritarian governments and supporting human rights in the ROK plus his summit meeting with Kim Jong Il, Kim Dae Jung received the Nobel Peace Prize in 1980 and remains one of the international community's distinguished elder statesmen.

KIM JONG IL

Kim Jong Il is the oldest son of Kim Il Sung and was born in the Soviet city of Khabarovsk on February 16, 1942 while his father was serving with the Soviet Red Army. The younger Kim and his mother moved to Pyongyang in late 1945 and joined the elder Kim who was beginning his political ascent under Soviet guidance. Kim Jong Il attended Kim Il Sung University in Pyongyang graduating in 1964 with a degree in political economy. In 1980, Kim Il Sung designated Kim Jong Il as his successor and then worked hard to prepare the groundwork for a successful succession by placing the younger Kim in increasingly important party, military, and governmental positions.

Kim Jong Il became known as the "Dear Leader" in North Korea as he assumed more responsibilities. Although many experts on North Korea doubted whether a hereditary succession could work in a communist political system, Kim Jong Il has solidified his power since the death of his father in 1994. Although Kim Il Sung remains the "eternal president" of North Korea, Kim Jong Il holds the positions of chairman of the Defense Commission, supreme commander of the KPA, and general secretary of KWP. There appears to be no serious challengers to Kim Jong Il at present, but there are some concerns that he has not worked to establish a succession plan as his father did for him. If Kim should die suddenly, and there are questions about his health, then the possibility for political conflict in the DPRK increases.

To maintain his political power, Kim has used the same extreme measures employed by his father. North Korea remains a police state with any opposition treated harshly through the gulag system and other repressive practices. In order to buy the loyalty of the military and political elite, Kim has initiated the "military first" policy whereby as much as 25 percent of North Korea's gross national product goes to the military. Bureau 39, under the KWP, controls the illicit activities supported by the Kim regime including illegal drugs, contraband cigarettes, and counterfeit currency that provide additional sources of payoffs for the elite. Kim Jong Il has also continued his father's programs of developing WMD and then using these weapons to force other countries to negotiate with the DPRK. Kim has used his nuclear weapons capability particularly effectively over the past several years to exact concessions from several countries.

One of the most severe challenges Kim Jong Il confronts is the poor performance of the North Korean economy. Kim bears much of the blame for this performance because of his own short-sighted policies. But these mistaken policies are compounded by the inherent problems Kim faces with employing economic reforms. For example, to modify the Juche principle of self-reliance that was begun by his father in 1955, Kim would have to take the chance of undermining his own political legitimacy because his power is so dependent on his father's legacy. The other major problem he faces with economic reforms is that Kim is very concerned about the possible political ramifications of opening up the economy. The KIC provides a good example because Kim Jong Il is aware of the many benefits that could accrue to North Korea by expanding this or other similar projects, but the thoughts of having many of his citizens intermingling with South Koreans cannot be a comforting thought based on his paranoia of maintaining political control. How Kim Jong Il and his successors deal with this basic dilemma will be very important to the long-term survivability of North Korea or its ultimate collapse.

ROH MOO HYUN

Roh Moo Hyun was born in Kimhae near the coast of southern Korea on September 1, 1946. A high school graduate, he did not attend college but successfully passed the bar examination in 1975 after studying on his own. Roh became a successful human rights lawyer in the ROK before entering politics. During the 1980s, he defended many students who were involved in demonstrations and other acts in support of the democratization process in South Korea. In 1988, Roh ran successfully for the National Assembly and served in the legislature until he was defeated in a reelection campaign in 2000. After that defeat, Kim Dae Jung appointed Roh minister of maritime affairs and fisheries, and Roh went on to win the nomination for president of the MDP in 2002. In December of that year, he defeated Lee Hoi Chang in a close election and assumed the presidency in February 2003.

When he came into office, Roh Moo Hyun brought with him a number of important programs he wanted to implement. He agreed with Kim Dae Jung's engagement strategy with North Korea, but changed the name of this initiative to the Peace and Prosperity Policy. The reason for this change was to signal that the DPRK would have to reciprocate more than had been its practice and that there would be more benefits to South Korea. Roh also introduced a number of reforms to decentralize the government, bring more transparency to the industrial sector, improve the educational performance in the ROK, and redefine the security relationship with the United States.

Unfortunately for Roh and his government, he ran into significant opposition to many of these plans. The most serious was an impeachment proceeding launched by the opposition in the National Assembly after the March 2004 legislative elections. Roh was charged with violating an election law that prohibits the president from active involvement in support of particular candidates in an election. The vote against Roh was an overwhelming 193-2 because many of his supporters abstained. As a result, Roh was forced to step down as president during his appeal. In May 2004, the Constitutional Court overturned Roh's impeachment and reinstated him as president. This process undermined Roh along with many of his initiatives, and further losses in the National Assembly through by-election defeats and defections of loyal legislators have contributed to his problems. A further effort to form a grand coalition in the National Assembly with the GNP also failed to come to fruition. As a result of all of these problems, Roh's polling numbers have fallen to below 20 percent late in his term.

The bilateral relationship with the United States gradually improved since Roh has been in office. Perhaps this improvement is relative because the 2002 presidential campaign in the ROK had a distinctly anti-American cast to it primarily because of controversies over the death of two South Korean school girls in an accident involving American soldiers. For some in the Bush administration, they viewed Roh's campaign as playing upon these anti-American sentiments. Nonetheless, Roh was able to pass legislation that provided for the sending of more than 3,500 ROK soldiers to northern Iraq in support of the United States. The two allies also have been able to work out some difficult issues involving troop relocations and plans transfer wartime operational control of South Korean forces to the ROK. The signing of the KORUSFTA was another major accomplishment although not yet ratified in either country. The North Korean nuclear weapons program and how best to respond to this challenge has presented some trying moments in the U.S.–South Korean relationship, and this will more than likely continue no matter what the outcome of the December 2007 presidential election in the ROK.

Documents

DOCUMENT 1

Joint Declaration of the Denuclearization of the Korean Peninsula

The South and the North

Desiring to eliminate the danger of nuclear war through denuclearization of the Korean peninsula, and thus to create an environment and conditions favorable for peace and peaceful unification of our country and contribute to peace and security in Asia and the world,

Declare as follows:

1. The South and the North shall not test, manufacture, produce, receive, possess, store, deploy, or use nuclear weapons.
2. The South and the North shall use nuclear energy solely for peaceful purposes.
3. The South and the North shall not possess nuclear reprocessing and uranium enrichment facilities.
4. The South and the North, in order to verify the denuclearization of the Korean peninsula, shall conduct inspection of the objects selected by the other side and agreed upon between the two sides in accordance with procedures and methods to be determined by the South–North Joint Nuclear Control Commission.
5. The South and the North, in order to implement this joint declaration, shall establish and operate a South–North Nuclear Control Commission within one (1) month of the effectiveness of this joint declaration.

6. This Joint Declaration shall enter into force as of the day the two sides exchange appropriate instruments following completion of their respective procedures for bringing it into effect.

Signed on January 20, 1992
Entered into force February 20, 1992

Chung Won Shik
Prime Minister of the Republic of Korea
Chief delegate of the South delegation to the South–North High-Level Talks

Yon Hyong Muk
Premier of the Administrative Council of the Democratic People's Republic of Korea
Head of the North delegation to the South–North High-Level Talks

DOCUMENT 2

Agreed Framework Between the United States of America and the Democratic People's Republic of Korea

Geneva, October 21, 1994

Delegations of the governments of the United States of America and the DPRK held talks in Geneva from September 23 to October 21, 1994, to negotiate an overall resolution of the nuclear issue on the Korean peninsula.

Both sides reaffirmed the importance of attaining the objectives contained in the August 12, 1994 Agreed Statement between the United States and the DPRK and upholding the principles of the June 11, 1993 Joint Statement of the United States and DPRK to achieve peace and security on a nuclear-free Korean peninsula. The United States and DPRK decided to take the following actions for the resolution of the nuclear issue:

I. Both sides will cooperate to replace the DPRK's graphite-moderated reactors and related facilities with LWR power plants.

1. In accordance with the October 20, 1994, letter of assurance from the U.S. President, the United States will undertake to make arrangements for the provision to the DPRK of a LWR project with a total generating capacity of approximately 2,000 MW(e) by a target date of 2003.

   • The United States will organize under its leadership an international consortium to finance and supply the LWR project to be provided to the DPRK. The United States representing the international consortium, will serve as the principal point of contact with the DPRK for the LWR project.

   • The United States, representing the consortium, will make its best efforts to secure the conclusion of a supply contract with the DPRK within 6 months of the date this Document for of the LWR project. Contract talks will begin as soon as possible after the date of this Document.

- As necessary, the United States and the DPRK will conclude a bilateral agreement for cooperation in the field of peaceful uses of nuclear energy.

2. In accordance with the October 20, 1994 letter of assurance from the U.S. President, the United States, representing the consortium, will make arrangements to offset the energy foregone due to the freeze of the DPRK's graphite-moderated reactors and related facilities, pending completion of the first LWR unit.

   - Alternative energy will be provided in the form of HFO for heating and electricity production.

   - Deliveries of heavy oil will begin within 3 months of the date of this Document and will reach a rate of 500,000 tons annually, in accordance with an agreed schedule of deliveries.

3. Upon receipt of the U.S. assurances for the provision of the LWRs and for arrangements for interim energy alternatives, the DPRK will freeze its graphite-moderated reactors and related facilities and will eventually dismantle these reactors and related facilities.

   - The freeze on the DPRK's graphite-moderated reactors and related facilities will be fully implemented within 1 month of the date of this Document. During the 1-month period, and throughout the freeze, the IAEA will be allowed to monitor this freeze, and the DPRK will provide full cooperation to the IAEA for this purpose.

   - Dismantlement of the DPRK's graphite-moderated reactors and related facilities will be completed when the LWR project is completed.

   - The United States and the DPRK will cooperate in finding a method to store safely the spent fuel from the 5 MW(e) experimental reactor during the construction of the LWR project, and to dispose of the fuel in a safe manner that does not involve reprocessing in the DPRK.

4. As soon as possible after the date of this Document, the United States and DPRK experts will hold two sets of expert talks.

   - At one set of talks, experts will discuss issues related to alternative energy and the replacement of the graphite-moderated reactor program with the LWR project.

   - At the other set of talks, experts will discuss specific arrangements for spent fuel storage and ultimate disposition.

II. The two sides will move toward full normalization of political and economic relations.

1. Within 3 months of the date of this Document, both sides will reduce barriers to trade and investment, including restrictions on telecommunications services and financial transactions.

2. Each side will open a liaison office in the other's capital following resolution of consular and other technical issues through expert level discussions.

3. As progress is made on issues of concern to each side, the United States and DPRK will upgrade bilateral relations to the Ambassadorial level.

III. Both sides will work together for peace and security on a nuclear-free Korean peninsula.

1. The United States will provide formal assurances to the DPRK against the threat or use of nuclear weapons by the United States

2. The DPRK will consistently take steps to implement the North–South Joint Declaration on the Denuclearization of the Korean peninsula.

3. The DPRK will engage in North–South dialogue as the Agreed Framework will help to create an atmosphere that promotes such dialogue.

IV. Both sides will work together to strengthen the international nuclear nonproliferation regime.

1. The DPRK will remain a party to the Treaty on the Non-Proliferation of Nuclear Weapons (NPT) and will allow implementation of its safeguards agreement under the Treaty.

2. Upon conclusion of the supply contract for the provision of the LWR project, ad hoc and routine inspections will resume under the DPRK's safeguards agreement with the IAEA with respect to the facilities not subject to the freeze. Pending conclusion of the supply contract, inspections required by the IAEA for the continuity of safeguards will continue at the facilities not subject to the freeze.

3. When a significant portion of the LWR project is completed, but before delivery of the key nuclear components, the DPRK will come into full compliance with its safeguards agreement with the IAEA, including taking all steps that may be deemed necessary by the IAEA, following consultations with the Agency with regard to verifying the accuracy and completeness of the DPRK's initial report on all nuclear material in the DPRK.

Robert L. Gallucci
Head of Delegation of the United States of America, Ambassador at Large of the United States of America

Kang Sok Ju
Head of the Delegation of the Democratic People's Republic of Korea, First Vice-Minister of Foreign Affairs of the Democratic People's Republic of Korea

DOCUMENT 3

Joint Statement of the Fourth Round of the Six-Party Talks

Beijing September 19, 2005
The Fourth Round of the Six-Party Talks was held in Beijing, China among the People's Republic of China, the Democratic People's Republic of Korea, Japan, the Republic of Korea, the Russian Federation, and the United States of America from July 26 to August 7 and from September 13 to 19 2005.

Mr. Wu Dawei, Vice Minister of Foreign Affairs of the PRC; Mr. Kim Gye Gwan, Vice Minister of Foreign Affairs of the DPRK; Mr. Kenichiro Sasae, Director-General for Asian and Oceanic Affairs, Ministry of Foreign Affairs of Japan; Mr. Song Min Soon, Deputy Minister of Foreign Affairs and Trade of the ROK; Mr. Alexandr Alekseyev, Deputy Minister of Foreign Affairs of the Russian Federation; and Mr. Christopher Hill, assistant secretary of state for East

Asian and Pacific Affairs of the United States attended the talks as heads of their respective delegations.

Vice Minister Wu Dawei chaired the talks.

For the cause of peace and stability on the Korean Peninsula and in Northeast Asia at large, the Six Parties held, in a spirit of mutual respect and equality, serious and practical talks concerning the denuclearization of the Korean Peninsula on the basis of the common understanding of the previous three rounds of talks, and agreed, in this context, to the following:

1. The Six Parties unanimously reaffirmed that the goal of the Six-Party Talks is the verifiable denuclearization of the Korean Peninsula in a peaceful manner. The DPRK committed to abandoning all nuclear weapons and existing nuclear programs and returning, at an early date, to the Treaty on the Non-Proliferation of Nuclear Weapons and to IAEA safeguards. The United States affirmed that it has no nuclear weapons on the Korean Peninsula and has no intention to attack or invade the DPRK with nuclear or conventional weapons. The ROK reaffirmed its commitment not to receive or deploy nuclear weapons in accordance with the 1992 Joint Declaration of the Denuclearization of the Korean Peninsula, while affirming that there exist no nuclear weapons within its territory. The 1992 Joint Declaration of the Denuclearization of the Korean Peninsula should be observed and implemented. The DPRK stated that it has the right to peaceful uses of nuclear energy. The other parties expressed their respect and agreed to discuss, at an appropriate time, the subject of the provision of a LWR to the DPRK.

2. The Six Parties undertook, in their relations, to abide by the purposes and principles of the Charter of the United Nations and recognized the norms of international relations. The DPRK and the United States undertook to respect each other's sovereignty, exist peacefully together, and take steps to normalize their relations subject to their respective bilateral policies. The DPRK and Japan undertook to take steps to normalize their relations in accordance with the Pyongyang Declaration on the basis of the settlement of the unfortunate past and the outstanding issues of concern.

3. The Six Parties undertook to promote economic cooperation in the fields of energy, trade, and investment, bilaterally, and/or multilaterally. China, Japan, ROK, Russia, and the United States stated their willingness to provide energy assistance to the DPRK. The ROK reaffirmed its proposal of July 12 2005 concerning the provision of 2 million kW of electric power to the DPRK.

4. The Six Parties committed to joint efforts for lasting peace and stability in Northeast Asia. The directly related parties will negotiate a permanent peace regime on the Korean Peninsula at an appropriate forum. The Six Parties agreed to explore ways and means for promoting security cooperation in Northeast Asia.

5. The Six Parties agreed to take coordinated steps to implement the aforementioned consensus in a phased manner in line with the principle of "commitment for commitment, action for action."

6. The Six Parties agreed to hold the Fifth Round of the Six-Party Talks in Beijing in early November 2005 at a date to be determined through consultations.

DOCUMENT 4

Initial Actions for the Implementation of the Joint Statement
(North Korea-Denuclearization Action Plan)

Beijing February 13, 2007

The Third Session of the Fifth Round of Six-Party Talks was held in Beijing among the People's Republic of China, the Democratic People's Republic of Korea, Japan, the Republic of Korea, the Russian Federation, and the United States of America from February 8 to 13, 2007.

Mr. Wu Dawei, Vice Minister of Foreign Affairs of the PRC; Mr. Kim Gye Gwan, Vice Minister of Foreign Affairs of the DPRK; Mr. Kenichiro Sasae, Director-General of Asian and Oceanic Affairs, Ministry of Foreign Affairs of Japan; Mr. Chun Yung Woo, Special Representative for Korean Peninsula Peace and Security Affairs of the ROK Ministry of Affairs and Trade; Mr. Alexander Losyukov, Deputy Minister of Foreign Affairs of the Russian Federation; and Mr. Christopher Hill, assistant secretary of state for East Asian and Pacific Affairs of the Department of State of the United States attended the talks and heads of their respective delegations.

Vice Foreign Minister Wu Dawei chaired the talks.

I. The Parties held serious and productive discussions on the actions each party will take in the initial phase for the implementation of the Joint Statement of September 19, 2005.

The parties reaffirmed their common goal and will to achieve early denuclearization of the Korean Peninsula in a peaceful manner and reiterated that they would earnestly fulfill their commitments in the Joint Statement. The Parties agreed to take coordinated steps to implement the Joint Statement in a phased manner in line with the principle of "action for action."

II. The Parties agreed to take the following actions in parallel in the initial Phase.

    1. The DPRK will shut down and seal for the purposes of eventual abandonment the Yongbyon nuclear facility, including the reprocessing facility and invite back IAEA personnel to conduct all necessary monitoring and verifications as agreed between the IAEA and the DPRK.

    2. The DPRK will discuss with other parties a list of all its nuclear programs as described in the Joint Statement, including plutonium extracted from used fuel rods, that would be abandoned pursuant to the Joint Statement.

    3. The DPRK and the United States will start bilateral talks aimed at resolving pending bilateral issues and moving toward full diplomatic relations. The United States will begin the process of removing the designation of the DPRK as a state-sponsor of terrorism and advance the process of terminating the application of the Trading With the Enemy Act with respect to the DPRK.

    4. The DPRK and Japan will start bilateral talks aimed at taking steps to normalize their relations, in accordance with the Pyongyang Declaration, on the basis of the settlement of unfortunate past and outstanding issues of concern.

5. Recalling Section 1 and 3 of the Joint Statement of September 19, 2005, the Parties agreed to cooperate in economic, energy, and humanitarian assistance to the DPRK. In this regard, the Parties agreed to the provision of emergency energy assistance to the DPRK in the initial phase. The initial shipment of emergency energy assistance equivalent to 50,000 tons of HFO will commence within the next 60 days. The Parties agreed that the abovementioned initial actions will be implemented within the next 60 days and that they will take coordinated steps toward this goal.

III. The Parties agreed on the establishment of the following WGs in order to carry out the initial action for the purpose of full implementation of the Joint Statement:

1. Denuclearization of the Korean Peninsula

2. Normalization of DPRK–United States relations

3. Normalization of DPRK–Japan relations

4. Economy and Energy Cooperation

5. Northeast Asia Peace and Security Mechanism The WGs will discuss and formulate specific plans for the implementation of the Joint Statement in their respective areas. The WGs shall report to the Six-Party Heads of Delegation Meeting on the progress of their work. In principle, progress in one WG shall not affect progress in other WGs. Plans made by the five WGs will be implemented as a whole in a coordinated manner. The Parties agreed that all WGs will meet within the next 30 days.

IV. During the period of the Initial Actions phase and the next phase—which includes provision by the DPRK of a complete declaration of all nuclear programs and disablement of all existing nuclear facilities, including graphite-moderated reactors and reprocessing plant—economic, energy, and humanitarian assistance up to the equivalent of 1 million tons of HFO, including the initial shipment equivalent to 50,000 tons of HFO, will be provided to the DPRK. The detailed modalities of the said assistance will be determined through consultations and appropriate assessments in the WG on Economic and Energy Cooperation.

V. Once the initial actions are implemented, the Six Parties will promptly hold a ministerial meeting to confirm implementation of the Joint Statement and explore ways and means for promoting security cooperation in Northeast Asia.

VI. The Parties reaffirmed that they will take positive steps to increase mutual trust and will make joint efforts for lasting peace and stability in Northeast Asia. The directly related parties will negotiate a permanent peace regime on the Korean Peninsula at an appropriate separate forum.

VII. The Parties agreed to hold the Sixth Round of the Six-Party Talks on March 19, 2007, to hear reports of WGs and discuss actions for the next phase.

Index

About the Author

Dr. WILLIAM E. BERRY, Jr. served 30 years in the U.S. Air Force before retiring as a colonel in 1997. During his career, he served in Vietnam, the Philippines, Korea, and Malaysia. He also taught at the Air Force Academy, the National War College, and the Asia-Pacific Center for Security Studies. A Cornell PhD, Dr. Berry has written and lectured extensively on topics related to American security interests in both Northeast and Southeast Asia. His previous book, *U.S. Bases in The Philippines: The Evolution of The Special Relationship,* is generally considered to be one of the seminal works on this subject. Dr. Berry is currently an independent consultant specializing in East Asian security issues and also an adjunct professor of political science at the Pueblo campus of Colorado State University. He and his wife, Noelle, live in Monument, Colorado.